SO-AEI-082

BIG THE PICTURE

Getting Perspective on What's Really Important in Life

Also by Ben Carson, M.D.

One Nation *(with Candy Carson)*

Gifted Hands *(with Cecil Murphey)*

Think Big *(with Cecil Murphey)*

Take the Risk *(with Gregg Lewis)*

The Big Picture *(with Gregg Lewis)*

You Have a Brain *(with Gregg Lewis and Rebecca Shaw Lewis)*

BIG THE PICTURE

Getting Perspective on What's Really Important in Life

BEN CARSON with Gregg Lewis

ZONDERVAN®

ZONDERVAN

The Big Picture
Copyright © 1999 by Benjamin Carson

Photo insert © 2000 by Benjamin Carson

Requests for information should be addressed to:

Zondervan, 3900 Sparks Dr. SE, Grand Rapids, Michigan 49546

ISBN 978-0-310-34195-6 (softcover)

Library of Congress Cataloging-in-Publication Data

Carson, Ben.
   The big picture: getting perspective on what's really important in life / Ben Carson with
Gregg Lewis.
      p. cm.
      ISBN-10: 0-310-23834-X (Softcover)
      ISBN-13: 978-0-310-23834-8 (Softcover)
   1. Christian life. 2. Carson, Ben. I. Lewis Gregg, 1951-. II. Title.
BV4501.2.C272   1999
617.4'8'0083—dc21   98-32033
                                                                                      CIP

All Scripture quotations, unless otherwise indicated, are taken from The Holy Bible, *New Interna-tional Version*®. *NIV*®. Copyright © 1973, 1978, 1984, 2011 by Biblica, Inc®. Used by permission. All rights reserved worldwide.

All rights reserved. No part of this publication may be reproduced, stored in a retrieval system, or transmitted in any form or by any means—electronic, mechanical, photocopy, recording, or any other—except for brief quotations in printed reviews, without the prior permission of the publisher.

Interior design by Sherri Hoffman

First printing 2000 / Printed in the United States of America

To Bill and Shirley Howard

and the Children's Cancer Foundation

for making my life easier,

and to Gary Roth,

a friend, a patient,

and an inspiration to me.

CONTENTS

Part One

SEEING THE BIG PICTURE

PROLOGUE

Two days after Christmas, on the evening of December 27, 1997, I kissed my wife and three sons good-bye, walked out the door of our suburban Maryland home, and headed for Baltimore-Washington International Airport. From there I flew to New York to connect with a transcontinental flight bound for South Africa.

As the 747 lumbered down the runway, lifted slowly into the air, and banked out over the Atlantic I knew I had sixteen long hours to rest and review my notes and finalize plans for what I hoped and prayed might be a history-making endeavor.

I leaned my head back, closed my eyes, and tried to remember everything I had learned about the case of Joseph and Luka Banda. The Banda boys were eleven-month-old Siamese twins joined at the top of the head, facing opposite directions.

All Siamese twins joined at the head are known as *craniopagus* twins (for the Greek *cranio,* meaning "helmet," and *pagus,* meaning "fixed"). Before 1987, only seventy-nine such cases were recorded in five hundred years of medical history. During that time, thirty attempts had been made to separate them. Only seven of the sixty children survived unscathed. Thirty had died during or soon after the surgeries, and seventeen were neurologically impaired. Reports on the remaining cases were incomplete.

Despite the historically bleak prognosis for separating craniopagus Siamese twins, I hoped to accomplish something with these boys that had never been done before. I wanted to give both Joseph and Luka Banda a chance to live normal lives. But I knew that in a few short hours that chance, like their lives and their futures, would rest in my hands. Literally.

This was not the first time I had faced such a challenge. Despite the extreme rarity of this condition, the Banda twins were my third personal encounter with craniopagus Siamese twins in less than a decade. In 1987 I had received a great deal of publicity from the national and international media when I led a team of surgeons at Johns Hopkins in the successful separation of twins who had been attached at the back of the head. Both boys had survived, although one of them sustained significant neurological damage. (Patrick and Benjamin Binder's story was previously told in the book *Gifted Hands*.)

The second set of Siamese twins I encountered in 1994, three years before the Banda twins were even born. It is the story of those two girls that follows.

One

THE SOUTH AFRICAN TWINS — WHY?

ONE DAY IN JANUARY 1994 I received a long-distance call at work. "I think you need to talk to this gentleman," my office manager told me. So I picked up the phone.

"Dr. Benjamin Carson?" I could not place the accent, but having spent a year living and working in Australia, I immediately recognized the "proper" British influence in the man's careful enunciation.

"This is Dr. Carson," I told him.

"I am so pleased to speak to you, Dr. Carson," the man said. "My name is Dr. Samuel Mokgokong. I am professor of neurosurgery at the Medical University of South Africa at Medunsa." Now the accent fit.

"How may I help you?"

Dr. Mokgokong quickly explained that he had under his care a set of South African Siamese twins whose case seemed similar to that of the Binder twins, whom I had helped separate seven years earlier. Because of that successful surgery, Dr. Mokgokong was hoping I would be willing to consult with him and perhaps even participate in the separation of his patients.

I told him that I would be glad to consult with him if he could provide me with copies of his case records. That immediate response was prompted by more than just the usual professional courtesy. My experience with the Binder twins had not only been a major turning point, a defining moment in my professional career, it had been one of the greatest medical challenges I had ever known. At the time I had considered it a once-in-a-lifetime opportunity.

And now, seven years later, from a call out of the blue and half a world away, I receive word about a second set of craniopagus Siamese twins. Of course I was interested. But I was not at all sure just how involved I should be or could be in a case as demanding and complex as this on the other side of the world.

Dr. Mokgokong informed me he would be making a trip to the United States within the month and could bring all the necessary records for me to review. I agreed to meet with him at Johns Hopkins in Baltimore, and we set a tentative date for his visit.

And so the South African neurosurgeon left Johannesburg in the heat of summer in the Southern Hemisphere to make his mid-winter journey to North America. Everything about him—from his deep resonant voice to his quick smile—conveyed such a friendly openness that I couldn't help but like Sam Mokgokong from the start. Slightly balding, about forty, he stood two or three inches short of my six feet yet outweighed me by more than fifty pounds. I could not help thinking that given his build and personality, he would make a wonderful African Santa Claus—all he needed was a white beard.

We struck up an almost immediate friendship. When we began discussing his case, I was soon as impressed with him professionally as I was personally, for he asked the right questions and seemed to have arrived at most of the right conclusions already.

The South African twin sisters did indeed have many similarities with the Binder brothers. Nthabiseng and Mahlatse Makwaeba appeared smaller in the photos than the Binders had been, but they presented about the same degree of attachment at the back of their heads. Using the basic procedures we had followed with the Binder twins and drawing from the experience gained from that surgery, I believed there was a pretty fair chance both little girls could be saved.

Encouraged by my optimism, Sam asked if I would be willing to come to Medunsa to lead the team that would perform the operation.

I hadn't been sure how I would react to this invitation when he had first called me. The operation on the Binder twins had taken months of careful planning, and our team had been composed of the best medical personnel Johns Hopkins had to offer, many of whom I had known, worked with, and operated alongside for years. Dr. Mokgokong assured me of the professional caliber of his colleagues, but I knew there was no way I could have the same level of trust operating among strangers with whom I had no personal history — inside or outside of an operating room.

But there was another problem. When we had performed our unprecedented surgery on the Binder twins, Johns Hopkins Hospital, consistently voted the number-one medical facility in America, had placed its resources at our disposal. Would a hospital in Medunsa, South Africa, have what would be needed to pull off such a dangerous procedure? Did they even have all the equipment necessary?

Once again, Sam tried to reassure me. He insisted that whatever equipment they did not have, he would acquire — if only he could make it known that I had agreed to head the operating team. As flattering as that was, I still was not completely convinced.

The more we talked and the harder Sam tried to persuade me, the better I began to understand what was being asked of me. And why. Sam told me how he had first learned of my work. One of his professional mentors back in 1987, a neurosurgeon named Dr. Robert Lipschitz, had cared for a set of Siamese twins around the time the Binder case had received so much publicity. Sam had heard my name at that time because Dr. Lipschitz had called and consulted with me before attempting an operation to separate his patients.

I remembered because Dr. Lipschitz and I had spoken long distance on more than one occasion — both before and after his surgery following which one twin died and the other suffered significant neurological damage.

Sam admitted he had had no idea at the time that the "Dr. Benjamin Carson" his friend and mentor was consulting with "was also a black man." When he had learned of my racial heritage some years later, Sam said he had taken a special interest in me and my career, and he had shortly thereafter read my autobiography, *Gifted Hands*. He had grown up under apartheid—overcoming astronomical odds to get where he was professionally. So Sam had closely identified with the hardships I had experienced. He told me that he and many of his South African colleagues and students had also read my book and had found great inspiration in my story, my medical achievements, and my example.

I quickly realized my new friend had more than one motive for inviting me to South Africa. Yes, he valued my surgical expertise for his patients' sake. But Sam also was hopeful that a successful separation of the twins would put Medunsa on the medical map. He explained that as the "black medical school" in South Africa, Medunsa had long been the stepchild in the country's university system. Compared to the world-renowned university hospital in Capetown, where Dr. Christiaan Barnard pioneered heart-transplant surgery, Medunsa was unfairly perceived by many as a second-class medical institution where black South Africans trained but had achieved little, if anything, of note.

Sam felt certain that would change with the successful separation of these Siamese twins. "Then everyone in South Africa and around the world will see what we are capable of at Medunsa."

As if that were not enough, Sam admitted he also wanted to bring me to his country as an encouragement to the black South African medical community. He seemed to think just by coming to South Africa I could strike a blow against the oppression of apartheid by serving as a highly visible role model for capable young blacks throughout his country. Perhaps more of them might consider a career in medicine if they could see the example and hear the story of the black American neurosurgeon who had come to Africa in an attempt to make history.

By itself, the medical challenge alone was heavy enough. The risks would be high. The chance of a successful separation of the twins was far from certain. As to all the other, broader goals Sam had in mind, I didn't immediately know what to think.

So I decided to do what I always do when I face a new challenge. Whenever I encounter uncertainty in my professional or personal life, whenever I find myself in need of wisdom (which happens regularly), I pray. I told Sam I would pray about his offer and ask for God's guidance.

Actually, I had been praying about the idea all along. But after meeting Sam, my continued prayers resulted in a strong sense that I should make the trip—that I *needed* to go. I believed God not only wanted me to get involved in this case but that great things would happen as a result. I had felt such leading in my life before, but this time the sense of direction I received seemed particularly clear and strong. It was convincing enough that I told a man I had known just a few hours I would fly halfway around the world—to a country that officially condoned a societal system bent on oppressing people like me solely on the basis of skin color—and try to help him accomplish something that had never before been successfully done on the continent of Africa.

Once I told Sam I would go, there was not a doubt I had made the right decision. I believed God was in it. And he was going to be with us.

Sam was thrilled. He went home to South Africa with the list of equipment I thought we would need for the operation and with my suggestions for assembling and preparing the fifty- to sixty-person, multidiscipline medical team required. Sam and I talked by phone several times over the next few weeks. My own hectic life pace continued—with my teaching, speaking, and traveling, my weekly clinics, my routine hospital rounds, and twelve-hour days in surgery several times a week. But as plans slowly and surely fell into place in South Africa for a surgery we scheduled to take place in April 1994, I began to anticipate what looked like an incredible second "once-in-a-lifetime" opportunity.

WHEN I ARRIVED IN South Africa, Sam met my flight at the international airport in Johannesburg. He had bad news. The twins were sick. Sam believed their condition serious enough to warrant postponing the surgery.

None of the doctors in Medunsa was sure what was wrong. Based on symptoms, they suspected some sort of viral illness, but their consensus was that we should wait a couple of months to give the girls a chance to regain their strength before subjecting them to the trauma of such a difficult and dangerous surgery.

After examining the Makwaeba twins myself, I concurred. As frustrated as I was not to be able to do the surgery I had come to do, I soon saw the bright side. My short visit would give me the chance to get acquainted with the surgical team and discuss strategies face-to-face, and my presence certainly gave me a far greater sense of the significance this operation had in the hearts and minds of the South African medical community.

I also got to take a firsthand look at the facilities in Medunsa. They were far different from any American medical schools I had visited. The administration offices and most of the classrooms were housed in fairly modern, multifloored buildings of masonry construction. The campus projected an airy, open feel with wide grassy lawns and multiple courtyards around which snaked a maze of interconnected, single-story brick buildings that made up the hospital's various wards and departments.

The openness extended indoors as well. I saw no private rooms. All patients were cared for in large, open-air wards, which housed twenty to thirty beds each. While I had no doubt that the fresh air circulating through the open windows probably did much to facilitate good health, even the gentlest of breezes sometimes carried in whatever was in the air outside—dust, leaves, pollen, and the more-than-occasional flying or crawling bug. Even the Intensive Care Unit was as open as most general hospital wards would be in a typical American hospital.

Another thing struck: the incredible variety of pathology I witnessed in the course of making hospital rounds. In the wards I visited, I saw patients with aneurysms, extensive vascular malformations, a multitude of different tumors and congenital malformations—all just sitting or lying in beds waiting for surgery. I couldn't help thinking what a fabulous experience it would be for any young American surgeon to work in that environment for even a few short months— honing his or her skills, providing much needed health care, and garnering experience which would take a lifetime to accumulate back in the States.

Everywhere I went in that hospital I was impressed by the compassion and competency of the obviously dedicated and well-trained staff. Given the challenges they faced and the limitations they lived with, I was extremely impressed with the caliber of health care provided at Medunsa.

Although I returned home sooner than originally planned, I actually felt a greater sense of confidence for the rescheduled procedure in June. And my focus upon this case seemed to fill my thoughts that first week home even though I was slated to receive a great honor in the U.S. For a number of years the publishers of *Essence* magazine had annually recognized African-American women they judged to have made a significant and notable contribution to the world. In 1994, for the first time, African-American males would also receive the prestigious *Essence* Award. I was one of the men chosen to be so honored in a nationally televised ceremony.

My wife, Candy, and I flew to New York for the gala, black-tie affair held in the Paramount Theater. Sitting at the front that night, I looked back at the well-dressed crowd and saw that half of Hollywood had turned out for the occasion. Then, glancing around me at the other honorees—Rev. Jesse Jackson, movie director Spike Lee, actor Denzel Washington, and comedian Eddie Murphy—I could not help feeling strangely out of place and thinking, *What in the world am I doing here?* I was no famous politician or entertainer. I was just a doctor. True, hundreds of thousands of people had read my autobiography. Many others knew the story of this poor inner-city kid from Detroit, second son of a single mother who had believed in me so much that she gave everything she had in life to love and push me out of the world she knew to pursue a dream that took me first to Yale, then to medical school at the University of Michigan, and finally out into the exciting and rewarding world of medicine. It was also true that I had made a name for myself within my profession when I became Chief of Pediatric Neurosurgery at Johns Hopkins by the age of thirty-three. But I also realized that the world of pediatric neurosurgery makes up a tiny part of a medical universe that remains so small it seldom even registers as anything more than a faint flash of light on the great telescope of public attention and scrutiny. I enjoyed neither the reputation nor the recognition of my genuinely famous fellow awardees. *What am I doing here?*

As I asked myself that question I realized I probably would not have been sitting at that awards ceremony, and none of these people would have come to honor and recognize me that evening, were it not for my involvement in the separation of the Binder twins back in 1987. That one operation, more than any other event in my medical career, had catapulted me to new and surprising prominence in my profession. It had opened doors throughout the world medical community. It had led to professional and personal opportunities I had never dreamed possible and provided me a platform from which to address audiences I would never have been able to reach before.

Looking around that auditorium full of well-dressed celebrities, none of whom knew about my upcoming trip to South Africa, I thought about all the repercussions of the Binder surgery seven years earlier. I wondered, *Could something like that be about to happen again? Did God want to use another separation of Siamese twins to go beyond changing my life—beyond changing some piece of medical history—to help change a country?*

If I have learned anything in this life, it is that we should never underestimate what God can do if we just allow him to work. I could hardly wait to see what would happen on my return trip to Medunsa.

Unfortunately, when I arrived in South Africa that June, the health of the Makwaeba twins was worse than it had been several weeks earlier. The girls' cardiovascular condition was deteriorating so rapidly that we all felt surgery would be their only hope. As tenuous as their situation seemed, we had no choice but to separate before they both died.

The team was quickly assembled and informed of our intention to proceed. Due to the condition of our patients, the atmosphere in the operating room was unusually intense, and the stress level seemed particularly high. To add to that, we began the operation under the unblinking eye of an American network television camera whose crew had followed me to South Africa in hopes of getting some dramatic video for a profile they were planning.

The primary surgical team assisting me consisted of Sam, his colleague Dr. Rissick Gopal, and another neurosurgeon from the Baragwanas Hospital in Soweto. There was also a cardiovascular surgery team led by Dr. Lukas Mathala, as well as the team of anesthesiologists under the leadership of a Dr. Bohmala, a plastic surgery team, pediatricians, and a host of nurses assigned to assist in the various procedures. This was going to be such a complex undertaking that the hospital had invested a great percentage of its resources in the hopes that a successful outcome would help make Medunsa a major player throughout Africa for other complex, multi-discipline surgeries.

The operating rooms had already been specially equipped in anticipation of this surgery. They boasted brand new ventilators, many new surgical tools, plus state-of-the-art monitors for the anesthesiologists and the cardiovascular surgeons.

We spent a good deal of time setting up the surgical tables so that they could be pulled apart at the moment of separation to allow the two different teams to quickly surround the individual twins in order to begin closing their skulls and scalps. I had learned a rather frightening lesson during the operation on the Binder twins when we had depleted Johns Hopkins' entire supply of their blood type—using more than sixty units. So we stockpiled what we hoped would surely be an adequate supply for this surgery.

The operation actually began as the plastic surgeons moved in and began carefully removing the scalp expanders they had put in place months earlier. These silicone balloon-like devices had been inserted under the babies' scalps and gradually pumped up with saline solution injected from time to time. The idea was to slowly stretch the scalp until we would have enough of a skin flap to close the huge surgical wounds at the completion of the operation.

As soon as the plastic surgeons removed their expanders, our neurosurgical team stepped in. With the scalp flaps folded back and out of the way, we drilled a series of burr holes near the junction of the two skulls. Then using Leksell *ronjeurs* (a kind of handheld clip-perlike device) we began biting the bone away bit by bit in an attempt to free the skulls and leave only the soft attachments underneath intact. The bone proved extraordinarily bloody, which meant we spent a great deal of time trying to control the blood loss by plugging the burr holes with purified beeswax. Even so, several units of blood had to be transfused during the bony resection — and this was but the first and one of the simplest steps of this operation.

Only after the fused sections of skull had been cut away could we see that the underlying *dura* (the thick leatherlike protective cover over the brain itself) was also complexly connected between the twins.

As we began carefully cutting and separating the dura covering, we encountered extensive *venous lakes* (typical channels running between different layers of the dura that help drain the normal blood flow out of the organ) and multiple venous connections between the brains themselves. At that point, more than a dozen hours into the surgery, it became obvious that we could not continue the operation without taking the twins into a carefully controlled hypothermic cardiac arrest.

To do this the cardiovascular team had to perform a thoracotomy in which they hooked up each twin to a heart-lung bypass machine that would slowly drain and cool their blood — from around 95 degrees Fahrenheit down to 68 degrees. Such a level of hypothermia would bring the babies' metabolic functions to a near halt. That would allow us to keep the heart from pumping or the blood from flowing for roughly an hour without fear of further brain damage. Within that time we hoped to separate all the interwoven venous structures and reconstruct any necessary and separate veins. This sort of suspended animation only works with infants under eighteen months of age whose brains are still developing and are flexible enough to recover from such a traumatic shock. The operation on the Binder twins was the first time anyone had used a combination of hypothermia, circulatory bypass, and deliberate cardiac arrest to preserve brain tissue for such a procedure. It had worked well when we had tried it with the Binder boys, so we could only pray we would be as successful with the Makwaeba sisters.

We were finally able to sort out all the connections and carefully divide the shared venous structures during the allotted time the girls were on total arrest. But no sooner had we gotten the twins separated and began pumping back in the blood, at the fifteen-hour mark of the surgery, than the smaller twin died immediately. The cardiovascular surgeons described the heart in that child as a "flabby bag of muscle with no potential whatsoever for pumping blood."

At that point we diverted all our attention to the second child, and she seemed in pretty good shape when we completed the operation a few hours later. It was not long until she could move a little and even exhibited some facial and eye movement in recovery. While the outcome certainly was not what we had hoped for, there was considerable joy among the medical staff and on the part of the little girls' family that one of the twins had been saved.

A few hours after surgery, however, the second child began exhibiting seizure activity and experiencing serious electrolyte disturbances in her blood. While the Medunsa staff tried to maintain brave faces despite this discouraging development, all of us were pretty depressed when her condition steadily worsened until she also died two days later.

The resulting autopsy revealed that the second child had no significant kidney function. It turned out these twins had been completely symbiotic and were only able to survive as long as they had because they had been joined together. As they had grown, the one with the cardiac function did not have the ability to provide adequate circulation for both. That is why their condition had deteriorated so much in the weeks prior to surgery. In retrospect it was clear nothing we could have done would have saved either twin. But that news did little to comfort the family or blunt the terrible disappointment among the surgical team and the Medunsa medical community who had placed such high hopes on the outcome of this surgery.

We conducted a postoperative press conference with the national media who had been following the case closely, and the morning before I flew home I made an appearance on *Good Morning, South Africa*, a morning network news show much like our *Good Morning, America*. During my interview, I tried to explain what had happened, to let people know that the difference in outcome between this case and that of the Binder twins had nothing to do with the how or the where of this operation. But knowing that no hospital in the world could have saved those two little girls did nothing to raise my spirits or those of the South Africans who had been praying for our success.

I do not know that I have ever felt lower than I did as my plane lifted off that day from Johannesburg and headed back over the Atlantic toward New York. As we climbed up into the heavens I began formulating questions in my mind. Questions for God.

Why did you get me involved in a situation like this where there was never any possibility for success?

Why did you let me spend so much valuable time and energy in something that could not possibly work out?

Why would you provide an opportunity like this only to allow us to fail? Why?

I was tired and frustrated and confused and angry. The whole unfortunate experience made no sense.

Two

A SET OF TWINS FROM ZAMBIA

So, FOR THE NEXT two and a half years I wondered, *Why?*

Then in December of 1996, Sam Mokgokong contacted me. He said the Medical University of South Africa at Medunsa wanted to present me with an Honorary Doctorate during their commencement ceremonies at the end of the current school year. I told him I was honored and would happily accept that honor as well as his gracious offer to host my wife, Candy, and me when we came to South Africa.

Sam then heightened my anticipation with yet another call the following spring. He informed me that another set of craniopagus Siamese twins had been born in Zambia. The doctors there knew of our attempted separation of the South African twins at Medunsa three years earlier, so they had contacted Sam to ask his advice on the possibility of separating Joseph and Luka Banda. Sam had flown to Zambia to examine the twins himself, and he told me he felt they were good prospects for a successful separation.

Sam had also told the twins' doctors I would be back in South Africa again in a few weeks. "Now the Zambian government would like you and your wife to come to their country while you are in Africa so that you can examine these twins and see if you think they are candidates for surgery."

So as we made arrangements for a short stopover in Zambia on our return flight, I began to think the timing was more than coincidence. Incredibly, this would be my third encounter in less than ten years with craniopagus Siamese twins.

The flight from New York to Johannesburg seemed as long as ever, although having Candy with me made this trip much more enjoyable. The cabin service on our South African Airline flight was exceptional, as it had been on earlier trips—even before the end of apartheid. I did notice a few curious looks from other passengers, who were perhaps surprised to see a black couple in the first class cabin of a 747 bound for South Africa.

I knew a lot had happened in that country during the three years since my last visit. The official end of apartheid had made a subtle yet noticeable change in the atmosphere on the campus at the Medical University of South Africa at Medunsa. The black students we passed on the sidewalks seemed to hold their heads a bit higher and walked with an increased sense of purpose and confidence. I felt certain that this was more than my imagination.

As Sam took us on a quick tour of the hospital to introduce us to old and new friends, I realized things had changed for me as well since my last visit. The disappointment I had experienced in this place had been tempered by time. So when Sam proudly recounted the many lives since saved by the equipment the hospital had acquired for our failed surgery on those little girls, I was reminded once again of God's infinite ability to redeem the most negative experiences. He can redeem even our biggest mistakes and greatest weaknesses.

I had already been privileged to receive eighteen honorary degrees from a broad spectrum of institutions of higher learning throughout North America, but never had I felt prouder or more honored than that day when the Medical University of South Africa at Medunsa awarded me a Doctor of Medical Science. I certainly had never experienced a more enjoyable ceremony.

Though conducted in the formal British educational tradition, the medical school's commencement exercises had a distinctive African flavor that made for a colorful ceremony marked by considerable pomp and circumstance. Having experienced more than my share of somber academic programs, I enjoyed the involvement of a large and exceedingly enthusiastic audience. The graduation exercises in Medunsa felt like a true celebration.

From the time Candy and I began planning this trip, we had anticipated a second highlight of our visit to South Africa, a safari at Krueger National Park, a day's drive north of Medunsa.

The night before this adventure I remember praying and reminding God that Candy and I had only one day scheduled to visit Krueger National Park—a natural wonderland people come from all over the world to see. I told the Lord I would be forever grateful if he would bless us with an opportunity to observe a wide variety of wildlife in the short time we had allotted. Having been fascinated by wildlife ever since stories and pictures had first triggered a love of books and learning when I was a small boy, I had always dreamed of someday getting a personal look at some of the more exotic African animals in the wild. I never dreamed just how literally my prayer would be answered.

Not only did we encounter lions, elephants, giraffes, zebras, and other hoped for animals, we also spotted rarer species such as green mambas and black mambas. We witnessed such a fascinating range of wildlife behavior that our guide told us he could not remember ever having another single day like it. He said he saw things he had witnessed only a few times in all of his years working in the park. At one point he pulled our four-wheel-drive Land Rover to a halt right in the middle of a roaming troop of baboons.

Looking around at the fascinating but boisterous and rowdy creatures surrounding us, I immediately recalled a television special about baboons I must have seen on the Discovery Channel. I had been both impressed and amazed to hear the host of that program say that an adult baboon's jaws were powerful enough to bite through a human skull.

Having a certain working appreciation for the strength of the human skull, and having grown quite attached to my own—not to mention those of Candy, Sam, and his wife, Polan, sitting with me in our open-topped vehicle—I calmly inquired of our driver as to the wisdom of stopping in that spot at that time.

Our experienced guide smiled at my obvious uneasiness and confidently informed me that these wild animals would never bother us.

Someone had evidently forgotten to tell that to the baboons. Because he had no sooner offered his assurance of our complete safety than the entire troop of baboons closed ranks and began climbing onto our all-terrain vehicle. A couple of the bolder creatures ascended to the roof and began climbing right into the vehicle with us.

Fortunately, a very quick-thinking Sam tossed out several slices of sandwich bread we had brought along for a picnic. And when our hairy friends leapt from our vehicle in pursuit of this free snack, we sped away to safety.

When our safari ended, we realized the shared experience of excitement and danger had served to further strengthen the bonds of friendship Candy and I both felt for the Mokgokongs who drove us back to Johannesburg the next day and saw us off at the airport the day following.

When we made our scheduled stop in Lusaka, Zambia, we were met at the airport by Dr. T. K. Lambart, that country's only neurosurgeon. He escorted us to a large two-thousand bed children's hospital to meet Joseph and Luka Banda. These boys exhibited the one quality I had detected in every set of Siamese twins I have ever encountered: they suffered from an extreme case of cuteness.

Like the Binder twins, Joseph and Luka appeared healthy, if not robust. That was a promising sign. Extensive tests had already been conducted to make certain both boys had functioning hearts, lungs, stomachs, livers, and kidneys. Unlike the South African girls we had operated on in 1994, all the boys' major systems seemed to work normally and independently. Of that we were certain.

Joseph and Luka had been eating well and developing right on schedule. They could cry and smile and reach out to grasp nearby objects. They kicked and squirmed with such energy and enthusiasm that they would certainly have rolled over right on schedule if only they could have coordinated their movements and turned in the same direction at the exact same time.

These otherwise healthy and charming boys had only one significant problem. They were attached to each other at the top of their heads.

The exact cause of craniopagus twins still is not known. The most widely accepted thinking holds that the development of con-joined identical twins results from the fission of a single fertilized ovum—though the when, the how, or the why of the incomplete division are uncertain. A less popular theory has been proposed by other experts who believe such twins become reunited during the fourth week after fertilization when the two rapidly growing embryos make direct contact and for some reason adhere to each other.

How it happened no longer mattered to Joseph and Luka Banda. To understand the extent of what had happened, imagine taking a tennis ball in each hand and mashing them against one another until the spheres are compressed to the point where a major portion of their surfaces are pressed tightly against the other. That is something like what the tops of these boys' heads looked like.

The shape of the connection was basically tubular. But it was the extent of the fusion that most concerned me; it encompassed the entire width and breadth of the top of their heads. How much had the two brains themselves been compressed together? To what degree were they overlapped and entangled? To what extent were they now interconnected? While I remained fairly optimistic about the poten-tial for success, I could tell just by looking at the broad fusion of their skulls that we would have our work cut out for us in trying to separate them.

As I carefully examined the twins' heads, feeling along the entire perimeter of their skulls' junction, I tried to imagine what prob-lems we might encounter once we opened them up and got a look inside. Then, while turning the boys gently back and forth in order to gain different perspectives and form a more complete picture, I suddenly realized there just might be a way to answer some of the most important questions I had about the case long before we actually operated on these twins.

Months earlier some researchers from the Johns Hopkins radiology department had invited me to their lab for a fascinating demonstration. Working in partnership with design experts and programmers from a high-tech research department at the National University of Singapore, they were in the process of developing a 3-D visual-imaging system. They hoped their creation would someday enable surgeons to study cases, examine patients in absentia, and perhaps even refine their knowledge and skills by conducting virtual reality surgery on their computerized work station.

After demonstrating the idea, they asked me for suggestions as to how their research might be used in the field of neurosurgery. I told them I would give their impressive invention some thought, and I filed the idea in the back of my mind. Now, months later in a hospital located in the heart of another continent, I saw a terrific application for this cutting-edge technology.

I explained to my Zambian colleague what I had in mind and told him I would be back in touch as soon as I got home. I needed to find out from the Johns Hopkins radiology-research team what form of data we needed to feed into their model.

Dr. Lambart had originally contacted Medunsa because he knew none of the hospitals in Zambia were equipped for the kind of procedure his young patients would require. Indeed he had informed me that there was only one respirator available for the entire population of his hospital. Once again I had been impressed by the high quality of care provided despite the severe limitations facing so many competent and compassionate medical personnel in the Third World. And Dr. Lambart seemed thrilled to think such state-of-the-art technology would be available to benefit his patients.

During the ensuing months, this resourceful Zambian neuro-surgeon and Sam managed to provide all the data the research team and I needed—CAT scans, angiograms, and MRIs sent on magnetic tape that could be specially formatted for the research team to feed the data into their virtual workbench model. I do not begin to know how the whole process works; so there is no way I can explain it in layman's terms. We were not talking brain surgery here—at least not real surgery. I could explain that.

However it worked, I can say it was the next best thing to brain surgery—at least in terms of my preparation and planning for the scheduled operation on the Banda twins. In a Johns Hopkins research lab in Baltimore, Maryland, I could don a special set of 3-D glasses and stare into a small, reflective screen which then projected an image into space so that I could virtually "see" inside the heads of two little Siamese twins who were actually lying in a hospital on another continent. Using simple hand controls I manipulated a series of virtual tools. A turning fork or spoke could actually move the image in space—rotating the interwoven brains of these two boys to observe them from any and all angles. I could magnify the image in order to examine the smallest details, erase outer segments of the brain to see what lay hidden underneath, and even slice through the brains to see what different cross-sections would reveal about the inner structure of the brains. This allowed me to isolate even the smallest of blood vessels and follow them along their interior or exterior surface without difficulty or danger of damaging the surrounding tissue. All of which, of course, would be impossible in an actual operating room.

The chief benefit of all this was knowledge. I could observe and study the inner structure of the twins' brains before we opened them up and began the actual procedure on the operating table. I could note abnormalities ahead of time and spot potential danger areas—which promised to reduce the number of surprises we would encounter in the real operation.

The biggest challenge during the surgical separation of the craniopagus Siamese twins I had worked with and the most delicate and time-consuming aspect of the previous surgeries had been the sorting out of overlapping, interconnected, and shared blood vessels. It required a tedious and meticulous separation and closing off, cutting through and sometimes reconstructing a massive tangle of veins.

Each vein had to be isolated and taken down in the right order—as carefully as if you were defusing a bomb. Make even a small mistake and the resulting blood loss could flood the surgical field and make it impossible to locate and control the problem in time to prevent serious brain damage or death.

Being able to see, study, and memorize the vascular anatomy—particularly in the crucial structure around the brainstem, the ventricular system, and the skull base—proved an incredible advantage. I've since tried to explain the benefit this way: a normal human brain is perhaps the single most marvelous and complex piece in the great three-dimensional master puzzle of creation. When you press two such complex organs together, the problems of orientation are compounded almost beyond belief. Finding your way around the abnormal venous structures of craniopagus twins is like being a cab driver dropped into the middle of a foreign city you have never been to before, where you do not speak the language and cannot even read the road signs—and still being expected to do your job. This time I at least had a detailed road map to study before I got there. In fact, I felt almost as if I had successfully performed the operation already.

AND SO I HAD a sense of confidence when I boarded that flight to South Africa two days after Christmas in 1997. We had had six months to plan for the surgery since I had first examined the Banda twins in Zambia. They'd had six months to grow stronger and be transferred to Medunsa. Now all indications were that Joseph and Luka could hardly be better candidates for what was still considered a very delicate and desperate surgical procedure. Separation remained the only hope these precious little boys had for an acceptable quality of life.

When I finished replaying in my mind all that had happened to bring me to this point again, I opened my eyes, pulled a folder out of my briefcase, and looked once again at the most recent photo of Joseph and Luka. Then, setting the picture aside, I reviewed my case notes for the umpteenth time.

When I concluded that review I closed my eyes and leaned my head back again to rest and to pray. Everything else had been done.

After flying through the night across a half-dozen time zones, I arrived in Johannesburg late Sunday afternoon. Sam once again met my flight. He took me right to the hospital where we spent what was left of the day examining our young patients, speaking to their mother, and catching up on everything that had been happening in our personal and professional lives in the months since we had been on safari together at Krueger National Park. Later that evening — which was just early afternoon according to my personal biological clock — Sam drove me several miles out into the country to a resort hotel where someone had made reservations for me to stay.

Most of Monday, December 29, 1997, was spent meeting and getting acquainted with the surgical team — several of whom had participated in the unsuccessful surgery on the Makwaeba girls back in 1994. We reviewed the Banda case together, discussed basic strategies, and then walked through the entire procedure, answering questions and listening to comments from anyone who had anything to say.

That night in my room, thinking about the surgery that was scheduled to begin at 6:30 the following morning, I spent time in personal meditation and prayer. This was not an unusual occurrence. I am in the habit of praying each evening — to thank God for the blessings of that day and to ask his strength, presence, and wisdom for tomorrow. And I always make a special point of praying for the patients I will be operating on — and for their families. When I make my rounds to visit with my young patients the day before their scheduled surgeries, I routinely challenge their parents by saying something like this: "If you will say your prayers tonight, and you ask your families and everyone you know to pray, I promise I will say mine. And then none of us will have to worry as much tomorrow." To exceedingly anxious parents I'll sometimes add, "I know you're going to worry some anyway. But I find when everyone is praying, you don't have to worry quite as much."

On this particular night, alone in my hotel room, thousands of miles from home, I spent several hours praying for Joseph and Luka Banda, their devoted mother, the rest of their family back in Zambia, the entire medical team—and for myself, asking God to grant me wisdom in knowing exactly what I needed to do during this surgery.

After offering that prayer and examining the angiograms one last time, I felt strongly convicted that the abnormal, semicircular sinus that the twins shared should be divided in the middle, even though conventional wisdom would have suggested giving the entire structure to one twin and then sequentially dividing the other twin from it. I began to think that if we started by giving half of that sinus to each twin we might then be better able to determine what other venous structures went to which boy and then utilize the remaining half-sinus as the main drainage conduit for each respective infant.

The traditional thinking would have avoided dividing a shared sinus. The fear was that such an acute interruption of a major drainage channel might cause all the vessels draining into that system to back up, engorge and result in massive swelling, hemorrhage, and death. Such occurrences have presented frequent problems during previous attempts at separating craniopagus Siamese twins.

Taking a new approach seemed a very dicey proposition. I had seen in my own experience just how much engorgement and bleeding could occur. Where the Binder operation had used sixty units of blood, the Makwaeba sisters had required even more.

Still I remained strongly convinced we should try dividing the shared sinus along the midpoint this time.

I took a long time to fall asleep that night. Not because I was worried—after all, I'd said my prayers. But I was wondering what would happen if I took a chance on a new, untried strategy the next morning.

Three

AN IMPOSSIBLE OPERATION

By THE TIME SAM and I arrived in the operating room before dawn on Tuesday morning, I was pleasantly surprised to see the entire medical team already assembled. They were conducting a preoperative prayer meeting and gospel-song service under a large banner that stretched across one wall and declared, "GOD BLESS JOSEPH AND LUKA." I too prayed that he would.

No sooner did the prayer meeting conclude than a bustle of activity began throughout the room. But things quieted quickly when someone turned on the stereo system I had requested be provided so we could listen to classical and inspirational music as we worked.

Once the babies were prepped, draped, positioned, and anesthetized, the plastic surgeons spent considerable time practicing the turning of the twins back and forth from one side to the other. They wanted to make sure they would be able to repeat the procedure safely at the crucial points of the operation. When the surgery itself began at 6:30 A.M., there was a level of excitement and overall feeling of confidence that everything would go well.

The plastic-surgery team removed their scalp expanders and stretched the skin back to expose the skull for us. At that point all four of the neurosurgeons moved in to surround the table. I asked Dr. Lambart, the Zambian neurosurgeon and the boys' primary doctor, if he would like to drill the first burr hole near the midpoint of the skulls' junction.

He did the honors with a hand perforator, a hard and sharp bit that is held tightly in place with one hand and rotated slowly in the same manner as the kind of manual drill carpenters and woodworkers used in the days before electricity and Black & Decker. With that burr hole as my starting point I used ronjeurs to begin chipping away the bone in a long line from the front to the back of the skull in the twin facing me. I proceeded very slowly with this chipping away process known as a *craniectomy*, and others controlled the bleeding by carefully treating all the raw bone edges with purified beeswax.

Having studied all the scans and conducted the virtual reality surgery, I realized that the actual junction between the two boys occurred on a diagonal, rather than a horizontal, plane. So our next step in the surgery was to cut through the dura and extend that opening in both directions, using scissors, along a line parallel to that junction. The idea was to expose the underlying vascular structures of the brain itself while making certain we didn't sever anything prematurely. This portion of the surgery required several hours of tedious dissection on both sides of the joining plane with extensive venous and arterial structures being encountered, controlled, and divided as necessary.

We extended this process until we finally reached both the frontal and posterior poles, or end points, of the connection joining the heads. A three-centimeter-thick overlap of the leatherlike covering of the boys' brains which also joined them—the dural reflection—was then cut midway, with half being reflected to one twin and half to the other. That decision was made according to how many and which blood vessels appeared to be associated with each twin. While there were numerous bridging veins running in opposite directions, I felt those could be sacrificed in a sequential manner, with great care being taken to observe the brain as each one was shut down, in order to detect whether or not any congestion and swelling occurred.

Toward the posterior pole of Joseph, who was facing me, and thus the anterior pole for Luka, we encountered a vascular area so complex that the veins looked like a huge tangled serving of spaghetti. We made the decision not to tackle that challenge until later in the surgery. Working instead with surgical spatulas, we lifted and separated the exposed brain tissue itself where the two boys' brains had actually adhered together.

At that point we neurosurgeons decided to temporarily sew the skin flap closed and take a break while the plastic surgeons flipped the babies over. Then they had to re-prep and re-drape the new field so we could repeat the entire process in reverse on the opposite side. While that took place, our entire neurosurgical team retreated to a conference room just down the hall from the operating suite, where we sat down to rest and eat a meal the "medical sisters," or nurses, had prepared for us.

While we ate, we could watch the progress in the operating room via closed-circuit video. But mostly we discussed what we had seen so far and agreed on what we planned to do next. On more than one occasion Sam had exclaimed to me, "I cannot believe how meticulous you are with each blood vessel." But I was convinced that such care was going to be crucial. And indeed there had been such little blood loss to this point we were all feeling extremely optimistic.

After lunch we spent all afternoon and much of the evening essentially repeating what we had done on the other side that morning, the major difference being that now we faced the side on which the joining of the boys' dura contained that abnormal sinus—which I'd been thinking and praying so much about the night before.

That structure did indeed appear less developed at the center than it did toward the poles. So I made the decision to proceed with the novel approach I felt I'd been led to consider. Using Weck clips and cautery to first pinch the sinus closed and control the bleeding, I cut through the dural reflection across the midline.

The clips held and bleeding remained minimal over the next few hours. We took down numerous additional blood vessels while allowing the part of the dura containing each half of the sinus to flap toward the respective twin that seemed to have the most superficial drainage associated with it.

Finally we were ready to tackle the less troublesome pole where the underlying venous structure merely resembled a *small* pile of spaghetti. After several more hours spent separating and taking down those engorged and entangled blood vessels, we finally finished at that first pole.

Now it was time to face the task we had put off to last — that massive tangle of blood vessels connecting the brains, which now looked even more imposing and hopeless than it had seemed when we had still been relatively fresh early that morning.

In addition to the huge knot of blood vessels, we encountered venous lakes or pools of blood within the dura that appeared to be under such pressure they threatened a massive hemorrhage at the slightest mistake with even the tiniest of veins. At home, in my own operating room at Johns Hopkins I wouldn't have dreamed of attempting such dangerous and delicate work without the use of my extremely powerful, $350,000 operating microscope. All I had there at Medunsa was simple loop magnification and my headlight.

When we reached the nineteen-hour mark I still could not see the end. Exhausted and increasingly discouraged, we closed the skin flap over that second side and took another break while the plastic-surgery team rotated the boys yet another time. I wanted a different angle on this remaining polar junction.

Collapsing into the chairs around the conference room table, I called in all the medical personnel who weren't needed in the operating room to discuss the status of the operation and share ideas. Everyone looked defeated. Spirits sagged and doubt registered on many of the faces.

"Perhaps we should consider stopping the operation at this point," I said. I wondered aloud if we should simply close up the wounds and give the boys and our medical team a chance to recover and regain the strength to go on. In the meantime, maybe we would even come up with a better strategy for solving the monster mess at the remaining pole. "What do you think?" I asked the assembled team.

Working our way around the room, everyone agreed about what we should do — and that was *not* to stop. We should go on. They told me they honestly didn't think they had the capability required to keep the boys alive and healthy in their current state of partial separation. As dangerous as it looked to proceed at this point, the feeling was virtually unanimous that to do anything else would be, in effect, a death sentence.

Given that verdict, I realized we had no choice but to press on. *Whatever will happen will happen.* As we walked back down the hall to the operating room, however, I began praying desperately that God would take over and simply use me to accomplish what only he could do.

I recalled one of the Bible verses I had read just the night before. In the fourteenth chapter of John's gospel, verses 12 and 13, Jesus made a rather remarkable promise to his followers. "I tell you the truth, anyone who has faith in me will do what I have been doing. He will do even greater things than these, because I am going to the Father. And I will do whatever you ask in my name, so that the Son may bring glory to the Father."

When we reentered the OR and stood again over those little boys, I prayed in Jesus' name that God would simply take over the operation. Since the Scriptures don't tell about Jesus ever separating Siamese twins, I thought this probably qualified as one of those "greater than these" things he promised we could do.

So that was what I kept praying as I began work on the engorged vascular structure that still stared us in the face. At home I would have had my operating microscope, an array of micro-instruments to work with, and a special operating chair with adjustable platforms to support and brace my arms and hands. Here I had only a scalpel with which I began painstakingly cutting between the transparently thin walls of those engorged vessels before ever so gingerly pulling them apart.

Despite the exhaustion that had almost paralyzed me a short time earlier, I now sensed a remarkable steadiness in my hands. I felt a strange calm, an almost detached awareness—as if I were merely watching my hands move and someone else had actually taken over the surgery.

I can't count the number of times during my surgical career when I've successfully completed some particularly difficult surgery, only to have a parent or some family member in the waiting room inform me that they, and everyone they knew, had been praying for me. And I could honestly tell them that I had genuinely felt that support. I have repeatedly experienced the undeniable and often tangible effects of prayer.

But I don't know that I have ever experienced anything quite like what happened in the Medunsa operating room that day. One after another, more than a hundred interconnected veins were isolated, separated, clipped off, or reconnected. When I separated the very last vein connecting Joseph and Luka, the stereo system at that very moment, began playing the "Hallelujah Chorus" from Handel's *Messiah*. I suspect every single person in that OR felt goosebumps and knew that something remarkable had taken place. And it was not our doing.

Twenty-five hours of surgery had passed. But there was no time to celebrate yet as the surgical tables were quickly pulled apart and we immediately subdivided into two teams of surgeons — one for each twin.

We still had a lot of work to do. But all of the neurosurgeons, despite our growing fatigue, were absolutely jubilant. Neither of the brains exhibited any serious swelling and there had been remarkably little blood loss to this point. We had used less than four units of blood for the entire operation.

Even more encouraging was the fact that we could see no remaining engorgement of any of the blood vessels. That meant circulation in both brains had been successfully restored and appropriate new pathways had clearly formed. There seemed to be every reason to believe Joseph and Luka had not only survived the surgery, but that both boys might actually wake up to live full and completely normal lives.

That prospect was almost too exciting to think about as we worked to close the open wounds and patch the protective covering of the dura with pieces of bovine pericardium (the heart-lining of a cow). That finally done, our neurosurgical team retreated once more to the conference room where, even before the plastic surgeons closed the scalps, we fell fast asleep sitting in our chairs.

Once the plastic surgeons finished their work, we returned to the OR and were absolutely flabbergasted to find one of the twins with his eyes open and gripping his endotracheal tube with both hands—trying to pull it out. By the time the boys reached the intensive care unit, the other twin was doing the exact same thing. After twenty-eight hours of surgery this was astounding!

Congratulatory phone calls from all over the country already flooded the hospital switchboard. Our entire surgical team had to be escorted across the campus for a hastily called press conference. The outdoor courtyards were packed with students and hospital staff singing and dancing in a massive, spontaneous celebration of joy, and everyone we encountered along the way wanted to shake our hands or pat our backs.

The press conference was jammed with television and radio reporters who had been at the hospital covering the story since the surgery began the previous morning. They had been filing hourly updates to their stations throughout the country. Millions of South Africans had followed this story in much the way the American public had responded to the McCaughey septuplets when they had been born the month before.

The story of the Banda boys had fascinated all of South Africa. Now the entire country wanted to celebrate the wonderful outcome of their surgery.

I spent a few minutes answering reporters' questions. The other doctors also took a turn. The boys' mother even made an appearance—a happier woman I have never seen. Hospital officials made official statements, and the Zambian ambassador delivered his country's official thanks to everyone involved. He told us we had been the subjects of prayer among all Zambian people, but particularly the prayers of his country's president and first lady. The ambassador invited us all to a special dinner of thanksgiving and celebration the next day in the Zambian embassy.

Unfortunately, I had to decline his invitation. My flight home would be leaving later that evening. I expected to be home in Maryland by the time the Zambian ambassador served the main course. In the meantime I was suddenly too exhausted to want to celebrate or to do anything but collapse in a bed.

Sam volunteered to drop me off back at my hotel to catch a couple hours of sleep before I had to pack my bags and head for the airport. It was mid-afternoon on Wednesday, New Year's Eve, when I reached the hotel I had last seen before dawn the day before. After saying good-bye to Sam and walking toward the lobby door, I thought the place seemed strangely quiet and dark. No one seemed to be inside either. I rang the bell at the front desk and waited. Nothing happened.

I wanted nothing but my room key and a little peace and quiet. But not this much quiet.

Suddenly a policewoman appeared at the front door. When she spotted me she reacted with surprise. "How did you get in?" she wanted to know.

"I walked in the front door," I told her. "I'm a guest here."

"That's impossible," she replied, looking me over suspiciously. "The hotel is closed for the holiday."

"Closed?" As surprised as I was to hear that, it explained why everything was deserted. "I didn't know," I told the officer. "I left early yesterday morning and didn't return last night. I've been in surgery for twenty-eight hours, and I just want to get a little sleep. I need to at least get into my room to collect my luggage because I have to catch a flight out of the country tonight."

A light dawned on the officer's face. She smiled broadly and asked, "You're that American doctor who operated on the Siamese twins aren't you?" By the time I began to nod she was shaking my hand and telling me to wait right there. She placed a quick call to the hotel's owner who rushed over within minutes, reopened the hotel, gave me my room key, and graciously promised to personally see that no one disturbed me until I needed to leave for the airport.

My sleep was short but sweet. And I knew I would be able to get a lot more on the flight home. Which I did.

But not before I scanned the headlines and began reading the account of the surgery in the special edition newspaper I picked up in the airport on the way to my gate:

LENGTHY OP FOR SIAMESE TWINS
Doctors confident intricate procedure to remove bone and separate brains a success

Zambian Siamese twins Luka and Joseph Banda, joined at the top of their heads, underwent a marathon operation...

Too tired to focus on the words, I set the paper down and closed my eyes. And as the soaring jumbo jet carried me home through the night toward the dawning of a whole new year, I could not help thinking how different this return flight was from the sad return flight from South Africa after the unsuccessful surgery in 1994. This time I felt like serenading my fellow passengers with my own rendition of Handel's *Hallelujah* Chorus in thanksgiving. Three-and-a-half years earlier I had had nothing but angry questions to launch toward heaven.

I had focused on the failure because I had not yet acquired the wisdom necessary to attain a better perspective. I had been too close to the experience to realize I needed that wisdom and perspective in order to see, let alone understand and appreciate, the Big Picture.

Four

GETTING THE BIG PICTURE

A COUPLE WEEKS AFTER returning home, I received word that the Banda boys had amazed their doctors by already beginning to crawl. For Joseph and Luka, the achievement of this simple developmental task, physically impossible before the surgery, convinced all of us that these two amazing little boys were well on their way to full and normal lives.

I received that wonderful news right about the time I flew to Birmingham, Alabama, where I had been asked to deliver the keynote speech at an annual convention for the executive directors of all the United Way Campaigns from more than 1,500 cities and towns across America.

Almost every week I am invited to speak somewhere. I have spoken in front of elementary school children crowded into assembly halls, to corporate leaders at business conventions, in church worship services, and before the most powerful politicians in our land at the National Prayer Breakfast in Washington, D.C. The audiences vary. But my basic message remains the same.

I always tell a little about my own experience and some of the biggest lessons I have learned over the years. I invariably try to encourage my listeners to make better use of the potential in the incredible human brains they have been given — even as I offer my own perspective on what is truly important in life. In one way or another I always seem to be talking about what I am writing about here.

Before I spoke that afternoon in Alabama, I actually spent several hours sitting in my hotel room beginning to outline this very book. And when it came time for me to walk across the street to the Birmingham Civic Center where the United Way conference was being held, I planned to touch on some of the same themes.

After a warm introduction by a United Way executive from my home state of Maryland, I walked out onto one of the most unusual convention hall stages I have ever seen. The entire platform had been designed to look like a working home kitchen. Instead of a podium in front of me there was a countertop. To one side was another counter with a built-in range. Wall cabinets mounted around a full-sized refrigerator served as my backdrop.

This unusual set helped underscore the conference theme: "Recipes for Success." So as I looked out at the television cameras and into the faces of the men and women sitting around the tables spread across the hall, I knew where I needed to start and where I wanted to take this group of people to give them at least a glimpse of *the Big Picture*.

IN MY BEGINNINGS

I BEGAN BY TELLING my audience:

"It's a great pleasure to be here today, with people like you who have discovered the joy of sharing with others and volunteering to try to improve the lives of other people. That is something that has always been very important to me — especially in making a career choice. In fact, it's why the first thing I ever seriously considered as a vocation was being a physician.

"That dream started when I was eight years old. At church I used to listen to the mission stories that frequently featured missionary doctors. They were people who, at great personal sacrifice, would go across the world taking not only physical but mental and spiritual healing to people. It seemed the most noble thing anyone could ever do. So I determined that was what I would become. I clung to that dream from the time I was eight until I was thirteen.

"At that time, having grown up in dire poverty, I decided I'd rather be rich. So the missionary doctor was out. I would be a psychiatrist instead.

"I didn't know any psychiatrists, but on television they all looked very rich. Have you ever noticed that? They all seem to live in fancy mansions, drive Jaguars, and work in big plush offices. And all they have to do is talk to crazy people all day.

"Since it seemed I was doing that anyway, I thought, *This is going to work out extremely well.* I started reading *Psychology Today*, majored in psychology in college, and took advanced psych in medical school. That's when I started meeting a lot of psychiatrists. I probably don't need to say anymore about that. (Actually, some of my best friends are psychiatrists.)

"I discovered what real-life psychiatrists do is quite different from what is portrayed on television. So I had to spend a little time analyzing myself and rethinking my life direction. I began asking myself, *What is it that I really ought to be doing? What am I really good at?* I started seriously evaluating my gifts and talents—an important step when choosing a career.

"I thought, *I'm really good at things that require eye-hand coordination. I'm a very careful person. I never knock things over and say, 'Oops.'* I loved to dissect things when I was a kid growing up; if there was a dead animal or a bug around, I knew what was inside. And I developed a fascination and love for the human brain during all those years studying psychology. Putting all this together I concluded, *I would make a fabulous brain surgeon!*

"That's how I came up with the idea to go into neurosurgery."

BRAIN SURGERY FOR DUMMIES

OF COURSE, IF YOU had seen me as a youngster and someone had told you that this guy would go on to be a brain surgeon, you might have laughed yourself to death. I was perhaps the worst student you can imagine. In fact, my nickname was *Dummy*."

Many people in my Birmingham audience chuckled at that. Lest they think I was merely exaggerating, I quickly summarized for them the story I've already told at length in my autobiography *Gifted Hands*.

"I remember once having an argument with several of my classmates over who was the dumbest person in the class. It really wasn't much of an argument. Everyone agreed it was me. But when somebody tried to extend that argument to who was the dumbest person in the world, I took exception. We debated vigorously about that.

"The teacher gave us a math quiz later that day. As usual I got a zero. And back in those days, you passed your test to the person behind you, and they would correct it as the teacher read out the answers. After you received your graded paper back, you had to report your score, out loud, when the teacher called your name.

"Sitting in my seat that day, I stared in despair at the big goose egg at the top of my paper. I began to wonder how in the world I would give the teacher my score without letting all those kids I'd been arguing with know I made a zero.

"I began to scheme. I thought, *Maybe if I mumble, she will misinterpret what I say*. So when the teacher called my name, I softly muttered, 'Nnnne.'

"The teacher exclaimed, 'Nine! Benjamin, you got nine right? How wonderful! Class can you see what Benjamin has done? Didn't I tell you if you just applied yourself you could do it. Oh, I am so happy! This is a wonderful day.' And she ranted and raved for about five minutes.

"The test had thirty questions—but nine right was so much better than my usual grade that the teacher went on and on.

"Finally the girl behind me couldn't take it. She stood up and said, 'He said, "None!"' The rest of the kids just roared at that and the teacher was so embarrassed she just sat down. And if I could have disappeared into thin air, never to be heard from again in the history of the world, I would gladly have done so.

"But I couldn't. I had to sit there and act like it didn't bother me—even though it did. Not enough to make me study, but it did bother me. Significantly. I remember my midterm report card in that class. I was doing so poorly I failed almost every subject.

"My poor mother was mortified. Here she was, with a third-grade education, working two or three jobs at a time as a domestic, cleaning other people's houses, knowing that life didn't hold much for her. And seeing my brother and me going down the same road.

"She didn't know what to do. So she prayed and asked God to give her wisdom. What could she do to get her young sons to understand the importance of education so that they could determine their own destinies?"

A MOTHER'S ANSWER

God gave her the wisdom — though my brother and I didn't think it was all that wise. It was to turn off the television. From that point on she would let us watch our choice of only two or three television programs during the week. With all that spare time, we were to read two books a week from the Detroit Public Library and submit to her written book reports. Which she couldn't read. But we didn't know that.

"I was extraordinarily unhappy about this new arrangement. All my friends were outside, having a good time. I remember my mother's friends coming to her and saying, 'You can't keep boys in the house reading. Boys are supposed to be outside playing and developing their muscles. When they grow up, they'll hate you. They will be sissies. You can't do that!'

"Sometimes I would overhear this and I would say, 'Listen to them, Mother.' But she would never listen. We were going to have to read those books.

"Sometimes, when I tell this story, people come up to me afterwards and ask, 'How was your mother able to get you to read those books? I can't get my kids to read or to ever turn off the television or Nintendo.'

"I just have to chuckle and say, 'Well, back in those day, the parents ran the house. They didn't have to get permission from the kids.' That seems to be a novel concept to a lot of people these days.

"At any rate, I started reading. And the nice thing was my mother did not dictate what we had to read. I loved animals, so I read every animal book in the Detroit Public Library. And when I finished those, I went on to plants. When I finished those, I went on to rocks because we lived in a dilapidated section of the city near the railroad tracks. And what is there along railroad tracks, but rocks? I would collect little boxes of rocks and take them home and get out my geology book. I would study until I could name virtually every rock, tell how it was formed, and identify where it came from.

"Months passed. I was still in fifth grade. Still the dummy in the class. Nobody knew about my reading project.

"One day the fifth grade science teacher walked in and held up a big shiny black rock. He asked, 'Can anybody tell me what this is?'

"Keep in mind that I never raised my hand. I never answered questions. So I waited for some of the smart kids to raise their hands. None of them did. So I waited for some of the dumb kids to raise their hands. When none of them did, I thought, *This is my big chance.* So I raised my hand ... and everyone turned around to look. Some of my classmates were poking each other and whispering, 'Look, look, Carson's got his hand up. This is gonna be good!'

"They couldn't wait to see what was going to happen. And the teacher was shocked. He said, 'Benjamin?'

"I said, 'Mr. Jaeck ... that's obsidian.' And there was silence in the room. Because it sounded good. But no one knew whether it was right or wrong. So the other kids didn't know if they should laugh or be impressed.

"Finally the teacher broke the silence and said, 'That's right! This is obsidian.'

"I went on to explain, 'Obsidian is formed after a volcanic eruption. Lava flows down and when it hits water there is a super-cooling process. The elements coalesce, air is forced out, the surface glazes over, and ...'

"I suddenly realized everyone was staring at me in amazement. They couldn't believe all this geological information spewing from the mouth of the dummy. But you know, I was perhaps the most amazed person in the room, because it dawned on me in that moment that I was no dummy.

"I thought, *Carson, the reason you knew the answer is because you were reading those books. What if you read books about all your subjects — science, math, history, geography, social studies? Couldn't you then know more than all these students who tease you and call you a dummy?* I must admit the idea appealed to me — to the extent that no book was safe from my grasp. I read everything I could get my hands on. If I had five minutes, I had a book. If I was in the bathroom I was reading a book. If I was waiting for the bus I was reading a book.

"Within a year and a half, I went from the bottom of the class to the top of the class — much to the consternation of all those students who used to tease me and call me Dummy. The same ones would come to me in seventh grade to ask, 'Hey, Benny, how do you work this problem?' And I would say, 'Sit at my feet, youngster, while I instruct you.'

"I was perhaps a little bit obnoxious. But after all those years it felt so good to say that to those who had tormented me.

"The important point here is that I had the same brain when I was still at the bottom of the class as I had when I reached the top of the class.

"The difference was this: in the fifth grade, I thought I was dumb so I acted like I was dumb, and I achieved like a dumb person. As a seventh grader I thought I was smart, so I acted and achieved accordingly. So what does that say about what a person thinks about his own abilities? What does this say about the importance of our self-image? What does it say about the incredible potential of the human brain our Creator has given us?"

THE INCREDIBLE HUMAN BRAIN

THINK ABOUT IT. No computer on earth can come close to the capacity of the average human brain. This brain that we all have is a tremendous gift from God—the most complex organ system in the entire universe. Your brain can take in two million bytes of information per second. If this room were completely full and ten times larger than it is, I could bring one of you up here on stage and have you look out at the crowd for one second and lead you away. Fifty years later I could perform an operation, take off the cranial bone, put in some depth electrodes, stimulate the appropriate area and this person could not only remember where everyone was sitting, but what they were wearing.

"That's how amazing and complex the human brain is. It's literally mind-boggling if you study the human brain. Yet we have people walking around talking about what they can't do.

"How many of you remember what you had for lunch today? Let me see your hands. Okay. That's pretty good for a group at this time of day.

"Let's think about what your brain had to do when I asked that question. First of all the sound waves had to leave my lips, travel through the air into your external auditory meatus, travel down to your tympanic membrane, set up a vibratory force which traveled across the ossicles of your inner ear to the oval round windows, generating a vibratory force in the endolymph, which mechanically distorts the microcilia, converting mechanical energy to electrical energy, which traveled across the cochlear nerve to the cochlear nucleus at the ponto-medullary junction, from there to the superior olivary nucleus ..."

The audience began to applaud as I tried to race through this recitation at the speed of an auctioneer. I held up my hand and said, "Wait a minute. We've got a ways to go." And then I continued.

"... ascending bilaterally up the brain stem through the lateral lemniscus, to the inferior colliculus and the medial jeniculate nucleus, across the thalamic radiations to the posterior temporal lobes to begin the auditory process, from there to the frontal lobes, coming down the tract of Vicq d'Azur, retrieving the memory from the medial hippocampal structures and the mammillary bodies, back to the frontal lobes to start the motor response at the Betz cell level, coming down the cortico-spinal tract, across the internal capsule into the cerebral peduncle, descending down to the cervicomedullary decussation into the spinal cord gray matter, synapsing, going out to the neuromuscular junction, stimulating the nerve and the muscle so you could raise your hand.

"Of course, that's the simplified version. I didn't want to get into all the inhibitory and coordinating influences or we would be here all day talking about that one thing.

"Your brain can do all that and you barely have to think about it, and it can be doing multiple, more complex things simultaneously. So with a brain like that, why would anyone ever utter the words, 'I can't'?

"Yet we live in a society where "I can't-ism" is rampant. We live in a culture where our young people aren't grasping the importance of education.

"The United States became a great nation built on industrial and agricultural might. We could outproduce anybody. But an interesting revolution has occurred in all of our lifetimes; we have moved from the industrial age to the information age. Now information more than industry has become the basis for power."

TROUBLE AHEAD

THINKING ABOUT OUR ARRIVAL in the information age was what alarmed me a few years ago when I read about a survey conducted to measure the ability of students in twenty-two nations to solve math and science problems. America ranked number twenty-one out of twenty-two.

"That should concern us all as we enter this information age. With scores like this, how can we ever expect to maintain our leadership position in the world?

"I have a lecture series at Johns Hopkins where we bring in seven to eight hundred school kids each month. I talk to them about medicine, neurosurgery, what I was like at their age, and their potential. Usually, near the end of our time together, I stop and ask them questions before I give them the opportunity to ask me questions.

"I ask, 'How many of you can name five NBA players?' All the hands go up. Even the girls. So I ask, 'Who can name for me five movie stars?' Not a problem in the world. 'Five singers?' No problem.

" 'How about five Nobel Prize winners?' Forget it. It's not gonna happen.

" 'What about the capital of Malaysia?' Can't do it.

" 'What's a microprocessor?' I asked not too long ago. One young fellow out of eight hundred raised his hand. He was so proud of himself. I said, 'Okay, tell us, what is it?'

"He said, 'A microprocessor is a tiny processor.' And that was the extent of his knowledge on the subject. Extraordinarily superficial knowledge. And you know, this is what we must battle, all of us who have had the opportunity and benefit of education.

"What are we fighting against in our culture? Look at what's emphasized. Sports. Entertainment. Lifestyles of the rich and famous. The very same things that other great nations in history became enamored with—before their falls. Greece. Rome. Egypt. Go back and read their histories—they did exactly the same things.

"I believe that it is possible for people and cultures to learn from historical mistakes. It's a difficult thing to do. But it is possible. We don't have to follow the same pathway. We can break out of that mold. But it's going to require a lot of people—concerned individuals like the ones sitting in this room—not only realizing their own potential but feeling a responsibility toward others, to help guide them into the right forms of thinking, to help them see the Big Picture."

That was only the first part of what I said in Birmingham that day.

Five

SEEING THE BIG PICTURE

LOOKING OUT OVER THAT convention audience of United Way directors from all over America, I thought of many other things I wanted to say, many more parts of the Big Picture I wanted to highlight for them.

"You may think that once I began to glimpse my own potential and what the future could hold, that life would be good to me and I would just zoom right to the top. Wrong!

"I had another problem. When I got to high school, I ran into perhaps the worst thing a young person can encounter. It's called *peers*. Negative peers. P−E−E−R−S. That stands for People who Encourage Errors, Rudeness, and Stupidity. And that is exactly what they did."

CRIMES OF FASHION

THEY TOLD ME, 'CARSON, you gotta wear these clothes.' In those days it was the Italian knit shirts and sharkskin pants. Some of you older guys may remember the sharkskins—you turn one way they look green, turn the other way and they're blue. Thick and thin socks, alligator shoes, stingy brim hats. Sounds like a clown suit now, but it was cool then.

"Isn't it nice that young people today don't concern themselves with fashion any more? Or at least you wouldn't know it by looking.

"I remember being on an elevator not long ago with an elderly woman who was quite properly dressed. The elevator stopped. Two young men got on and they had on these baggy pants. You've seen these pants. You don't wear them around your hips, you wear them around your thighs. It looks like you could fly in them.

"This elderly woman was very concerned. She said, 'Young men, I believe your pants are coming off.' And they looked at her and said, 'Dey s'poseda look like dat.'

"I could barely contain myself until the elevator stopped on my floor and I got off. It was so funny. And yet it wasn't. Because these young men don't have a clue. Where did that fashion come from? It came from the state penitentiary. You see, in prison men are not allowed to wear belts—so consequently their pants hang down. One day someone said, 'Let's make a fashion out of this. All we have to do is say that it's cool and it'll sell.' And it did.

"You know, the nice thing is that women are a lot smarter than men when it comes to fashion—right? They would never fall for anything like that—would they? You don't see them walking around with those baggy pants do you? Well, I beg to differ. It just takes a little different form.

"Think back with me a few years. Some fashion moguls and clothing business people got together and they said, 'We're so powerful we can make people wear anything we want. So to see how far we can take this, let's have some fun, and make some money at the same time.' So they go out and recruit these skinny little models that look like they just escaped from a concentration camp. (First, they convinced women they are supposed to look like that.) And then they said, 'Let's put these jeans on these models and tell people they are *high fashion* jeans.'

"Now if you've ever been to Malaysia you know about all the jean factories they have there. They manufacture jeans by the ship-load. They sell some to Yves St. Laurent who charges $500, and they sell some to K-Mart who sells them for $15.

"The fashion moguls said, 'Let's make these glamour jeans. But wait a minute. Let's rip holes in the jeans. Then we can put our models on the front of *Cosmopolitan* with these holey jeans, and we'll tell people it's sexy.' Then someone added, 'Let's charge more for the ones with holes in them than we do for the ones without holes. And I bet people will still buy them.'

"Were they right? Of course they were. People will buy anything that someone tells them is fashionable.

"How is that engaging that sophisticated brain that we were talking about?

"What about the young men with the gym shoes? You've seen these gym shoes haven't you? Fifty dollars for one pair. You've seen that?"

As is always the case when I use this example in a speech, people in the audience began calling out higher prices. So I respond ...

"Oh, a hundred dollars? One hundred and fifty? For one pair? Actually I knew that. I just wanted to see if you knew that." And everybody laughed.

A FOOLISH EQUATION

I THINK THIS IS fascinating, because in 1994 my wife Candy and I went to South Korea. And I found out that South Koreans don't seem to be obsessed with sports and entertainment the same way Americans are. They are more enamored by intellectualism.

"When I was there, just by coincidence, my picture was on that month's cover of the South Korean edition of *Reader's Digest*. Now there's no way in the world my picture is ever going to be on the cover of, say, *Ebony* or *Jet* magazine—unless I learn how to bounce a ball or sing rap music. But things are very different over in Korea.

"You remember that survey that said American students ranked twenty-one out of twenty-two when it came to math and science? Know who was number one? South Korea. I found out something else very interesting.

"South Korea is where they make many of those gym shoes. For six dollars a pair. Do you find that as fascinating as I do? They make the shoes for six dollars; we buy them for a hundred-and-fifty. They're number one; we're number twenty-one.

"Somewhere in that equation is a fool. And I don't think you have to be a brain surgeon to figure out where the fool is.

"Some basketball player will stand in front of a television camera, shoot a twenty-five-foot jump shot, point to his shoes, and say, 'That's why I can do it.' If you believe that, you deserve to pay a hundred-and-fifty dollars for a six-dollar pair of gym shoes. Because you are not using the tremendous brainpower that our Creator endowed us with. And this is the kind of message we need to get across to our young people today."

THE DREAMS THAT COME IN DIVERSITY

At this point I changed course — to another subject I wanted to address with this audience.

"If you really want to be inspired in this nation — all you have to do is look around and see all the different kinds of people there are here.

"I remember when I was in high school I wanted to be a contestant on the television show *GE College Bowl*. In the hopes of making it onto that program, I studied all kinds of different subjects — including classical music and art.

"At the time I was going to Southwestern High School, an inner-city high school in Detroit. I came into a lot of criticism for my unusual interests. People would say, 'Classical music? Art? That's European stuff. That's not culturally relevant to you! What's wrong with you?'

"What is culturally relevant to an American?

"Take a trip to Ellis Island out in New York Harbor. Walk through those galleries to see the pictorial history of that place. Study the photos. Look into the eyes of those people, those immigrants who came here from all corners of the earth, many of them with only the things they could carry on their backs. Note the determination on those faces. Consider the way they worked. Not for eight hours a day. But for ten, twelve, sixteen, eighteen hours a day. Not five days a week, but six or seven. When there was no such thing as a minimum wage.

"They did it not for themselves, but so that their sons and daughters, their grandsons and granddaughters, might have an opportunity for success in this land. Those people became the backbone of America.

"Hundreds of years before that, other immigrants came here in the bottom of slave ships. They worked even harder for longer hours for even less. They too had a dream. That one day their great-grandchildren could pursue the dream of freedom and happiness in this land.

"You know, of all the nations in this world, this was the only one big enough and great enough for all of those people from all of those backgrounds to realize their dreams. And some people say that our diversity is a problem? It's not a problem. It's a blessing.

"Drawing from and building on that diversity is how America got to be the most powerful nation in the world faster than any other nation in history. We had so many people, from so many backgrounds, with so many different talents. With those kinds of resources we were able to focus tremendous energy on our problems. That was and is a wonderful thing. And that's what the United Way should be about today.

"Think about it. How many people would go to the National Aquarium and pay to get in if every fish inside was a goldfish? It wouldn't be that interesting, would it? Who would go to the National Zoo if every animal in it was a Thompson's Gazelle? It might be interesting for about five minutes, but that's it. Who would want a bouquet of flowers if every one was identical? And really, who would want to get up in the morning if everyone looked exactly like you? Think about it. In some cases it would be a national disaster. So I think we all should be thankful that God gave us diversity and variety.

"We all have our own talents and strengths to contribute. And once I discovered that truth for myself, I experienced a rapid rise in my medical career. I found myself Director of Pediatric Neurosurgery at the number one hospital in America when I was thirty-three years old.

"People would come from great distances with their sick children to see Dr. Ben Carson. Then I would walk into the room, and they would ask, 'Is Dr. Carson coming?' When I would say, 'I'm Dr. Carson,' some of them would just about have a seizure. Which was how I got interested in seizure surgery—just kidding.

"But it was interesting to see people's reactions. But you know, no one ever walked out. Once I began to explain what we were going to do and it became apparent that I knew what I was talking about, people seemed perfectly happy with the idea of me being their surgeon.

"Time went on for me—doing surgery on difficult brain tumors, pioneering hemispherectomies for seizure, intrauterine surgery to correct problems even before birth. And then in 1987 the Binder Siamese twins blew the roof off, and things have never been back to 'normal' since.

"The challenges continue. Just the week before last I had the opportunity to travel to South Africa to lead a team which separated what we call type two vertical craniopagus Siamese twins. After a twenty-eight-hour operation we did manage to separate them. It was the first time twins like that have ever been successfully separated in one operation. Not only are both surviving, but it appears that they are both one hundred percent normal.

"Having that kind of experience doesn't make me a special person—it makes me privileged. And a privileged person is any individual who has been given an opportunity and a platform to positively affect the lives of others. That is my definition of success."

THINKING BIG

My CONCLUDING THOUGHT TODAY is THINK BIG—my philosophy for success in life."

I once wrote an entire book titled *Think Big,* which spelled out this philosophy in detail. But I wanted to summarize the main points for these United Way executives as my "recipe for success" at the close of their conference. So I explained my recipe, which is also an acronym.

"The T is for Talent, which God gave to every individual. Not just the ability to sing and dance and throw a ball—not that there is anything wrong with that by the way. I have nothing against sports and entertainment—don't get me wrong. It's just that I think things have been blown out of proportion today.

"We tell our young people that education is so important. Yet we pay an average major-league baseball player as much as we pay a hundred school teachers put together.

"Our young people aren't stupid. They look at what we do, what we produce, rather than what we say. And we have got to do whatever it takes to make them understand that academic achievement is every bit as important as sports and entertainment.

"H is for Honesty. If you live a clean and honest life, you don't have to worry about any skeletons in the closet. Because if you put them there, they will come back to haunt you for sure.

"And if you always tell the truth, you don't have to try to remember what you said three months ago. That makes it much easier to concentrate on the task at hand.

"The I is for Insight, which comes in part from listening to those people who have already been where you are trying to go. Solomon, the wisest man who ever lived, said, 'Wise is the man who can learn from someone else's triumphs and mistakes. The person who cannot is a fool.'

"N is for Nice. Be nice to people. Once they get over their suspicions about why you're being nice, they'll be nice to you. And you can get so much more done when people are being nice to you and you're nice to them. If you're not a nice person, I challenge you to try it for one week. Be nice to everyone you encounter for one solid week.

"It's seven minutes after four on Saturday. Until seven minutes after four next Saturday, be nice to everybody. That includes your spouse. Everyone you encounter.

"What will that mean? That means not talking about people behind their backs. I know that's going to be hard for some people. It means not talking about people in front of their backs. That means if you see somebody struggling with something, help them. It requires putting yourself in the other person's place before you begin to criticize.

"If the elevator door is open and there is only one space left, let someone else get on. It means when you're driving your car and someone puts a blinker on, don't speed up; slow down and let them in. It means speaking to people in the morning. When you get in the elevator say 'Good morning.' Once people get over their initial shock, they'll be happy to talk to you.

"Because that's what we are created to be — social beings. Human beings were not meant to be isolated individuals who are always suspicious of everyone else. We're meant to be loving, relating, interacting creatures.

"Which you will soon discover if you try this experiment. You'll find that being nice gets to be contagious if you do it.

"The K is for Knowledge, which can make you a more valuable person. Yes, I do have a big house. I have lots of cars. I have many of the things that Robin Leach thinks are important. But are they important? Of course not. If somebody comes along and takes it all away, it's no big deal. I can get it all back almost immediately using what's inside my head. (Or at least I could before Managed Care.)

"That's what Solomon meant when he said, 'Gold is nice, silver is nice, rubies are nice. But to be treasured far above all those things are knowledge, wisdom, and understanding.' Because with knowledge, wisdom, and understanding you can get all the gold, silver, and rubies you want. But more importantly, you come to realize that gold and silver and rubies aren't really very important. It's a far more valuable thing to develop your God-given talents to the point where you become valuable to the people around you.

"B is for books. They are an invaluable mechanism for obtaining that success. I've already talked about what reading did for me.

"The second I is for In-depth learning—learning for the sake of knowledge and understanding as opposed to superficial learning. Superficial learners are people who cram, cram, cram before a test, sometimes do okay, and three weeks later know nothing.

"Superficial learning is why we're number twenty-one of twenty-two. We can, and it is imperative that we do so, change the emphasis and do better in our educational system when it comes to in-depth learning.

"The last letter, G is for God. There is nothing wrong with God. We live in a society where people are always saying, 'You can't talk about God in public,' as if somehow that violates the concept of separation of church and state. How can anyone say that in this country?

"Thomas Jefferson, one of our founding fathers, had 190 religious volumes in his library. The preamble to our constitution talks about certain inalienable rights that our Creator endowed us with. The pledge of allegiance to our flag says we are 'one nation, under God.' Almost every courtroom in the land has on its walls, 'In God We Trust.' Every coin in our pocket, every bill in our wallets also says, 'In God We Trust.'

"If it's in our constitution, if it's in our pledge, if it's in our courts, and it's on our money, yet we can't talk about it, what condition are we in as a country? In medicine we call it *schizophrenia*. And doesn't that describe a lot of what is going on in our society today?

"We need to make it clear to people that it's all right to live by godly principles—loving your fellow man, caring for your neighbor, and living a life of service by developing your God-given talents to the point that you become invaluable to the people around you. We need to remind each other there is nothing judgmental about having values and principles, and there's nothing wrong with standing for something.

"If we apply these truths to our own lives, if we instill these values in the next generation, then, and only then, will America be truly united and become the greatest nation the world has ever known."

THE REST OF THE STORY

I CAME AWAY FROM my speaking engagement that day in Birmingham thinking the same thing I think wherever I speak. When it comes to getting a Big-Picture perspective on life, there's no way I can say everything I want to say, no way to say everything I think needs to be said on this subject, in any one speech.

I am not even sure it can all be said in one book. But I am going to try.

Every day I go to work I have to make life-and-death decisions. For that reason, and because so many of the people and families I work with have suddenly been forced to reconsider what's really important in life, I have spent a lot of my own time searching for perspective on the Big Picture. So I want to share some more of those thoughts in the remainder of this book.

We will begin in Part Two talking about some Big-Picture perspectives with very personal implications and important lessons I have learned that can and should make a difference in the way each of us live out our daily lives. Then we will widen the angle a bit more in Part Three to examine some major current societal issues that could benefit from some different, Big-Picture perspectives.

I have written this book because I believe what I said to my United Way audience in Birmingham. For me, success is defined by what I do with every opportunity, every platform I have been given, to positively affect the lives of others. I can only hope and pray that the lessons I have learned can make a difference in my life and the lives of others. And I am writing this book for other people who want to make a difference.

That is always a lot easier to do if we first get the Big Picture.

Part Two

A CLOSE-UP VIEW OF THE BIG PICTURE

Six

SEEING HARDSHIP AS ADVANTAGE

Whenever I tell my own story, I seldom do more than touch on my mother's personal history. But I want to say a little more here because my mother, Sonya Carson, knows a thing or two about hardship.

Born into a large and extremely poor rural Southern family, the next-to-the-youngest of twenty-four children, she knew only thirteen of her siblings—because she spent most of her lonely and unhappy childhood moving from one foster home to another.

When she was just thirteen years old, she met and married my father, an older man who promised to rescue her from poverty, take her north to Detroit, where he would show her a life of affluence and adventure. The warning signs were there from the beginning. He was an engaging man, an able provider. But he loved partying and showing off his young wife on whom he regularly bestowed lavish gifts of fashionable clothing and jewelry. He always seemed to spend money at least as fast as he earned it.

Despite my mother's ongoing concerns about their financial security, my parents seemed happy, especially in those early years after my brother Curtis and I were born. But the longer she wondered where my father was getting his extra money, the more she suspected his involvement in illegal sales of alcohol—and perhaps even drugs. When she found out he was a bigamist—with another wife and family—that was the last straw.

Curtis and I did not learn the reasons until we were older. At ages ten and eight, all we knew was that our father had suddenly gone and was no longer part of our lives.

When my father left, he took the modest financial nest egg my mother had scrimped and saved for years to put together. She was left with nothing but a crackerbox of a little house, on which she could no longer afford to pay the mortgage, and two active sons to raise completely on her own. Plus she had never held a paying job, had no marketable job skills, and possessed less than a third-grade education.

Though we did have to accept food stamps from time to time, Mother proudly determined she would not depend on welfare. She worked two, sometimes three jobs at a time as a domestic, just to keep a roof over our heads and clothes on our backs. Yet she also managed to put a little something aside—a nickel here, a dime there.

When she drove her car until it fell apart, she had enough nickels and dimes stowed away to go out and buy a new one—astounding friends and neighbors who wondered how in the world an uneducated, poverty-stricken, single mother of two boys, who cleaned other people's homes for a "living," could possibly afford a new car. Vicious rumors abounded. But Mother never paid much attention to what the neighbors were saying. She had her eyes fixed on an overriding goal: to do whatever it took to provide her sons with the environment and the attitude that would insure their success in life.

Our neighbors didn't understand her motivation any more than they understood her thrift—or her gritty determination. My mother was one tough lady.

I remember a day when, as a boy of ten, I was riding in the car with her. The traffic stopped suddenly, and a tailgating driver bumped us from behind. The man quickly drove away without even getting out of the car. My mother chased him clear across Detroit before he finally gave up, pulled over, and got out to exchange insurance information.

She was just as tough and demanding with her sons. She had high expectations for Curtis and me, and she never let us forget it. We may have lived in poverty, but she convinced us that was only a temporary predicament. She observed the lives and the habits of the successful and wealthy folks whose homes she cleaned every day. "They're no different from us," she insisted. "Anything they can do, you can do. And you can do it better!"

In her vision, education would provide our escape, and when other parents questioned the academic demands she placed on us, she told them: "Say what you want, but my boys are going to be something. They're going to be self-supporting and learn how to love other folks. And no matter what they decide to do, they're going to be the best in the world at it!"

I pay tribute to my remarkable mother's influence almost every time I speak. And I have to agree with the countless people who approach me afterwards to tell me, "You are fortunate to have a mother like that."

They are right! I would not be where I am in the world today without her influence and her example of overcoming hardship.

A FRIEND WITHOUT FAMILY

THE SECOND EXAMPLE I want to share is that of a friend who overcame far more hardship than I ever faced. And she managed it without a mother's help.

Colene Daniel was eight years old, living in a two-room basement apartment in a Cincinnati ghetto, when police broke in and pulled her and her four brothers and sisters from their beds in the middle of the night. The children were sent to separate foster homes without ever being told why they had been taken away from their mother.

Within six months, Colene's first foster parents gave up trying to get through to this little girl who suddenly feared and hated the world. So the next few years Colene lived with a hundred other children at "The Colored Orphanage of Cincinnati." There, an uneducated, overworked, and frustrated staff once punished her for engaging in a pillow fight by locking her alone, overnight, in the dark closet of an attic they told her was haunted by ghosts of patients who had died in the building during its previous days as a hospital.

When, after four years, the orphanage was closed and bulldozed, Colene went through a series of foster-home experiences in which she was repeatedly told she was dumb and would never amount to anything. At fifteen, she returned to her mother, but soon ran away and rented her own basement "apartment" for $54.00 a month. She supported herself by working nights and weekends as an accountant for a local bookie. Using a false ID to get food stamps to supplement her income, she enrolled in one of the top public high schools in the city. When school officials began to ask questions about her home life and her parental guidance, she hired two winos from the neighborhood, cleaned them up, coached them, and took them with her to a school function where she introduced them to teachers and staff as her "parents."

When her secret finally did get out, that she was underage and living alone, she had to go to court to convince a judge not to put her back in foster care. Two teachers who believed in her agreed to be her official guardians so she could continue to live on her own while she finished high school. By her senior year Colene made the honor society, took an active role in a student achievement program, and served on the student government—while holding down three part-time jobs.

Colene then worked her way through college and not only graduated with a Bachelor of Science degree in Speech Pathology and Audiology, she was listed in *Who's Who in American Colleges and Universities.* After receiving a Masters in Health Care Administration, Colene advanced up the corporate ladder while working at hospitals in Saudi Arabia, China, Kenya, Houston, and Chicago. In 1991 Johns Hopkins Hospital hired her as Vice President of Corporate Services— which put her in charge of much of the day-to-day operation of our institution by giving her oversight of all the hospital's service staff.

A short time later, after she was named head of a newly formed Department of Community Services, Colene went back to school and earned a second master's degree—this one in public health. In addition to her extensive hospital duties, she now spearheads our corporate involvement with neighborhood activists and residents working to revitalize the East Baltimore inner-city community where Johns Hopkins is located. Not long ago she was appointed to the new Baltimore City School Board of Commissioners to improve public education in our city.

Her incredible energy and dedication have earned Colene widespread recognition as a first-rate communicator, leader, and executive who certainly knows what it takes to overcome hardship in life. Her story, her personal faith in God, and her example have so inspired me that I am proud and grateful to consider Colene Daniel a respected colleague and a treasured friend.

As I consider the life stories of these and other people who have overcome hardship, and as I think back on my own personal experience, I have come to (what may seem to some people) a startling conclusion: hardship can actually be an advantage.

Let me give a few of my reasons for thinking that.

HARDSHIP TAUGHT ME FINANCIAL RESPONSIBILITY

BEING POOR, MY BROTHER and I learned to save money. For instance, we could have gone to school on a city bus, but that would have cost twenty cents a day. You could buy a loaf of bread for twenty cents in those days. So we rode our bikes instead, and in that way we contributed to the family grocery budget.

Any penny saved was truly a penny earned, so we made certain we never turned in a library book a day late—otherwise we would have had to pay a two-cent fine. We never walked past an alley without looking to see if there was a bottle to turn in for a penny deposit. No amount of money was too small when it came to spending—or to saving.

I remember as an adult going back to Detroit's Southwestern High School and talking to one of my old science teachers who had helped me prepare my financial statement when I was applying to Yale. He smiled and shook his head as he told me, "I couldn't imagine how a family of three people could possibly survive on your mother's income!" We did it by thrift—an attitude as well as a skill my mother exemplified and instilled in Curtis and me.

That deeply ingrained trait has served me well over the years. Indeed, I find the thriftiness I learned as a financial survival skill when I was a boy comes in handy today as I oversee an enormous and complex pediatric neurosurgery budget that never seems to stretch far enough. The constant tension of dealing with severe financial limitations seems a familiar burden I can manage without being crippled by frustration, developing an ulcer, or even losing too much sleep. Yet without my years of hardship, I am not certain I could cope with that pressure.

HARDSHIP SHOWED ME THE SECRET TO HAPPINESS

Many adults say that only when they look back on their childhoods do they understand how poor they were. They had not considered themselves poor at the time because they had loving families to provide a tremendous sense of security and happiness.

I can only partially relate to those feelings. The love we experienced in our family did indeed provide security and happiness, but perhaps we were simply too impoverished *not* to know we were poor. As a result I learned early in life that happiness does not depend on having money.

This lesson was reinforced not just by my mother but by the life and example of an elderly acquaintance by the name of "Sister Scott." While Mother worked hard to make our family life happy, she could not always manage to be happy herself. The cumulative strain of her lifetime of hardship sometimes took its toll. For a few days, sometimes weeks at a time, my mother would have to leave us. She always told us when to expect her back, and she never failed to return when she said she would. So we didn't worry.

We did not learn until years later that she suffered terrible depression, and whenever she felt as if she were approaching a breaking point, Mother would check herself into a hospital just long enough to regain her emotional equilibrium and strength.

Sister Scott, an elderly Canadian woman we knew from church, came to stay at our house and take care of Curtis and me on several of those occasions. She fed us, washed our clothes, and cared for any number of other needs young boys have.

Even though Sister Scott seemed even poorer than we were, she was one of the happiest people I have ever known. She stood about five-feet-six-inches tall, a little on the thin side, medium brown complexion, with her white hair pulled back tight in a bun. A dignified woman who spoke proper English, she was also an extremely animated listener. With incredible interest, she would focus on any story we would tell her, punctuating every other sentence or two with the appreciative exclamation "Oh, my!" There was never a doubt in my mind that Sister Scott's love for life and for people included us and the time she spent taking care of my brother and me.

I have two enduring memories of those times she took care of us. The first was the time Sister Scott found out Curtis and I wanted to learn how to roller skate.

"No problem!" she told us. "If you want to skate, I can teach you." We assured her we did, so she strapped on a pair of those old fashioned, one-size-fits-all skates that lash onto your shoes and adjust with a metal key. Then she gave us a quick demonstration.

Looking back I realize she must have created quite a sensation in our neighborhood: an eighty-year-old woman roller skating up and down the sidewalks of inner-city Detroit with two awkward, prepubescent boys in tow. But at the time we never gave a thought to what we looked like. We were too busy trying to keep pace with Sister Scott and thinking, *If an old lady like her can roller skate, surely we can do it.* And before long we could.

The other lasting memory of Sister Scott is her singing. She must have been a big Ethel Waters fan because she was always singing "His eyes are on the sparrow ... so I know He watches me." She was also the one who taught me the words to "Jesus Is All the World to Me" by singing it over and over again as she cooked dinner, did the dishes, cleaned the house, and tucked us into bed.

Knowing Sister Scott convinced me that you cannot buy happiness. She, like my mother, believed true happiness results less from money than from our relationships — with ourselves, with other people, and with God. It comes not as much from what we have and acquire but from what we accomplish in the way of attaining our goals. Happiness doesn't result from what we get but from what we give.

And those lessons learned early in life were driven home again during the early years of my marriage when Candy and I were both in school. We had very little money. Life was hard. But we were never happier. And the experience reminded us that happiness doesn't depend nearly as much on our circumstances as it does our relationships, our attitudes, and our beliefs.

HARDSHIP GAVE ME PERSPECTIVE ON MONEY

ONE DAY IN 1995, I was going through my mail when I noticed the return address of Yale University on a formal, official-looking letter. Even as I opened the envelope I remember thinking, *Do I still owe something on one of my old student loans? I thought I paid those off years ago!*

It came as a surprise — more like an absolute shock — when I began to read the personal letter inside. The president of Yale had written, informing me that I had been selected to receive an honorary degree from my *alma mater*. I could not think of a greater honor.

I remembered the fall of 1969 when a skinny young kid from inner-city Detroit first walked onto that historic campus, awed both by the setting and the people surrounding him. My modest and ordinary dorm room offered the nicest living conditions I had known my entire life. So I will never forget the feelings I experienced visiting the homes of my professors and fellow students who came from some of the wealthiest families in America.

My first reaction wasn't so much envy as fascination. I saw it as a learning opportunity, a chance to observe how people from different backgrounds live and conduct themselves. Rather than becoming jealous of my affluent classmates, my exposure to their world gave me an understanding of what kind of lifestyle it was possible to achieve—if I was willing to work for it.

This is not to say that I think the greatest goal in life, or even the best reason to work hard, is to acquire expensive things or to live in a comfortable home. Having experienced poverty already, however, this exposure to a life of comfort quickly convinced me that, given a choice, I much preferred the comforts.

Also, through this new exposure to the people around me, it became increasingly clear that what my mother had been trying to drill into me for years was true: I could be like these people if I wanted to. But that would never happen simply by wishing my circumstances were different; I had to work hard, and that meant academically, to make myself valuable to society and the people around me.

At the same time, I quickly learned that affluence can actually be a detriment. It certainly proved to be for some of my fellow students who spent a seemingly endless stream of money buying and installing state-of-the-art stereo systems for their dorm rooms, availing themselves of the myriad of entertainment opportunities in nearby New York City, and impressing the best-looking coeds with extravagantly expensive dates every weekend. For them, money created distractions they failed to overcome. A number of them flunked out of school that first year.

In a sense, my lack of money actually contributed to my academic success. Without the opportunities and distractions money could buy, I found it much easier to focus on my studies.

HARDSHIP FORCED ME TO SET AND PURSUE GOALS

OUR FAMILY WAS SO poor that nothing we ever wanted came easily—or immediately. My brother and I were forced to learn the value of that critically important, life-impacting principle that behavioral scientists refer to as *delayed gratification*. Because this principle held true in regard to everything our family ever purchased—from big-ticket items like a new car for my mother or a used bike for Curtis and me—it also carried over to those bigger, less-tangible life goals.

When our mother assured us we would not always be poor, we understood that our family's financial progress would require time and effort. For example, when Mother was finally able to afford to move us back into the home we had lived in before my father left (after years of renting), we saw that as just one step, albeit a milestone worth celebrating, on a long and arduous journey.

In the same way, our mother convinced Curtis and me that we could and would find success some day if we just followed the road of education to its natural end. Once we believed that, the increasingly difficult steps on that road became quite manageable legs of our journey toward that higher, ultimate goal. In the process we learned the importance of having a workable strategy for achieving any major goal in life.

I find that formula for achieving success, which I learned growing up in hardship, usually holds true today. Invariably, the most effective strategies for achieving our highest goals always involve education, time, and one other important benefit I gained through those early years of hardship ...

HARDSHIP INSTILLED A STRONG WORK ETHIC

I HELD A LOT of jobs growing up. I needed to in order to pull my own weight in the family and help earn money to pay for anything extra I wanted to have—from records to spending money. And that prior experience with hard work made me a better medical student and, in turn, a better resident and a more successful surgeon.

During medical school at the University of Michigan, I once overheard two residents talking about me. They didn't know I was listening. "That Carson is a workhorse!" one of them exclaimed.

I suppose it was true. I was so used to working on various part-time jobs through high school and college that neither my work ethic nor the long, hard hours required of doctors-in-training seemed at all unusual. The 100- to 120-hour work weeks expected of a junior resident were never easy. But I found them far less difficult than did many of my friends who had not needed to work so hard growing up.

Hard work has always been, and I expect always will be, a way of life for me. Sometimes (but not always) learned *through* hardship, hard work is the surest path I know *out of* hardship.

HARDSHIP MOTIVATED ME TO DEVELOP MY IMAGINATION

ONE OF THE ANNUAL highlights of my growing-up years was our family trip to the Michigan State Fair each summer in Detroit. Mother always managed to save up just enough money for admission, which would get us in to all the educational, agricultural, and art exhibits. But there was never enough money left over to purchase tickets for the rides. We had to enjoy those attractions vicariously as we strolled down the midway, reading the excitement on other people's faces and listening to their screams as they were jerked and spun and whirled through the air.

I don't recall ever feeling resentful of the people who could afford the rides, the games, or the shooting galleries, although I was a bit envious — especially of the children I saw bumping and banging around in those dodge-em cars. For years I dreamed of driving one of those bumper cars. Yet I thoroughly enjoyed watching other people have their fun, trying to imagine what it would be like to do all those things myself.

The midway of the Michigan State Fair wasn't the only stimulus for my imagination. There were other seemingly commonplace life events other people around us enjoyed, which we were too poor to experience—except vicariously. Until I went away to college, I had never once flown in an airplane or even seen a luxury cruise ship, let alone sailed on one. I had never been inside a limousine. I had never so much as eaten out in a sit-down restaurant.

I had certainly watched people on television doing all those things and more. But for years I had to content myself with creating vivid and elaborate pictures in my mind of what it would be like to do each of those things—and a zillion others—which I fully expected to experience some day after I achieved success as a result of my own hard work and efforts.

I now believe that *not* experiencing those things for so long, except in my imagination, made them shine a little brighter in my mind and seem a "prize" all the more tantalizing. I am also convinced that regular exercise of my imagination enhanced my natural creativity and actually improved the skills of mental visualization that are so important for any good surgeon.

Sometimes I worry about my own three sons, who have been to the White House to meet the President, sailed aboard cruise ships, ridden in stretch limos, and traveled around the world. Since they have already done so many things and have not been "limited" to vicarious experiences, I worry they may be handicapped, or at least challenged, in terms of creativity and imagination.

So my wife and I deliberately create some hardships for them! (More on that in Chapter 8.)

HARDSHIP TRAINED ME TO LOOK FOR THE GOOD IN THE WORST SITUATIONS

THREE QUICK EXAMPLES OF how negative experiences and even "failure" can have positive implications:

First, I, like far too many "underprivileged" students in our society, went to a series of subpar schools with poor educational standards and an even poorer learning environment. I certainly did not have access to the quality education afforded most of my classmates at Yale.

So you could fairly and accurately call my educational background "disadvantaged."

My school experience, however, turned out to be a great *advantage* in at least one crucial way. Because there were not a large number of academic superstars where I went to high school, I was able to stand out enough to develop tremendous self-esteem and confidence in my scholastic abilities. My early academic prowess probably resulted in what was sometimes unjustified cockiness, but if my ego had not been quite so inflated, if I had not been able to call on those memories of how incredibly intelligent everyone thought I was, I might have given up when I encountered the much higher academic standards and when I felt humbled by the intellect of some of my truly brilliant classmates at Yale. Without the confidence born of so many years being considered among the best and brightest back in high school, I certainly would have quit when my medical school advisor told me he thought I should drop out and consider another career.

Without my "disadvantaged" education, I am not sure I would be where I am today.

Given a Big-Picture perspective, even some of the worst experiences in our memories, incidents we would consider total "failures," can, in retrospect, be seen to have had a positive effect on our lives.

For example, one summer during college the economy took a downturn. Jobs were scarce. Yet I desperately needed to earn money for the coming school year. After all other doors closed, I signed up to sell encyclopedias door-to-door. With two days of training, my well-memorized sales pitch, and my sales manager's promises of big commissions ringing in my ears, I arrived in my appointed sales territory primed for success.

I quit after half a day. I was embarrassed to do so because I had never been a quitter. I had always worked hard enough to impress my superiors and be a success at every job I had ever held. But the humiliation I felt about giving up my very first day was not enough motivation to continue what had been one of the most painfully difficult mornings of my life. Reciting my spiel in a training classroom had been a piece of cake. Knocking on the doors of complete strangers and trying to get them to listen was torture. I hated the whole routine—especially the sense of rejection when door after door closed in my face. I felt like a complete failure. It was one of the absolute worst experiences of my life.

Yet now I look back on the entire affair with real appreciation for what it taught me. I learned an invaluable lesson about myself that day that has helped to keep me focused and out of any number of potentially disastrous experiences since. That brief, one-time inoculation cured me for all time of ever wanting to become a salesman. I don't like asking people for things; I have a particularly strong disdain for bothering people.

Realizing this about myself has kept me from ever succumbing to the temptation of politics—because politicians have to raise enormous amounts of money by asking for support and favors from too many people. I could never do that.

I do, however, participate regularly on the Children's Miracle Television Network to solicit funds for the Johns Hopkins Children's Center, and I gladly take part in fund-raising events for the Children's Cancer Foundation, which has been so supportive of me and my work over the years. Recently I even began my own charity—the Carson Scholars Fund—which I eventually hope will give our nation's academic achievers the same level of recognition and encouragement that athletic achievers enjoy during their high school years. So I don't mind asking on behalf of others.

Taken along with our successes, such failures can teach us what we are good at and what we are not, what we enjoy and what we hate. (There is usually a strong correlation there.) Once we know that, we can use those huge frontal lobes God gave us to better plan our lives.

So it is that even our hardships can help us. If we just learn the lessons those experiences hold, we can make short-term decisions and establish long-term plans that will utilize our strengths and avoid exposing whatever weaknesses we have. Then someday, way down the road, we can look back—as I do on my encyclopedia endeavor—and laugh.

Even failures that are so painful we cannot laugh about them can have their positive sides. I think about the first two patients I ever had who died—both during hemispherectomies—an operation which I had performed successfully several times before. (For more details on hemispherectomies, see Chapter 15.)

The first patient was a baby girl, a little less than a year old. She suffered cardiac arrhythmia and died in the ICU after we thought she had come through the surgery just fine. Her death hit me especially hard because she was the very first patient I had lost either during or after surgery in my five years as a surgeon.

When the second patient, a little boy about the same age, died on the operating table during the same procedure less than a year later, I became more distressed. Two such similar deaths so close to each other—I couldn't accept this as something that "just happens."

I spent hour after hour in meetings with my staff and with my colleague and mentor, Dr. John Freeman, who was the Chief of Pediatric Neurology at Johns Hopkins. We pored over notes and reviewed charts again and again, asking each other and ourselves a thousand times, "Why? Why did these children die?"

We never could pin down a specific cause or explanation, but we had a suspicion, which we decided to act on in an attempt to keep it from happening again.

Up to that time, my pediatric neurosurgery cases were assigned to adult anesthesiologists rather than anesthesia teams that specialized in pediatric cases. But we now wondered if perhaps there were some factors in these two cases which a pediatric anesthesia team might have paid a little closer attention to—that adult anesthesia teams did not, simply because they didn't have to with adults. Subtle changes and nuances in the neurological system that only a seasoned pediatric anesthesiologist might pick up on.

A third child died after we began changing our OR procedures to make sure I had a pediatric anesthesia team working with me any time I did a hemispherectomy. Although we never did know exactly what the problems might have been, we have not lost another hemispherectomy patient in almost ten years. The new protocol was so successful that I now have a fully equipped pediatric operating room for all of my neurosurgical cases. And that includes a pediatric anesthesiologist working with me whenever I operate on a child.

So even what was a devastating failure for me, and a terrible tragedy for three grief-stricken families, has been a blessing to many other families since. Those three failures, as painful as they were, led directly to procedural changes that have probably saved many, many more children's lives.

Hardship has taught me to search for the positive even in the most negative situations. I have found the good often enough over the years to finally believe the promise the apostle Paul cited in his letter to the Romans when he wrote, "We know that in all things God works for the good of those who love him, who have been called according to his purpose" (8:28).

LOOKING AHEAD

BUT HOW DO WE learn these lessons so often taught by hardship? How do we help more people turn hardship to an advantage? How do we get, and then give others, this Big-Picture perspective on the troubles we all face in life?

Those are some of the questions I will try to answer in Chapter 7.

Seven

MOVING BEYOND A VICTIM MENTALITY

In the spring of 1994, the same year I operated unsuccessfully on the Makwaeba sisters in South Africa, I received one of the greatest honors of my life: I was selected as one of ten individuals inducted by the Horatio Alger Society at that organization's annual meeting in Washington, D.C. Only in retrospect can I appreciate the irony: that the sad death of those Siamese twins, which I considered among the most discouraging failures in my professional career, should come so close to the time I was invited to join an organization created for the purpose of recognizing and honoring "success."

Only after being informed of my selection did I learn that the Horatio Alger Society is comprised of about two hundred or so distinguished Americans—all of whom have achieved the highest recognition in their fields after starting out on the lowest rungs of the socioeconomic ladder. I was both amazed and humbled at my induction ceremony as I listened to the inspiring personal stories of my fellow inductees (some of which I will tell a little later). By the time society member Johnny Cash personally presented me with my own Horatio Alger Award, the evening was already one of the great highlights of my life.

Every year since then, I have counted our Alger Society annual get-togethers among my personal high points. Each induction ceremony is just as inspiring as my first, and the more members I have gotten to know over the years, the more

I am impressed by their remarkable stories and can-do spirit—and the more I have found myself thinking about how all of these accomplished and successful individuals have found their own ways to turn hardship to advantage.

How? What is their secret? How did they get and then give others this Big-Picture perspective?

CALLING ALL VICTIMS

THE BASIC PROBLEM IS one of attitude. That is always a key. The first step to overcoming hardship has to be a change in attitude. Far too many people today have a victim's mentality. They have a small-picture perspective on hardship—because that is what a victim mentality is. It is a short-range, self-centered, limited outlook, where the zoom lens of your attention stays so focused on the closest, most immediate obstacles that nothing else can be seen.

People with this focus get so overwhelmed by their hardship that they feel paralyzed and powerless. Then, since they aren't responsible for the seemingly insurmountable obstacles surrounding them, they assume little if any responsibility for tackling those problems. After all, they are "victims"—so someone else has to set things right.

I saw this victim mentality epitomized a few years ago at one of the televised "town meetings" conducted by President Clinton during his first term of office. During the question-and-answer time, a woman stood up to announce that, due to circumstances beyond her control, she had recently lost her job. She had a family to feed and no income. And she wanted to know what the president could do for her.

The President of the United States could have encouraged, challenged, maybe even inspired and empowered this woman if he had told her she seemed to be an able-bodied individual, that she was obviously an intelligent and articulate person, and that he felt confident that given a little time, effort, and determination she would find another job—possibly a better one.

Did he say that? Of course not.

In our day, few politicians would. The media would probably have a field day if they did. An answer like that from a politician would be viewed not as *encouraging* but *uncaring*. It certainly would not have shown the president "feeling the pain" of this victim.

Yet I couldn't help contrasting that woman's attitude with my own mother's after she was left destitute—with two boys to raise, no education, and no job skills. What a difference! The whole world today—from the President on down—seems to accept without question this "victim mentality."

It is not just an American phenomenon (although we have probably exported plenty of it). I see it every week in the personal letters I receive from all over the world asking me for financial aid. For some reason, probably because they have heard or read my personal story of overcoming hardship, quite a large number of people seem to assume I have the financial resources to put them through college or medical school.

Some of the letters are heartwrenching. People from underdeveloped countries write eloquently of their lifelong dreams of becoming a doctor, describing the hardships their families face, telling how they have to support their brothers and sisters, and promising to pay me back once they achieve their professional status. I feel for these people who write me asking for my financial sponsorship, but I receive so many of these letters that if I responded to them all I would be bankrupt within the month.

Instead, I wish I could convince them of what I truly believe—that if they would put the same amount of initiative, thought, and time into devising a strategy for achieving their goals themselves that they have already invested in trying to get me (and who knows how many others) to help them, they would be a lot further along in the game. But that is a tough concept to sell to those who have already adopted a self-fulfilling victim mentality that says they are neither responsible for, nor capable of, solving their own problems.

So how do we change this attitude? How do we counter the victim mentality that pervades our world?

WHERE HAVE ALL THE HEROES GONE?

MY ONLY WISDOM ON this question comes from personal experience and observation, though I am convinced what I have seen in my own life has broader applications.

For me, the single biggest factor in developing the attitude necessary to overcoming hardship was having positive role models. That started with the people I knew who I could look up to and learn from. Fortunately, I did not have far to look for such inspiration and guidance. I have already noted my mother's influence. She refused to see herself as a victim and determined not to let us think of ourselves that way either.

One of the primary ways she did this was refusing to accept excuses from me or my brother Curtis. That may have been one of the best things she ever did for us. Simply because we knew there would never be an excuse good enough to explain why we had not done some chore or brought home a better report card, we quit giving excuses and figured out how to do what was expected.

Victims often look for excuses and explanations for why things are the way they are. Overcomers, as my mother's example taught me, look for solutions that will change things.

That attitude made all the difference in that encounter with my medical-school advisor I alluded to earlier. Despite the academic success I had experienced in my undergraduate days at Yale, when I struggled during my first year at the University of Michigan Medical School, my advisor assumed the problem was lack of ability, or at least an inadequate preparation for the rigors of the program. He actually recommended I drop out. When I refused, he then suggested that I consider cutting my class load in half and allowing myself four years to complete the first two years of medical school. He thought maybe that way I could get by.

Had I allowed myself to feel and think like a victim, I might have accepted that advice, and I am certain the rest of my life would have been very different. Instead, I concluded that my advisor's assessment of my intelligence and potential was wrong. I was an intelligent person who had proven myself in the past. So there was no reason why I couldn't analyze the reasons for my failure and come up with a workable strategy for solving this problem.

And that is what I did. The real issue was not whether I could learn — but how. In considering my predicament and comparing it with my previous academic experience, I realized I had never been a very good auditory learner. Yet here I was spending six to eight hours a day sitting in classrooms listening to dull, dry lectures. Nothing was sinking in.

I had always absorbed knowledge best and fastest by reading. Why not capitalize on that strength?

For the rest of my medical school training I skipped probably eighty percent of the classroom lectures. Instead, I spent those hours — and a lot more — in my room or at the library reading the textbook and all sorts of related resources for myself. Then I made sure to be in all the labs for any hands-on learning. My new strategy resulted in a rapid reversal of my academic performance that not only shocked my advisor but surprised myself.

Had I ever before been inclined to think of myself as a victim, I would certainly have slipped back into that mentality. I would have told myself, "You've had too much to overcome to hope to succeed in medical school. You just haven't been prepared adequately to make the grade. Maybe you do need to reduce your class load, forget trying to excel, and set your sights on *just getting by.*"

Fortunately, I not only had my mother's example to draw on, but I found other role models around my community (Sister Scott was just one) and beyond. Looking back and remembering those who influenced me convinces me that anyone hoping to overcome hardship today needs to look for such role models. And any of us who are concerned about the crippling effect the victim mentality is having on this generation and the next had better work at being a positive example to the people around us.

HISTORIC HEROES

History has provided me with other examples. Booker T. Washington particularly impressed me. Born as a slave, he risked severe punishment by learning to read. Through reading he educated himself to the point where he became a friend and advisor to presidents. His example reinforced what I was learning in my own life about the power of reading not just to educate but to transport you temporarily out of your circumstances, to broaden your perspective, and to give you a clear enough view of the bigger picture to find your way past the biggest obstacles and overcome whatever hardship you face.

Church also offered me Biblical role models of faithful overcomers. The story of Joseph from the book of Genesis was always one of my favorites. A dreamer even as a small boy, Joseph certainly knew how to think big. And he learned a great deal about turning hardship into advantage.

Instead of accepting the victim role when his jealous brothers sold him into slavery, Joseph determined to be the best slave he could possibly be and ended up as his master's head servant. When he was unjustly imprisoned on account of the false accusations of the master's wife, he refused to become bitter or feel victimized. By determining to be the best prisoner he could be, he was made overseer of the prisoners. By continuing to make the most of the seemingly limited opportunities, Joseph eventually became prime minister of the most powerful nation on earth. He could have given up and become a victim at a number of difficult points of his life. Instead, Joseph's choices made him a victor—and a powerful example to millions of people like me down through history.

MODELS IN MEDIA

When I was growing up, my "overcoming" role models were not limited to examples at home or from the community. Neither were they only historic or Biblical heroes. All of society—including literature, media, and entertainment—highlighted and celebrated the lives and stories of many such individuals worthy of emulation.

The basic plot was the same in so many old movies I watched on television as a boy—the trials and adventures of admirable people who worked and fought and struggled until they emerged victorious over whatever circumstance they faced. The same overcoming theme repeated itself in countless settings—whether historic tales about pioneers braving the frontier, immigrants arriving in a new world with nothing but a dream and the clothes on their backs, orphans growing up to become major industrialists, outnumbered soldiers somehow accomplishing their mission. Many such movies were based on true stories. A lot seemed more sappy and sentimental than realistic. But the spirit they embodied and the message they instilled both reflected and shaped a real societal belief in the positive power of such character traits as determination, integrity, intelligence, courage, faith, and a willingness to work to succeed against all odds.

Well, a lot of things have changed since then—not all for the better. Though there was once an uplifting power in such stories, Hollywood today seems neither to recognize their value or assume responsibility to tell them. A great place to start might be to create a weekly television series telling the inspiring, true stories of the remarkable people I have met through the Horatio Alger Society.

Three quick examples from the nine other Alger Society members who were inducted with me in the class of 1994:

ALONE TO AMERICA

JOSEPH NEUBAUER WAS FOURTEEN when his parents put him on a boat and sent him to America in 1956—alone. Before then, he had never traveled out of his native Israel. The only English he knew was what he learned in one year of school and picked up from watching John Wayne movies, which explains why he answered the immigration officials' questions with a simple "Yup" or "Nope."

Still, he was excited about life in this new country when his ship steamed past the Statue of Liberty to dock at Ellis Island on a cold winter day. "I had on a pair of shorts and one sweater. That was it," he recalls. "But I was determined to make it."

Life in America certainly looked more hopeful than the violent and explosive environment he had left behind. He remembers before the foundation of Israel, when it was still a mandated territory called Palestine. "I remember British soldiers with red berets stringing barbed wire across the street, and there was fighting right outside our windows. I remember the house being strafed and having to tape up the windows so they wouldn't blow out. There were shortages of food and fuel. I remember standing in bread lines and running out between air raids to get food. It was tumultuous."

Joseph's father decided to send his son to America to complete his education. An aunt and uncle, already established in Massachu- setts, agreed to take him in—provided he pay his way by working in the family's roadside store after school and on weekends.

Joseph's uncle met him in New York, flew back to Boston with him the next day, and enrolled him in school. The principal took a special interest in this first and only foreign student in his Danvers, Massachusetts, high school. So did one of the English teachers who spent hours working with him after school. That was fortunate for Joseph who says, "Reading Shakespeare when it's not your native tongue is a little difficult. So Miss Williams was a very, very important person in my life. She contributed her free time to help me succeed."

He not only learned a new language but had to adjust to a whole different culture. "I'd never seen American football. I didn't know anything about American customs, holidays, cars, girls, or clothes. I had to learn it all from scratch."

With the help of those concerned educators, his aunt and uncle, and a number of new friends, Joe graduated from high school and was admitted to Tufts University. There he discovered an even more diverse world through his association with kids from around the United States—New York, Philadelphia, Chicago.

To help pay his way, Joe landed a part-time job as a waiter in a fraternity house—eventually working his way up to the position of food steward. As a senior he was nominated for, and won, a scholarship for graduate study at the prestigious University of Chicago Business School, where he sat under the tutelage of some of the most elite and influential economists in the world.

When he graduated with his MBA, Joe joined Chase Manhattan Bank to learn about finance. His performance there soon caught the eye of his superiors, including David Rockefeller, who took a special interest in becoming Joe's mentor and friend. At the age of twenty-seven, Joe became the youngest vice president in the bank's history. After taking other positions at PepsiCo (where he became the youngest treasurer of a *Fortune 500* company) and Wilson Sporting Goods, a company called ARA Services lured Joe to Philadelphia. Two years later, the board named him president, and in 1983 he became CEO. When his publicly traded company was put up for sale, Joe recruited seventy of the company's other top executives for a successful management buyout.

A decade later, when Joe was inducted into the Horatio Alger Society, his privately owned company (with over a thousand employee-owners) had grown into one of the largest and financially strongest service companies in the world, with more than 120,000 employees, and worldwide revenues exceeding $5 billion. In addition to providing food services for everything from college campuses to hospitals and airports, ARA's reputation for quality had won Joe's company the honor of being the official food-service manager of the Olympic Games since 1968.

I count it a privilege to call Joe my friend. Despite his tremendous success in the often cutthroat world of business, he has remained a man of compassion who says he feels compelled to try to help others because so many people helped him. This former immigrant kid, who walked off a boat in 1956 with literally nothing but the clothes on his back to become head of a multibillion dollar international business venture, has some valuable advice about overcoming hardship: "Set your sights high," he says. "Stick to them. And work at it very, very hard. Invest in others and allow people to invest in you."

CHANGING COURSES IN MIDSTREAM

A SECOND PERSON INDUCTED into the Horatio Alger Society with me in 1994 was Terry Giles. His too is an inspiring story.

Terry remembers spending much of his childhood trying to help his loving but financially struggling family keep food on the table. He started out picking up bottles along roadsides, then ran paper routes, and when he got a little older, working as a busboy and dishwasher. His father failed at a long string of small business ventures. The family moved so frequently — often to avoid creditors — that Terry attended twenty-one different schools in ten years.

The family could never afford to buy their own home and routinely fell behind in rent and utilities. Whenever the electric company turned off the power or the landlord threatened to evict them, the Giles simply moved to another rental house. The strain took a toll on his parents' marriage; Terry and his sister endured a series of separations and then a divorce.

"When I look back on it, I don't ever feel like I was a kid," Terry says. "I loved my time with my mother and sister, but I feel like I always looked forward to growing up."

That is certainly understandable given his disjointed and sometimes traumatic childhood. Everywhere he went, poverty and his constant new-kid status made him an easy target for the verbal and physical abuse of the school bully. His baseball skills were a good equalizer for him. But by the time Terry could prove himself on the playing field, begin making friends and being accepted, he says, "My family would move on and the cycle would begin all over again."

On the positive side — Terry learned to be adaptable. A nomadic life helped him develop at least one skill that served him well in a later career: "I found out early that it was far more satisfying to talk your way out of trouble than to handle it physically," he says.

An eighth-grade teacher, noting some raw communications skills during an oral book report, insisted Terry enroll in a speech class in ninth grade. He went on to compete in high school speech and debate, and eventually won a debating scholarship to the University of California in Fullerton.

From grade school on, Terry says he dreamed of becoming a lawyer. "Probably a lot of it had to do with the fact that I grew up watching *Perry Mason* and *Owen Marshall*." So it wasn't surprising that when he graduated from Pepperdine University Law School with honors, he decided to open his own firm specializing in criminal law.

Five years later he supervised a staff of eighty-five, including twenty-nine lawyers, making his partnership the largest criminal law firm in the state of California. He was both a busy and talented defense attorney.

Despite his astounding success and a great love for the law, Terry gave up his booming practice in 1983. He made the difficult decision after a former client was arrested and charged with two murders he had committed within six months after Terry had gotten him acquitted on an earlier "conspiracy to commit murder" charge.

Terry says that for some time he had been wrestling with nagging questions about his career. When this former client showed up with two new murder charges, Terry asked himself, "Is the world a better place to live because I do what I do for a living?" And he says, "I didn't like the answer to that question. So I realized at that point I was going to have to quit."

It wasn't easy just to walk away from a lifelong dream when he was at the top of his field. But his early life experiences of starting over so many times helped ease the transition. "Because of what I dealt with growing up, I'm not afraid of the unknown. As a result, I'll try new things quicker than someone else might. I relate that to my childhood."

Wanting to do something beneficial to society, something productive, Terry and his wife decided to venture into business. He bought a small Toyota dealership in Garden Grove, California, which was selling thirty cars a month and ranked 1,150 out of 1,200

Toyota dealers in the United States. In two years, he built it into the fifth-largest Toyota dealership in the world—averaging nine hundred new-car sales per month.

With profits from his auto dealership Terry bought into a distributorship for Canon copiers. Within a couple of months, the first fax machines hit the market. Capitalizing on that new technology, that company became the third-largest Canon distributorship in the country.

In 1987, worried about fluctuations in the Japanese economy and the United States' uneasy trade relations with that country, Terry sold his interests in Toyota and Canon to invest heavily in West German real estate. Only to have the value of those holdings multiply when the Berlin Wall came down a short time later.

Over that same period, the owner of ComputerLand, Inc., who Terry had once represented in a civil suit, asked him to help handle the legal details in the sale of his company which was the largest computer sales business in the world. Once that sale was completed, Terry became one of the largest individual shareholders of that company and was named to ComputerLand's board of directors.

With the proceeds from all these business successes, Terry and his wife established the Giles Family Foundation through which they distribute their many charitable contributions—most of which are anonymous. Their foundation also developed and funds a nonprofit corporation called the American Institute for Life Technologies, which acquires patents and manufactures products designed especially for use by disabled people.

Now when he asks himself the question, "Is the world a better place to live because I do what I do for a living?" Terry feels great about the answer. And whenever he gets the opportunity to talk to young people, he tells them what his life has taught him about facing obstacles. He advises them to "reach for the stars. Decide what you want to be and don't settle for anything less. Believe that you can live your dream, and then work toward that goal, and it will happen. The worst mistake you can make is when you give up on yourself."

HERO ON PARADE

THEN THERE IS WALTER Anderson, the third person I want to tell you about, who joined the ranks of the Horatio Alger Society the same year I did. I felt a special kinship to him as I heard his story—for reasons that will be obvious as I relate it here.

Walter grew up in a four-room railroad flat on the wrong side of the tracks in Mt. Vernon, New York, in an atmosphere made volatile and violent by an illiterate, abusive, alcoholic father. "I lived with fear every day, nearly every minute of my childhood," Walter remembers. "Often my father would beat me for things I *might* do, not for things I had done. I felt safer on the street corner than in my own home."

Like me, my friend Walter credits his mother and reading as key influences in his life. His mom always tried to shield him from his father's abuse. "I never doubted my mother's love," Walter says. "She encouraged me to read despite the fact my father would beat me if he found me reading. Years later, after my father's death, I asked her why she would do so when she knew my father would beat me, and she said, 'I believed that if you would learn to read, somehow you would find your way out. And you did.'"

The Mt. Vernon Public Library became a secret sanctuary where Walter regularly escaped the abuse of his father and the cruel ridicule of classmates who would laugh at the holes in his ragged clothes. "I read myself out of poverty long before I worked myself out of poverty," he says. "By reading I could go anywhere, I could be anybody. I could imagine myself out of a slum."

Six days after his seventeenth birthday, he found another way out. He joined the Marines. That decision altered his perspective, his values, and his life forever. "I was able to develop self-respect, self-esteem, and a belief in noble motives and noble purposes. I learned about honor and dignity." In 1965, just months before he was to complete his active duty, Walter volunteered for Vietnam.

When he returned home from overseas and was discharged, Walter first took a job as a laboratory assistant, then as a sales trainee.

But what he really wanted to do more than anything else was to write. "Ever since I was fourteen or fifteen years old, I had a tremendous need to express myself."

Carrying the only thing he had ever had published, an emotional and articulate "letter to the editor" he had written from the front lines in Vietnam, Walter walked into a newspaper office to plead with the editor for a job. After reading Walter's one-clipping portfolio (his hometown paper, the *Mt. Vernon Daily Argus* had printed his letter on page one under the title "Just What Is Vietnam?") the editor of the *Reporter Dispatch* in White Plains, New York, hired him for $90.00 a week.

While working as a reporter in White Plains, Walter enrolled in a local community college and graduated two years later—first in his class of six hundred students. By that time he was "night editor" of his paper and had started his own action-line column, which was syndicated in seven other newspapers. Nearby Mercy College awarded him a full scholarship to continue his education. He graduated from there summa cum laude, once again class valedictorian.

After serving as editor and general manager of two daily newspapers, first in New Rochelle and then back in White Plains where he began his career, he moved to *Parade* magazine. He served as managing editor there before being promoted to editor of the largest circulation Sunday magazine in the world at the age of thirty-five.

From the time he took over the editorial reins of *Parade* in 1980, until he was inducted into the Alger Society with me, circulation of his magazine had risen from 21 million copies in 129 Sunday newspapers to more than 37 million copies in 353 papers.

During the course of his journalistic success, Walter met and interviewed a lot of famous people from whom he learned some valuable lessons. "I thought for the longest time that I was the only human being who worried that others would find out that I was inferior, that I was vulnerable, that I deserved to be rejected. I now know that every sane human being worries that others will find out that they are not quite good enough, that they can be hurt, that maybe they don't belong."

So, from his own life and from what he has learned from talking to some of the most successful people in our society, Walter has compiled his Seven Rules to Live By. I think they make a pretty good prescription for curing the victim mentality I have been talking about.

Here are Walter's seven rules:

Know who is responsible. "I am responsible." When you begin with these three words, you can build a new life, even a new world.

Believe in something big. When we commit to high ideals, we succeed before the outcome is known. Your life is worth a noble motive.

Practice tolerance. You'll like yourself a lot more and so will others.

Be brave. Remember, courage is acting with fear, not without it. If the challenge is important to you, you're supposed to be nervous; we only worry about things we care about.

Love someone. Because you should know joy.

Be ambitious. No single effort will solve all of your problems, achieve all of your dreams, or even be enough—and that's okay. To want to be more than we are is real and normal and healthy.

Smile. Because no one else can do this for you.

Examples like Joe's and Terry's and Walter's can not only inspire us to move beyond a victim mentality, they can also provide a Big-Picture view that may show us the advantages to be found in our own hardship, which I discussed in Chapter 6. Plus they can teach us a thing or two about our need for a Big-Picture perspective on the kinds of priorities and choices I will be talking about in Chapter 9.

A ONE-OF-A-KIND PAIR

But before I move on I would like to share one more example of two incredible individuals who had every reason to consider themselves victims and give up on life. Although never members of the Horatio Alger Society, they would have been, if the organization had existed in their day. Because their lives, or perhaps I should say *life*, better epitomizes what the Horatio Alger Society stands for than any other example I have ever seen or heard.

When I first became involved in the case of the Binder twins back in 1987, I began to research the history of congenitally conjoined twins. That was when I became interested in learning all the details I could find about Chang and Eng. Born in Thailand when it was called Siam (thus the origin of the term Siamese twins), in the year 1811, Chang and Eng were *thoracopagus* twins. That means they were conjoined at the chest.

They not only survived and grew to adulthood, they made a name for themselves and for their employer traveling around the world as star attractions in the Barnum & Bailey Circus. Tiring of travel and gawking crowds, Chang and Eng decided to retire from carnival life, settled in North Carolina, and took up farming.

Here is where their story becomes incredible. In our society today we find people who injure their little pinky and expect to receive disability payments for the rest of their lives. But back in the 1800s these two individuals, joined together at the chest, never able to get away from each other, capable only of limited mobility, not only became successful farmers, they each married and between them fathered somewhere between eleven and twenty-one children. (The historic records are incomplete.)

Unfortunately their wives couldn't stand each other, so the men lived with one woman one week and the other woman the next. That meant they actually managed two successful farms until they finally died in their sixties. Which was quite a bit longer than the average life span in those days.

I often recount the story of Chang and Eng when I speak because their example inspires me—and because I think it has so much to say on the subject of this chapter.

In fact, when I tell people about these original Siamese twins, I often conclude the story with the same basic question I ask after talking about the most incredible resource God has given all of us to help face and overcome the hardships of life. With the incomparable human brains all of us possess, with inspiring examples like Chang and Eng, *How can any of us ever utter those two most tragic words in the English language: "I can't"?*

I can't—and neither should you.

Their story exemplifies a saying I have also begun sharing with audiences recently. For me, it sums up everything we have been talking about: *A victim walking through sand looks down and sees dirt, a victor sees the ingredients for building a castle.*

Eight

PARENTING: LIFE'S MOST IMPORTANT RESPONSIBILITY

In Baltimore, one day in the winter of 1998, a tragedy occurred. Though it was no different than many other such tragedies in other cities around our country, it happened in our community. On Friday afternoon, February 6, a teenage boy was gunned down and killed in broad daylight while walking home from school on a North Baltimore sidewalk. Witnesses reported seeing several teenagers brazenly beating Wayne Martin Rabb Jr. with a baseball bat, then chasing him along the busy city street before shooting him twice from behind. Police suspected those teens were the same ones who had hospitalized the boy in another baseball-bat beating outside of Northern High School just three weeks earlier. Reports indicated that the first altercation had stemmed from a lunchroom incident involving spilled milk. By all accounts the fifteen-year-old victim was a good kid with no gang affiliation, who, being fearful, had been asking for a transfer to another school for several weeks.

The story made headlines and was featured on the television news. The brutality of the crime horrified the entire city. Those people who lived near the school reacted with a confused mixture of anger and fear, while concerned parents and community groups loudly lamented the tragedy and demanded that something be done "to protect our children."

At the time, I had already been invited by the general manager of WJZ-TV, a local Baltimore station that had a booster-type partnership with Northern High, to speak at a "For Our Kids" school rally early the next week. Although I had a couple of surgeries scheduled that day, including a ten-to-twelve-hour hemispherectomy, I had promised I would try to make the evening meeting in time.

After this young man was killed on Friday, I received another call asking me to make a special effort to be there because the mayor and a number of government officials had also been asked to address what now promised to be a large gathering of upset parents and concerned citizens. Again, I said I would try.

The operation went well, and after instructing my surgical resident to close, I raced twenty minutes across town to Northern High School, arriving just after the program was scheduled to begin. As I parked my car and hurried into the building, I noticed a large and visible police presence—both outside and inside the school. An escort met me in the lobby and whisked me down a closed-off hallway and through a side door to the auditorium stage just as the school choir and band concluded the musical portion of the program.

On stage I joined Baltimore mayor Kurt Schmoke, the Maryland state's attorney, various school officials, PTA officials, Marcellus Alexander as general manager of WJZ Channel 13 TV, and television actor Charles Dutton, star of the sitcom *Roc,* who had grown up in that North Baltimore neighborhood. Together we faced a restless standing-room-only audience of more than a thousand concerned parents (including the father of the slain boy).

As I listened to the other speakers, I realized we were all there for the same purpose—to express our sympathy to the family and friends of the murdered teenager, to acknowledge people's concern, to solidify their commitment to work for change, and to offer whatever encouragement and hope we could. But as I looked out at the somber, worried faces of the parents, I wanted to do more. I wanted to challenge them—to remind them of the incredible responsibility that was theirs—and to say something that might make a difference, if not for the city of Baltimore or even Northern High School, at least in the life of one family, at least in the heart of one mother or father sitting in that auditorium. As I waited to speak, I prayed, asking God to give me words.

Finally, stepping to the podium, I began by referring to another teenage boy: "I spent most of this day removing half the brain of a young man who suffers from intractable seizures." That got their attention. When the "Oh my!"s and the other murmurs of surprise tapered off, I went on.

"Now I come here tonight to talk to you about using our brains..." I tried to impress them with the capability of the human brain by using the same example I gave the United Way folks in Birmingham, explaining how I could bring someone up on stage, let them look out at that crowd for just one second, and in fifty years retrieve that memory, complete with descriptions of everyone's attire and seat placement. After pausing for the exclamations of amazement, I said, "We're not talking about Einstein's brain here. We're talking about an average human brain that is capable of processing two million bytes of information per second. We need to understand that what we have been given is so precious...

"I stand here before you tonight, principally because my mother understood that. She recognized the potential that God has placed in each one of us.

"I'm not going to spend our time tonight reciting my story—about growing up in inner-city poverty, the son of a single mother with a third-grade education, and being the dummy of my class until I discovered reading and found out I wasn't so dumb after all. We are going to fast forward through all that to get to something a little more relevant to what we are talking about here tonight—my experience in high school..."

And I talked about how I had begun to make straight A's until tenth grade—when I ran into those "P-E-E-R-S—People who Encourage Errors, Rudeness, and Stupidity. And that's exactly what they were doing. I started to listen to them telling me how I should act; that if I wasn't out until late at night playing basketball I clearly had some sort of hormonal imbalance.

"I listened and went along and my grades went from A down to B. I listened some more and the B's became C's. The more I listened the farther my grades plummeted. But I didn't care. You know why? Because I was *cool*." I described the fashions my teenage peers had convinced me were so important. A lot of people in the audience that night laughed because they remembered those iridescent sharkskin pants.

"I wanted so badly to be considered *cool* that I began complaining about my clothes to my mother and begging her to buy me an Italian knit shirt. She let me know she was very disappointed to hear what I was saying; she thought she'd raised me to be different. Not to be the kind of person who always had to do the same things everyone else did. Not to cast my lot with people who weren't using their brains.

"When I responded by telling her I really did need an Italian knit shirt to be happy, she made me a deal. She said, 'I'll bring home all the money I make next week and turn it over to you, Ben. You'll be in charge of all the family finances. You can buy all the groceries, pay the bills, take care of the necessities. And whatever you have left over at the end of the week, you can spend on Italian knit shirts or whatever else you want.'

"I thought, *This is going to be great.* I bought the groceries and then began going through the bills. Of course I ran completely out of money long before they were all paid.

"In the process I realized that my mother, with her third-grade education, was a financial genius—just to keep food on our table and *any* kind of clothes on our backs. I also realized I'd been a fool. I had been complaining and wanting her to buy me a seventy-five-dollar shirt when she only made a hundred dollars a week, working her fingers to the bone, scrubbing other people's floors, and cleaning other people's toilets.

"I took a hard look at my behavior and wondered, *How could I be so selfish!*

"I started studying again. My grades went back up to A's. Some of those old peers laughed and called me *nerd* and *Poindexter*. But I refused to let that bother me. Because I had a goal.

"Plus I could always shut them up by saying one thing: 'Let's see what I'm doing in twenty years, and then let's see what you're doing in twenty years.' That's what we have to get our young people to understand—the concept of delayed gratification. The average person today lives to be about seventy-five years old. You have twenty to twenty-five years to prepare yourself. If you spend it appropriately you have fifty years to reap the benefit. If you spend it inappropriately you have fifty years to suffer the consequences.

"This is *Wisdom*. This is something we need to pray and ask God to give us and help us communicate to our young people.

"I need to close tonight by telling you about another problem I had as a teenager. My terrible temper. I was one of those people who thought they had a lot of *rights*. Ever know anyone like that? They think the world owes them something, that no one better cross them or . . ."

I told how I had gotten so angry one day that I lunged at a friend with a knife. "I aimed at his stomach, but I hit his belt buckle instead. Rather than slicing open my friend's abdomen, the blade broke off, and my friend ran away terrified but otherwise unhurt. Afterward, I was almost as frightened as my friend by the realization of what had almost happened. I could have very well ended up in jail instead of Yale. Instead, God used that incident to help turn my life around. I began to understand that when you get angry and react, that doesn't make you a strong person. It means you are a weak person; you are letting other people dictate your behavior.

"God didn't give us these incredible brains so that we could go off and act like maniacs every time we think somebody is looking at us the wrong way. That kind of behavior indicates incredible weakness. We need to let our young people know, 'You are stronger than that.' And we need to show them by our own examples.

"Our *examples* as parents are critical. Because kids are born with a built-in hypocrisy antenna. When we say one thing but do something else, that antenna pops up and blocks out everything else we tell them. We need to remember that.

"And there's one last thing. Let's not forget God. I know this is a public school and some people think we shouldn't bring up God here . . ."

Then I said what I often do, about God already being mentioned in our Constitution, our Pledge, in our courts, and on our money—which, I pointed out, makes it mighty strange that we cannot even mention him in a public school.

". . . so we need to make it absolutely clear to our young people, through our examples, that there is nothing wrong with living life by godly principles, caring about our neighbors, loving our fellow man, using our divinely designed human brains, and developing our God-given talents to their utmost, so that we can become useful and valuable to the people around us.

"If we as parents do that, not only will Northern High School be great, but the city will be great, the state will be great, and our country will be great. God bless you all."

TOUGHER THAN BRAIN SURGERY

I WANTED TO SAY so much more to those parents in the Northern High auditorium that evening, but then, I feel that way almost every time I speak to a group of parents. Not just because parents are some of my favorite people but because I think parenting is the most important job in the world.

I know that in the eyes of many people, my profession as a neurosurgeon gives me a certain amount of prestige. That is part of the reason I am invited to speak at places like Northern High. It is why publishers ask me to write books. They feel I have credibility simply because I am Ben Carson, pediatric neurosurgeon.

Yet, at the age of forty-seven, looking at the Big Picture, I have come to the conclusion that what I do as a parent in my own home is far more important than anything I can accomplish in the operating room at Johns Hopkins Hospital—and I think the same can be said for all of us. No matter what we do for a living, when it comes to how we can best impact the world today and shape its future tomorrow, chances are our parenting will have the greatest, most lasting influence on others. I know the difference parenting can make.

Though I operate mostly on children, I also work with parents under crisis conditions every day. They come in all shapes, sizes, colors, and temperaments. One of the hardest things I have to do is to face parents whom I know have abused their children. To realize what horrible damage they are doing to their children, not just physically but emotionally and spiritually. To be civil with them when I really feel more like punching them — that's tough.

Fortunately, I see a lot more parents from the other end of the spectrum — parents whose loving dedication to their children inspires me. I think of a young patient whose medical problems were so complex that the parents moved the family all the way from Florida to Baltimore so they could be near their child as she got the specialized care she needed. I find that kind of sacrificial love impressive — though it is not unusual in the families I see.

More often than not, mothers inspire me most. I think of a young patient — a little girl named Brooke — who had a severe craniofacial deformity which was part of a syndrome that also affected all four of her extremities as well. This two-year-old had so many physical problems that she had literally been in and out of hospitals all of her life — sometimes for as long as three and four months at a time.

Fortunately this little girl had the most loving, patient mother I have ever seen. If anyone ever had the right to be tired and frustrated and angry and irritable with her circumstances and with the people around her, it was this mother. If she had broken down in despair or blown up at the staff, none of us would have blamed her. But she was always so upbeat, so pleasant to be around, so kind and loving — not just with her poor child but with all of us who helped care for Brooke — that we would go out of our way during rounds to make sure we could see and talk with her each day. She encouraged and ministered to us.

Each time I think of Brooke's mom, I remember what a difference she made in my life and in the lives of the other medical staff in the weeks and months she was with us. Then I realize what impact a lifetime of such love will have on her daughter. That truly inspires me.

MOTHER MODEL

Of COURSE, MY CONVICTIONS about the importance of parenting did not start with my profession. My own growing-up experience is all the proof I need. I not only saw and felt the difference my mother made in my life, I am still living out that difference as a man.

A lot of people think their mother is the greatest in the world, but it is particularly meaningful when other people recognize your mother as special—which is why my brother Curtis and I were especially proud when, for its 1997 Mother's Day issue, *Parade* magazine featured our mom in an article telling our family story. They put her picture, taken with the two of us, on the cover, accompanied by the title "What Mom Knew."

> Sonya Carson missed school as a child, married at thirteen, and was eventually abandoned by her husband. She raised her two boys alone and in desperate poverty. Today, one of her sons is a renowned surgeon, the other a successful engineer.

Though she always had our vote for "Mother of the Year," it was still a thrill to see her get a little of the credit she deserves.

DEBUNKING PARENTHOOD?

Because I SEE PROOF of parenting's impact every day in my profession and because I have experienced it personally in my life, I was more than a little disturbed by the media attention given to a recent book on the subject—a book that hit the market with a huge splash at the very time I was working on this chapter. I have not read Judith Rich

Harris's book *The Nurture Assumption; Why Children Turn Out the Way They Do, Parents Matter Less Than You Think and Peers Matter More.*

The title, the book's premise, and the author's stated motivation for writing it, are more than enough to keep me from adding it to my personal "must read" list. *Newsweek* (September 7, 1998) identified what they called Harris's "central claim" this way:

The belief "that what influences children's development ... is the way their parents bring them up ... is wrong." After parents contribute an egg or a sperm filled with DNA, she argues, virtually nothing they do or say, no kind words or hugs, slaps, or tirades; neither permissiveness nor authoritarianism; neither encouragement nor scorn — makes a smidgen of difference to what kind of adult the child becomes. Nothing parents do will affect his behavior, mental health, ability to form relationships, sense of self-worth, intelligence, or personality. What genes don't do, peers do.

What truly troubles me isn't Harris's opinions. Everyone is entitled to opinions. What troubles me is the credibility the media gave her ideas by treating the book, which flies in the face of research (not to mention common sense), as "serious science." *Newsweek* went so far as to make it their cover story. They hyped it by proclaiming, "Do Parents Matter? A New Heated Debate About How Kids Develop." Many other national publications reported on Harris and reviewed her book. Then of course the author made the rounds of the television networks' morning shows.

That bothers me because for every grateful and concerned parent of a "problem" child for whom Harris's book means a little *less* unwarranted guilt and blame, I believe there are ten, or a hundred, parents in our society today who desperately need to be challenged to assume *more* responsibility for the nurture and development of their children. And not all those adults who need such reminding are to be found in neighborhoods like those around Northern High in Baltimore.

What Harris' book preaches is the opposite of what I tried to say to those concerned parents at Northern High that night. It goes against everything I say wherever I speak. It contradicts what I have seen from the parents I encounter as a pediatric neurosurgeon. And it denies what my own life has taught me: that when we consider and begin to get the Big Picture, we discover that parenting matters *more*, not less, than anything else we do in life.

THREE THEMES FOR PARENTING

So, DESPITE THE MEDIA coverage, the tidal wave of attention given this latest "hot-title" attack on parenthood will quickly fade. The vast majority of parents, I think, instinctively understand their important role in the lives of their children. As I continue to accept speaking invitations, I keep coming back to the same basic themes. They aren't profound—and they certainly aren't new. They are, to use the *Parade* magazine's words, *What Mom Knew*.

The first thing I wish every parent understood is that our children gain their sense of who they are, and who they will be, from their family. At least they should. If we provide an appropriate environment—where communication is open and values are espoused— then our children will be far less likely to seek outside influences to determine who they are and how to behave.

The second thing I want to communicate to parents is a warning: Children really do have a built-in hypocrisy antenna. Trust me. I'm a brain surgeon; I look inside kids' heads. I have seen it—well, okay, I've never actually *seen* it—but I definitely know it is there.

We cannot say one thing and do something else. We cannot tell our kids to "get your homework done on time" or "get ready for your test," if we always pay our bills late, receive late notices, and have our utilities cut off for nonpayment. We cannot expect children to keep their rooms clean if our bedroom looks like a pigsty. It does little good to lecture our children on the value and reward of hard work and commitment if they do not see us working hard to accomplish something important to us.

My mother knew that. She told *Parade,* "Every mom knows that a child isn't going to hear too much of what she *says*. It's what she *does* that is important. You have to start living what you say."

The third most important thing parents need to remember is *love.* Children need love. No matter what the circumstances, love and acceptance make all the difference. No matter who we are or what we do, we all need someone to give us unconditional love. This doesn't mean we don't punish or provide appropriate discipline; love, in fact, should be our motivation for those things. We need to love our kids and do it so convincingly and consistently that they will never doubt it.

That is the greatest single challenge of parenthood.

TEN STRATEGIES FOR IMPROVED PARENTING

I ADMIT THAT WHEN I encounter children whose parents do not take their roles seriously and do a less-than-adequate job, I lament that the most important job in the world is entrusted to people who have little or no training. As a physician, I have to be licensed. Every medical person I work with has to be licensed—doctors, physician assistants, nurses, medical technicians. Any plumber or electrician I call to repair something in my home has a license. The mechanic who works on my car is licensed.

Yet the only requirement for parenting is to have someone to parent—and you don't even have to plan or want a child. I am not advocating the licensing of parents, however. Nor am I recommending prerequisite training. I am not yet so discouraged by the prognosis for parenting in our society that I would consider granting the government more regulatory authority over families. In fact, despite my ongoing concern about the state of parenting, I see reason for optimism. Parenting books continue to sell in record numbers; people seem to both care and sense their need for help in the task every mother and father has been given.

I am also optimistic because I have seen so many people whom I thought had no business having children—being too troubled, immature, or young—grow with the job and become admirable parents. In my practice, I have encountered many a teenage mother with nothing but her love for her child. She may begin with no parenting skills whatsoever, yet with time, good examples, appropriate reporting systems for encouragement and accountability, and some sort of support system, she grows and matures into a wonderfully effective mother. It happens time and again.

Nearly all the parents I meet have the necessary love and the desire to be good parents. They are convinced of the importance of their task, and a lot of them instinctively know about the importance of family in establishing identity, the need to be an example, and a key being unconditional love. They grasp the *what* and the *why,* they just need a little help with the *how to.* They are the reason I share the following simple strategies. Some I have picked up by example. Others I have learned the hard way—by trial and error.

1. Remember your own childhood

This is a such a simple concept, yet an invaluable parenting skill.

Children today come programmed with the same basic emotions children have always had. Those feelings are part of the software bundle our Creator includes on every make and model of humanity.

Because there are no "new" feelings, not even any "updated" versions of old emotions, we can better parent our children simply by thinking back to our childhood—remembering what we thought was fair and unfair, what we worried about, what hurt or embarrassed us, even what we thought we might be able to get away with.

Remembering helps us empathize. It can help us be more patient. It may even raise a warning flag that will help us spot potential trouble in time to head it off.

Three quick practical examples drawn from experience with my boys:

I remember how much I hated doing chores as a boy. And I remember what finally made the difference in motivating me to begin doing them without my mother's nagging was realizing just how hard my mother worked to support our family. Only then did I recognize how unfair and selfish it really was for me to think I should always be out playing catch and never doing my share.

Because I remember that, I have made a point to make sure my boys recognize the enormous time I put into my job for their benefit. I want them to understand that the fact we are able to live the way we do, without financial problems, is the result of their parents' hard work. Hopefully that realization will foster their own sense of responsibility.

Remembering my own struggle with anger helps me better interact with my son who is most like me in that regard. I am constantly reminding him that it is a sign of weakness to let other people's actions and attitudes dictate your response.

I also remember how much my own personal faith meant to me growing up—in everything from controlling my anger to giving me purpose and reducing my fears and uncertainty about the future. That memory is one of the things that prompts me to bring up and encourage each of my boys' spiritual growth at least once every week.

2. Let kids make the rules

This is not the same as relinquishing our authority as parents. I am not suggesting that children be in charge of the home. But I have found that when we let children have a voice in establishing expectations, we have a lot less trouble getting them to meet those expectations. This was one of my mother's best strategies.

One day when Curtis and I complained about everything she asked us to do, she told us that if we were tired of her being in charge, if her requirements were so unfair, she would let us decide what needed to be done and who would do it. We could come up with a fairer plan.

So we did. It was our plan, so we had no more reason to complain. And in our attempt to be fair, we had given ourselves more responsibilities than our mother had. So she was pleased to let that arrangement continue as long as we wanted.

Recently Candy and I tried this tactic with our boys. We sat down with them and asked, "What things do you think you should be responsible for?" They quickly generated a list of household chores, routine yardwork, homework, music practice, and so on. Then we let them help determine both the rewards for fulfilling those responsibilities and the penalties for failure to do so. Which leads me to my next point.

3. Make certain your children experience consequences

Once we established what was expected, we all determined how many points they received for each expectation. We actually give them chips—like poker chips—for completing their responsibilities in a timely fashion. They were rewarded for getting all their homework done, practicing their music without being reminded, and even for having a good attitude. They get chips taken away for bad attitudes, having to be nagged about a responsibility, leaving something undone, or doing an incomplete or inadequate job. The system works with report cards as well. They get twenty chips for every A, five chips for every B—and they owe us twenty for any C.

They can trade chips for dollars to earn spending money, to buy Christmas presents, to purchase something special they want, or to go into their bank account. We have pointed out to them that just by completing their responsibilities, maintaining a good attitude, and bringing home great report cards, they can expect to have enough money accumulated to buy their own car by the time they are seventeen or eighteen years old.

I know some people would disagree with this strategy. They think, *As long as my children live under my roof I shouldn't have to pay them to accept their share of family responsibilities.* That's fine. Every family needs to tailor their consequences and rewards to their own circumstances. But we find this plan works for us because one of our primary goals as parents is to help our boys learn what the real world is like: if you do a super job, you can expect better compensation; if you do a lousy job, you cannot expect much.

One more related comment: another important way to make certain your children experience the consequences of their actions is to resist the urge to always bail them out when they get themselves into trouble. Remember that hardship can be good. This is one of the most difficult things to do as a parent, but sometimes we need to exhibit a little tough love and let our kids suffer the natural results of their behavior. The older they get and the more serious the mistakes they make, the tougher this is. So the sooner this lesson is learned, the better.

4. Parenting can be a group effort

In previous generations, kids were not only accountable to their parents but to older relatives, their parents' friends, neighbors, and even the occasional adult stranger, who all took responsibility for supervising and instructing the community's children. That was true not just in small-town America but in the inner city where I grew up.

If a boy was making mischief—whether it was throwing rocks at passing train cars or carelessly bumping into an elderly person on the sidewalk—there was always some adult around who would speak up to tell you, "That's not right!"—or to make a phone call to report your transgression to your parents or maybe even to take you by the arm and march you home to make the charges in person.

That doesn't happen very often today. It seems that as our population grows and we are forced to live closer together, we no longer know our neighbors well enough to assume such responsibility. Or maybe we are reluctant to say anything in a society that holds to no moral absolutes because we are reluctant to judge anyone's behavior as *right* and *wrong*.

Whatever the reason, parents today are poorer as a result. For while I am convinced that parents are far more important than a village when it comes to raising a child, having others in the village to count on can be a tremendous help.

Parents today need to band together. We must find groups of other concerned parents—in neighborhoods, schools, and churches—so we can support each other, share concerns, exchange strategies, and sharpen each other's parenting skills. None of us should try to tackle such a high-stakes exploit alone or without a safety net.

5. Know your child

Treating two distinctly different children fairly does not necessarily mean always treating them exactly the same. Different personalities may require different strategies to achieve the same results. This is especially true when it comes to disciplinary techniques. Some children respond to punishment, others may be motivated by positive reinforcement. Some respond to spanking, others to temporary isolation or loss of privileges. A loving parent who knows his or her children is better equipped to choose the most effective disciplinary techniques.

A quick word about corporal punishment. The American Academy of Pediatrics recently condemned the practice, completely discounting the wisdom to be found in the Biblical book of Proverbs (13:24) that says: "He who spares the rod hates his son, but he who loves him is careful to discipline him."

I think "careful" is a key word any time we are talking about discipline. Despite those who would condemn all corporal punishment, I think it can be used in moderation, especially with children who are too young to be reasoned with. I recognize the dangers if we are not careful—especially when parents punish in anger and frustration. That is when most abuse occurs. But I think it unfair and unwise to lump abusers into the same category as loving, caring parents who administer corporal punishment with reluctance, even sadness, in appropriate measures and at appropriate times.

Having said that, I can probably count on the fingers of my hands the number of times I have had to administer corporal punishment to my three sons. Yet I know what sort of correction they each respond to, and they are generally disciplined and obedient kids.

6. Set high standards

My own mother was my best model for this strategy. I have already talked about her constant declarations that Curtis and I should expect to "be the best." So we always knew she would accept no excuses if we didn't *do our best*.

I apply the same sort of high expectations with my sons—not just academically, but also in terms of their standards of behavior. For example, now that our older two sons are teenagers, we talk to them about girls and dating. This is one more instance when it is helpful to think back and remember what and how I felt growing up.

I warn them about the dangers of raging hormones and the little subtle tricks some teenage girls will use to get them involved. Many people might think I am being unrealistic at best and perhaps even paranoid. But I would prefer my sons steer clear of all serious relationships as teenagers. Little good comes from them, yet the temptations are great.

Candy and I make it clear that the fact (which isn't a *fact* at all) that "everyone is doing it" is not a good excuse—when it comes to sex or any other behavior. We expect our sons to be strong enough to be different. To have higher expectations of themselves than they do the crowd.

7. Make time together

I work late far too many evenings. But on any night I get home before 9:00 P.M. we eat together as a family. That practice is something the boys themselves established and insist on continuing. As long as there is any chance I can be home by 9:00, they wait so we can all share supper together. Though early mornings are hectic at our house, we often manage to eat together then as well, and those shared meals provide some important time together.

Another valuable way to foster time together is to adopt some family project that requires cooperation between children and parents. In our family we have a string quartet—comprised of Candy (who was an accomplished musician at Yale when I met her) and our three boys. *The Carson Four* play two violins, a viola, and a cello. They have now become so accomplished that they accompany me on some of my speaking engagements, and a number of organizations have asked them to perform.

Of course, not every family could—or would even want to—have a string quartet, but I think any family could benefit by finding something they enjoy doing together that gives each person a chance to contribute to the whole.

8. Talk is cheap ... and invaluable

We are always looking for times in our schedule when we can be together and talk. Mealtimes are good starting points. We also regularly try to sit down as a family and read from the book of Proverbs, which contains a lot of practical wisdom—on anger for example. As we apply the verses to our lives, invariably the talk turns to things that have happened during the past few days or weeks. Someone will share how they handled a situation and what they might do differently next time.

Kids today have a lot of things going on in their lives, a lot of issues to deal with. Unless you sit down with them regularly to give them unpressured time to talk, you may never know what those issues are. Most of us know that listening is a key element in any communication, but it is doubly important for parents to remember to listen to their kids.

One morning recently I could tell my son BJ was angry. So I asked what he was mad about.

"I'm not mad," he quickly replied.

"Well," I told him, "You certainly have an interesting way of demonstrating happiness." It turns out he and his mother were not seeing eye-to-eye about some matter. So I said, "Let me hear it from your perspective."

And you know, just my willingness to hear his side was enough to diffuse his anger. Which is what I find often happens. Sometimes when they are in the wrong, kids will realize the weakness of their case as they talk and the argument naturally dies out without your having to say a word.

9. Marry the right person

This is the single best strategy I know for insuring that you raise healthy, happy kids to productive adulthood. It is amazing to me how many people choose a mate for life without ever considering the fact that the children produced by their marriage are going to be profoundly and permanently affected by the examples they see. Too many adults seem to think they are going to somehow change their mate. And they too often fail to realize if that mate manifests some worrisome characteristics they wouldn't want to see in their children, they had better think long and hard as to whether or not they have found the right person to marry. Why? Because children who have one good and one bad example stand no better than a fifty-fifty chance of following the good one—probably less.

I will talk more about the importance of making marriage a priority in Chapter 9. One of the best reasons I know for doing so is the positive ramifications it can have on our task as parents. I have said enough about my mother to indicate that a single person can do an outstanding job of parenting. But I also think when God set up the universe so that our procreation required a male and female, he had the same ideal in mind for parenting. Our task is much easier when we make it a two-person job.

Even then, no matter how equally you try to divide the responsibility, one or the other often has to assume more than their fair load. In our family, when it comes to the daily nitty-gritty of hands-on parenting, Candy carries the lion's share. For her great competence and willingness to do so, I am forever grateful.

10. Make parenting a true priority

Because one of the best indicators of any priority is our time, I wrestle with guilt on this score almost every day. One of the occupational downsides to being a surgeon is the hours required. Combine that with the fact I work at one of the biggest and busiest medical centers in the world and I just have to accept the fact that I am not going to get as much time with my family as I want. There is, for example, no way I can attend my sons' soccer games or tennis matches at four or five in the afternoon. It hasn't happened yet—and it may never happen.

That is one of the key areas where Candy takes up the slack. When it comes to after-school sports events, she is always there for our boys.

It is occasionally easier for me to make an evening concert or performance, so any night the boys participate in something like that, I try to attend.

Fortunately I have been blessed by God with the ability to switch gears quickly. When I leave the hospital, whatever time that might be, I am able to turn off all my professional problems and concerns so that when I walk in the door at home I can immediately focus on family. I seldom let the hospital intrude on my relationship with Candy and the boys. I think one can only switch gears like that if both gears are critically important for him. And being able to do that helps make up a little for all the hours I am not there.

Perhaps the biggest way I try to compensate for the times I cannot show my priorities by being with my family, is to take Candy and all three boys with me on many of my trips and speaking engagements. The kids know how much the plane tickets cost, which gives them some idea just how important a priority I consider them to be. Fortunately I can usually require those people who want me to speak to pay for my family's travel expenses as well. If the organizers of an event happen to think the cost required to bring my family is too great, or that my family is not that important, I usually decide their event is not important enough to warrant my participation.

FAMILY IS FUTURE

I AM CONVINCED THAT the future of the American family—black, white, and any other color—will determine the future of our nation. If we have weak and broken families that provide neither love nor a working moral compass, then we can expect no improvement in our country and our world.

If the leaders of America really believed and understood this Big Picture, perhaps more of them would understand the importance of creating new national policies and strategies to help traditional families thrive and once more become what God designed families to be—the moral, spiritual, emotional, social, and educational foundation on which a better world can be built. (We might start by rethinking our tax structures, which place such a disproportionate burden on average families, and addressing our economic environment that requires both parents to work.)

But until we begin that kind of national debate, I expect to concentrate my attention on parents themselves. I will keep sharing *What Mom Knew* with concerned parents like those at Baltimore's Northern High School, because this is such a critical personal issue for all of us.

Children are the greatest natural resource in the world. Our God-given job as parents is to develop those resources to their greatest potential. In the Big Picture, it is the most important job in the world.

Nine

DETERMINING PRIORITIES AND MAKING CHOICES

I DO NOT SPEAK only to parent groups. I spend a lot of time with students, such as those I encountered not long ago on a memorable visit to Wendell Phillips High School, an inner-city school on Chicago's south side.

Before I spoke, the people who invited me to the Windy City held a reception in my honor. There I met and talked with school officials and local religious leaders, many of whom informed me about the troubled neighborhood where the school is located. They indicated that gang influence was prevalent, living conditions were deplorable in the surrounding public housing developments, dropout statistics were high, and SAT scores were low.

It sounded like a lot of other high schools I have visited around the country. Yet so dire were these warnings that, on the cross-town drive to the school, I could not help wondering what kind of reception I would receive from the students.

I need not have worried. When I walked into Wendell Phillips High School, its long deserted hallways gave the building a cavernous, empty feel. The entire student body (1,500–2,000 strong) had already been excused from class and was assembled quietly in the school's auditorium. A school administrator, who was addressing the audience, noted my entrance through a back door and abruptly interrupted his remarks to announce, "And here's Dr. Carson now!"

All eyes turned my way. Immediately students began to applaud. Some stood. Suddenly they were all standing, clapping, and cheering. The applause continued the entire time I walked down the aisle and climbed the steps onto the auditorium stage. I couldn't remember ever receiving a warmer, more enthusiastic, or more spontaneous reception anywhere in my entire life.

I found out later that a local bank had purchased and distributed paperback copies of my autobiography, *Gifted Hands*, to every student at Wendell Phillips. A lot of those teenagers had evidently read the book and felt they already knew me. By the time I reached the microphone, the noise faded away. I felt overwhelmed by their welcome.

I did what I often do when facing such a young audience. I wanted them thinking seriously about their lives and futures. So I quickly summarized my earliest years as a child, about my own student days back at Southwestern High School in Detroit. I referred briefly to the incident when my anger nearly caused a tragedy that would have altered my life forever. I recounted my struggles with peer pressure, which sidetracked me for a time.

Then I talked about the difference between being viewed as *cool* and being classified as a lowly *nerd*. I find that serves as a graphically relevant illustration for my message on *delayed gratification*—a theme I hit almost every time I speak to young people.

The *cool* guys in every school are the ones who have earned a varsity letter in some sport—maybe several sports. They wear the latest fashions. They know all the hit tunes. They can converse about the latest blockbuster movies. They drive sharp cars and seem to collect a bevy of beautiful girlfriends.

The *nerds* are the guys always hauling around an armload of books, with more in their backpack. They wear clean clothes—and often big, thick glasses. They even understand the science experiments. They ride the school bus, or worse yet, their parents drive them to school. Most of the popular girls would not be caught dead speaking to them in the hallway between classes.

The years go by, and graduation draws near. Often the cool guy has not done well in school, but his personality wins him a job at the local fast-food franchise, flipping hamburgers and waiting on customers. The nerd, who has won a scholarship, goes off to college.

A few more years go by. The cool guy is still flipping burgers. Maybe he has even moved up to Assistant Shift Manager by now. The girls who come in to eat lunch may notice and smile at him. He is still cool.

The nerd finishes up at college and does very well. Upon graduation he accepts a job offer from a Fortune 500 company. With his first paycheck, he goes to the eye doctor, who replaces those big, old, thick glasses with a pair of contacts. He stops at the tailor and picks out a couple of nice suits to wear. After saving a big chunk of his first few paychecks, he makes a down payment on a new Lexus. When he drives home to visit his parents, all the young women in the old neighborhood say, "Hey, don't I know you?" Suddenly, they do not want to talk to the guy behind the fast-food counter anymore.

The first guy—the cool guy—had everything back in high school. So what did he get for all that?

The other guy was not cool at all—but he was focused. Where did he go in the long run?

"And that," I told my audience, "is how we have to learn to think about life! With a long-term view. A Big-Picture perspective!"

Those students at Chicago's Wendell Phillips High School could not have been more attentive as I recounted the things this former *nerd* has seen and done. They listened to me explain and illustrate the incredible potential that resides in the average human brain. They even seemed receptive to my challenge that they begin to use those brains to plan and prepare for the future. So, as I wrapped up my talk by daring them to THINK BIG, I did something I had never done before, though I realized it could backfire if I had read this audience wrong. But since they had been such a responsive group, I decided to risk it.

I concluded by asking that auditorium full of high school

students for a show of hands. "How many of you are ready, here today, to raise your hands and say to me, to your teachers, and to your peers, 'I want to be a nerd.'"

Although many of them laughed, almost all the students of Wendell Phillips High School raised their hands as they stood and applauded and cheered even louder than when I had walked in.

DO-IT-YOURSELF FRONTAL LOBOTOMY

WHEREVER AND WHENEVER I speak, I try to challenge my listeners to make changes in their beliefs, thinking, and behavior that will have a positive impact on their world. I especially try to motivate young people to consider the future seriously. Because I am a scientist who has spent a good deal of my life studying, working with, and marveling at the human brain, I frequently remind my listeners that we are the only creatures on earth to whom God gave such huge frontal lobes.

What does that mean?

Frontal lobes are used for rational thought. As human beings we come programmed with the ability to extract information from the past, gather information from the present, integrate that data, and project it into the future. In other words, we can plan. That means we are the only creatures on earth capable of seeing and actually affecting the Big Picture. And the significance of that is: we do not have to live like animals.

Other animals only react to their circumstances—which makes them victims of those circumstances. As human beings we have been given the capacity to analyze, strategize, and prioritize so that we can alter our circumstances. We can anticipate and plan and take action that will even affect our future.

Too many people give up this divine inheritance. Instead, they act like animals and just react. They go from day to day simply responding to circumstances rather than creating different ones.

I am convinced that the average person spends more time planning his or her next birthday party than planning his or her life. Most of us are wasting those amazing frontal lobes.

How many people do you know who actually sit down with a pen and paper and specifically plot out a strategy for where they want to go in life and how they intend to get there? The most successful people I know have gotten where they are, at least in part, because they have done that. They have spent time thinking about the future, setting goals, and developing deliberate plans to get there. It takes time and effort to use our frontal lobes, which is why so many people find it easier just to go with the flow, do whatever everyone else is doing, and take life as it comes.

How many students at Wendell Phillips High School who raised their hands that day are like that? How many will actually follow through on their stated intention to take a long-range, Big-Picture perspective and become academically successful *nerds*?

I don't know.

But I do know this. Each one of those students, like each one of us, has been given the remarkable capacity to determine the direction of his or her life. What we do with that potential will largely depend on three factors: our priorities, our principles, and our choices.

WHERE THERE'S A PRIORITY . . .

SUPPOSE YOU WERE TO walk up to a panhandler on the sidewalk in downtown Baltimore. He has been telling everyone that he is out of work and needs money just to buy supper. You promise him if he can get to Bismarck, North Dakota, within twenty-four hours, a very nice job will be waiting for him there. What happens? Chances are he will look at you as though you are crazy and inform you he has no way of getting to Bismarck. He has no resources. He might well complain that he isn't interested in living in North Dakota. If you are lucky, he may politely thank you for the kind offer, before he insists there is just no way he could take advantage of it.

Now just suppose that, instead of a job offer, you could absolutely guarantee that same panhandler $1 million if he would meet you in Bismarck, North Dakota, within twenty-four hours. What do you think would happen? In all likelihood, you would not hear a single excuse. He would be there—with time to spare. You can bet on that.

My point is this: people always find the time and the means to do what they really want.

Priorities get done. Priorities are ... well ... PRIORITIES!

A lot of people complain that their priorities get crowded out, or at least shoved onto the back burners, of their lives. If that is true, I believe, then those things are not *priorities*.

Certainly, if we are not careful and deliberate about planning, preserving, and maintaining our priorities, they can easily get bumped off the front burner. Then whatever is most urgent, whatever seems most pressing, automatically becomes our priority. At that point we are no better than animals; we are just reacting.

REAL PRIORITIES

IN CHAPTER 8 I acknowledged the struggle I have allotting the time required to make parenting the priority I believe it should be in my life. I face the same struggle with the other half of my "family priority"—my marriage.

Any relationship takes time and effort to survive and grow—a marriage more than any. When two different personalities bump against each other day after day, month after month, year after year, the inevitable friction can spark little resentments that smolder and spread until they burst into flames.

These days a lot of marital conflict seems to develop around roles, power, and authority issues—who is the boss and who is supposed to be submissive. Unfortunately, when such struggles get played out in front of the children, it can create discomfort, insecurity, and confusion, which is why some church denominations have even weighed in with official statements intended to settle the issue.

While a certain amount of tension and disagreement are inevitable in any relationship, most marital power struggles can be avoided.

We need to look at marriage as a complete partnership in which two loving individuals attempt to make one another happy by submitting to each other in love and creating a wholesome, cheerful environment for the family. But that is impossible without making marriage and family a priority.

That takes time and energy, both of which require planning. One of the things Candy and I do to keep our relationship a priority is to celebrate two days every month — which we call our *month-aversaries*. On the sixth of each month we commemorate July 6, 1975, the date of our wedding. And on the twenty-eighth of each month we remember November 28, 1972. That was when we began going together after we had both been nearly killed in an automobile mishap. Whenever possible, we try to do something special together on our month-aversaries, even if it is just exchanging cards or talking about what the years have brought to us and acknowledging the tremendous blessings we have experienced through our marriage.

I am fortunate to have a loving wife who is incredibly patient and understanding about my long hours at the hospital. She is always careful and considerate never to place excessive demands of her own on my schedule.

Before we were married I warned her that because I was not only going to be a doctor but a neurosurgeon, I probably was not going to be at home nearly as much as most husbands are. She grinned and asked, "Is that a promise?"

Candy not only has a great sense of humor, but she is such an independent individual that she enjoys my company when I am there but doesn't ever fall apart when I am not. During my residency, she decided since I was never home, she would go back to graduate school and earn an MBA. She not only manages our family finances, she has her own small business and plays an active role in overseeing the work and growth of the foundation we started, the Carson Scholars Fund.

In addition to regularly traveling together to my speaking engagements, Candy and I have adopted another important strategy for keeping our marriage a priority. This too involves planning. I keep my administrative assistant in almost daily contact with Candy so that marriage and family time can be written into my official work schedule. Otherwise the daily demands would crowd out my family, and I would be reacting to my circumstances instead of maintaining my real priorities.

A BALANCING ACT

But FAMILY IS NOT my only priority, of course. Two other interacting and oft-competing priorities have to be balanced on a weekly, if not daily, basis.

My first priority most weekdays, from 7:00 or 7:30 A.M. until whatever time I get away from the hospital each night, is my work. In choosing neurosurgery as a career, I made the decision many years ago to devote my professional life to ameliorating the lives of neuro-logically ill children. That priority carries with it many ramifications.

My particular career demands sacrifice, effort, and an enormous amount of time. I wish I could do what I do working eight, ten, even twelve hour days, knowing I will have evenings and weekends free. But that simply doesn't happen. That is okay because it is the by-product of my priority — to help as many children as I possibly can. Like the bum getting to Bismarck, I manage to find the time and the means to do what I really want to do.

I find that one of my toughest challenges in life, however, is balancing my professional priority and its effect on the people around me. Over the years I have come to realize that my work ethic and my priorities sometimes make my staff miserable. My administrative assistant and physician assistants especially have to spend enormous time away from their families in order for me to do what I do.

I never feel good about forcing my priorities on others. They have to make their own choices; and I have lost some good staff people because of it. So I am always trying to find ways to better compensate the talented and dedicated people who continue to work with me. I wish I had money in the budget to pay them for all the extra hours they put in, but I don't. I try to be more flexible with their vacation time, but that is not always possible either.

It is tough when our priorities impinge on the lives of others. Even careful planning cannot always prevent that.

PUBLIC PRIORITIES

I HAVE ANOTHER MAJOR priority that has to be constantly balanced with my family and professional roles: the role I have accepted in public life.

This public role is what takes me to places like Wendell Phillips High School and Baltimore's Northern High School and the United Way conference in Birmingham. I average one to two speaking engagements a week because I make it a priority. In this public role I also serve on the corporate boards of both Yale University and the Kellogg Company, and have founded the Carson Scholars Fund to help foster academic achievement in our nation's public schools.

The media attention and national visibility resulting from all my extracurricular involvement has led some of my professional colleagues to question my motivations. They assume I must be a glory-seeking publicity hound.

But on numerous occasions since I became a pediatric neurosurgeon, I have arrived at crossroads in my life that required me to make choices about my professional as well as personal priorities. For example, I could have decided to focus more of my efforts into medical research.

I have great admiration and affection for my friend and Johns Hopkins colleague, Dr. Henry Brem, who is one of the world's most outstanding academic neurosurgeons. Henry has recently developed a procedure integrating time-released chemotherapy into biodegradable wafers that can be implanted into brain tumors. It is the first new brain-tumor therapy approved by the FDA in twenty-five years and promises to improve both the quality and length of life for patients with malignant brain tumors. I am grateful that there are people such as Dr. Brem who benefit all mankind by making medical research such a high priority in their careers.

I also appreciate those colleagues who channel most of their professional energies into the academic arena. I enjoy giving lectures as a faculty member at the Johns Hopkins University School of Medicine, just as I find great satisfaction in my instructional role of training the surgical residents assigned to work with me in the operating room. But those are not my own highest priorities.

I am also grateful that some of my colleagues invest considerable time and energy in our national professional organization, the American Society of Pediatric Neurosurgery (ASPN). But again, that is not my priority.

Instead of devoting more energy to any of these things, I decided some years ago that neurosurgery provided me a platform from which to exert a much wider influence. I realized I have been given an extraordinary opportunity. Few people have gone through what I have to get where I am. And even fewer people in my position have been privileged to have cases like I have had — separating Siamese twins, for example — which bring them some degree of prominence and notoriety.

God has given me so much that I feel it would be a tremendous shirking of responsibility not to try to use my unusual platform to do and say more, to give something back. So it has become a major priority in my life to try to make a broader positive impact on society as a whole. That is why I do so much public speaking, serve on corporate boards, give of my time to my church, and do whatever else I can to establish a public image I can use to advance the cause of academic achievement and excellence.

THE PRINCIPLE DIFFERENCE

EVERYONE HAS PRIORITIES. IF we fail to establish our own, someone else — or circumstances — certainly will. And it is a lot easier to establish them and to maintain them when we found our priorities upon strong underlying principles.

Where do we find those principles? How do we learn them?

If we are fortunate, we learn principles by which we can set our priorities from our families. I have talked a lot about my mother's influence already. Many of the values and principles she taught by her words and her actions underlie my own major priorities of family, work, and public service.

In an age teeming with dysfunctional families, I realize not everyone benefits from a family heritage that instills such principles. But those of us with children could better shape the values and principles our kids learn from us if we would give a little more serious consideration to our own and then try to articulate those principles to our children at every opportunity.

ANOTHER PRINCIPLE SOURCE

Families are not the only place we learn values and principles, however. Most of us also pick up principles from other people. Though I often talk about the detrimental influence of peers, I discovered the positive influence peers can have when I got into a high school ROTC program. There I met people from whom I learned such valuable, lasting principles as discipline, hard work, and teamwork.

Peers continue to influence us even beyond our childhood and youth. In my book *Think Big,* I paid tribute to a number of mentors and colleagues who have been instrumental in my personal and professional success. I am constantly adding to that list as I continue to learn important lessons from people I work with from the Horatio Alger Society friends I mentioned in Chapter 7.

As we approach the new millennium, the ancient wisdom of Solomon (Proverbs 13:20) still holds true: "He who walks with the wise grows wise, but a companion of fools suffers harm." In other words, the people we associate with influence those core principles on which we base our priorities.

WHAT'S WRONG WITH THIS PICTURE?

We ALSO ADOPT SOME of our principles from the world around us—in the form of social and cultural values. As with families and peers, this can be good or bad. Our national heritage includes such great historic principles as independence, self-determination, freedom of choice, and many other fundamental values that have shaped the thinking and lives of Americans. Traditionally, our educational, religious, civic, and governmental institutions have promoted such widely held principles.

Today, however, it seems the most predominant cultural principles are conveyed through media and entertainment. One that I take issue with almost every time I speak is our culture's rather recent validation of *instant gratification* as an acceptable and appropriate expectation. Television is probably the worst purveyor of this idea. *We see it, we gotta have it, and we gotta have it now!*

Hollywood also gives us the impression that we are total failures if we are not millionaires by the age of forty. We celebrate *Lifestyles of the Rich and Famous*—proving that even widescreen TV offers only a small-picture view of the world. I think Robin Leach should also host a show called *Lifestyles of the Formerly Rich and Famous*. Maybe that would give a Big-Picture perspective and help us better understand the need for priorities based on solid principles.

I don't hold out much hope that is going to happen. Too many of us have already bought into the small-picture thinking that is so prevalent on the tube and throughout our society today.

THE FAITH FILTER

So HOW DO WE counter such small-picture thinking? If the principles we learn from our typical sources—family, peers, and society—are all potentially flawed, where do we find better ones we can count on?

I believe this is where religious faith can play a critical role. For me as a Christian, the priorities and principles that direct my life grow out of my relationship with God. Since I was a teenager, I have made a daily habit of prayer and Bible reading—always including, but not limited to, the book of Proverbs in which Solomon, supposedly the wisest man in history, shares his advice and principles for successful living.

Many people think the Bible is a fuddy-duddy book—irrelevant, outdated. But most of the people who say that are not reading it. They certainly could not be reading Proverbs, a particularly practical collection of wisdom principles that apply to the biggest personal issues we wrestle with every day.

When I struggled with anger as a teenager, many of Solomon's sayings on that subject spoke to me—Proverbs such as: "A gentle answer turns away wrath, but a harsh word stirs up anger" (15:1); or "An angry man stirs up dissension, and a hot-tempered one commits many sins" (29:22).

Other Proverbs took on greater meaning as I grew older: "My son ... do not forsake your mother's teaching. Bind them upon your heart forever; fasten them around your neck. When you walk, they will guide you; when you sleep, they will watch over you; when you awake, they will speak to you. For these commands are a lamp, this teaching is a light, and the corrections of discipline are the way to life ..." (6:20–23); "Pride goes before destruction, a haughty spirit before a fall" (16:18); "The tongue has the power of life and death, and those who love it will eat its fruit" (18:21).

LESSONS FOR LIFE

WHEN WE UNDERSTAND SUCH wisdom and have thoughtfully adopted life priorities based on lasting principles, even the toughest situations and decisions we face become a lot easier. Some quick examples:

Once as a boy when I bought something at the store, the clerk made a mistake and gave me too much change. Instead of a one-dollar bill she gave me ten dollars.

I walked out of that store elated. I began to fantasize about all the things I could do with *my* extra nine dollars. But by the time I reached home I had a knot in my stomach twice the size of the fist in which I still held the money. I was no longer feeling so good about my "good fortune."

I recognized the feeling I experienced as guilt. I knew keeping the money wouldn't be honest; and honesty was a principle I had learned from my mother as well as at church.

So I walked back to the store and returned the ten-dollar bill to the clerk with an explanation of what happened. She gave me the correct change and I strode out of that store nine dollars poorer but feeling on top of the world. That reinforced for me an even more important truth than the virtue of honesty. It reminded me that there is such a thing as right and wrong, and when you do what is right, based on the principles you believe in, the satisfaction that results is better than having money.

Not long ago I faced a different situation, involving a larger amount of money. I had signed a contract to co-author a book of special concern to people of the African-American community who suffer from certain health problems in numbers disproportionate to the general population. Because many of these health problems — heart disease, stroke, hypertension, certain types of cancer, and so on — can be greatly affected by lifestyle choices, our book suggested practical and specific lifestyle changes that could greatly improve the percentages.

The publisher complained of too much moralizing for a book on "medical issues." For example, in a discussion of sexually transmitted diseases I suggested abstinence was a highly effective and reasonable means of combating the problem. I even suggested that any young man who was thinking about getting into a sexual relationship should ask himself, "Would I want someone to do to my sister what I am planning on doing with this young woman?" The publisher considered my promotion of abstinence moralizing and did not want to include it for fear it would offend or turn off readers. But I refused to take it out. Not only did I feel it was valid medical advice, but it reflected my own strong convictions.

As a result, the publisher and I parted ways, and I lost the money because I was not willing to compromise my principles and publish a book simply for monetary gain. Again Solomon's wisdom in Proverbs 22:1 fits here: "A good name is more desirable than great riches; to be esteemed is better than silver or gold."

It was an unpleasant decision because I had invested a lot of time in the book. But it was not a difficult decision, because I still believe decisions and priorities need to be based on principles.

I faced another thorny predicament several years ago. I was invited by a Maryland right-to-life group to tape a television commercial for their cause. Since I have made it a priority to try to preserve, rather than take, life, I happily agreed to help.

The television commercial drew much positive response. But as the weeks passed I noticed something that began to bother me in the overall campaign to persuade voters to end elective abortions in Maryland. Some of the information disseminated, and many of the arguments being made, were not entirely accurate. The more I saw of what seemed like scare tactics and misleading statements in this campaign, the more uneasy I felt about my name being associated with it. So I called the group's headquarters and asked that my commercial be withdrawn.

Considerable public debate ensued when word got out. Many people concluded that Johns Hopkins had forced me to recant my position. But no one from Hopkins ever did, or ever would do, such a thing. In fact, the authorities at the university have always been extremely supportive of my public role.

The decision was only difficult in the sense that I did not want to hurt a cause I believed in by withdrawing my public support. Making the decision itself was easy enough—because I saw it as a matter of principle. If I wanted to stand for the principle of truth, I could not in any way allow my name to be publicly associated with statements that were only part true and misleading. It was as simple as that.

SAFE SEX

Firm principles can also serve us well by keeping us out of many difficult situations altogether. And this is never more true than in the realm of adultery and affairs.

I have known a number of individuals over the years who have been involved in adulterous affairs; I have yet to witness a happy outcome. Time and again I have seen the emotional and spiritual distractions resulting from affairs so complicate the lives of the people involved that their value to society and the people around them is severely diminished. The national scandal Americans have had to endure over the months I have been working on this manuscript is just one painfully public case in point. It is a sad and regrettable case that only proves what King Solomon, who was also a powerful ruler, learned long ago, "A man who commits adultery lacks judgment; whoever does so destroys himself. Blows and disgrace are his lot, and his shame will never be wiped away" (Proverbs 6: 32–33).

But lest I be charged again with too much moralizing, I hasten to add that I try not to be judgmental. Better men (and women) than I have tripped and fallen into sexual temptation. The moment we begin to believe we are invincible we actually become most vulnerable.

That is why I have concluded that the best protection from sexual temptation is principle. The kind of principle Solomon talked about in chapters 5–7 of Proverbs when he warned, "Do not lust in your heart after her beauty or let her captivate you with her eyes, for the prostitute reduces you to a loaf of bread, and the adulteress preys upon your very life. Can a man scoop fire into his lap without his clothes being burned? Can a man walk on hot coals without his feet being scorched? So is he who sleeps with another man's wife" (6:25–29).

A couple of years ago I learned the value of heeding such advice (moralizing or not), holding firm to my principles, and making my marriage a major priority. I myself was accused of adultery by a woman in Florida who claimed I was the father of her child. I learned of this embarrassing charge when one of the university lawyers called my office to inform me that Florida's social services department wanted to attach my wages for child support.

Because I have lived by my principles and made my marriage the priority it is, I didn't have to scratch my head and wonder if I had slipped up sometime. I never had to ask myself, "Is it possible ... ?" Because I know that my wife is the only woman I have ever slept with, I could issue an absolutely confident denial. When I instructed my own lawyer to find out what was going on, I had no idea what we would learn about this woman, but I knew with certainty that he would find no truth to her charge.

Indeed, we soon learned that the only "proof" Florida officials could cite was the paperwork the woman had filed — including my current title, a magazine photo of me in scrubs, a record of where I had attended high school, college, and medical school, and the fact that I had spent a year of residency in Australia. My lawyer promptly threatened the state of Florida with a lawsuit for making these charges based solely on information anyone could have gotten from one of my books. The woman, when forced to provide additional details, could only claim I had been living in an Atlanta high-rise with a number of other doctors back in 1982 when this alleged sexual encounter, in which her child was conceived, occurred.

It was a simple matter to refute that contention. One of my superiors wrote the State of Florida a letter pointing out that I was chief resident in neurosurgery at Johns Hopkins University in Baltimore, Maryland, in 1982. My employment required me to reside within thirty minutes of the hospital, and it would have been physically impossible for me to live a double life in Maryland and Georgia.

I never heard another word from Florida. After the case was dropped, a number of people who knew the story questioned why I had not taken civil action against the woman or at least the state governmental agency that had subjected me to such a disturbing allegation.

I was tempted to do so — not because of the embarrassment as much as the aggravation. The day I was first called and informed of the charges, I was about to begin a complex operation on a baby with a huge brain tumor. Visibly upset by what I had just learned, I had to try to ignore the distraction of my own personal thoughts and feelings, to concentrate on successfully removing what fortunately turned out to be a benign tumor. Part of me would have loved to exact a little revenge for what I had to go through. But my belief in another principle—the principle of forgiveness—ultimately determined my decision not to pursue a legal response.

LIFE IS A MULTIPLE CHOICE TEST

THE REASON WE NEED to consider our priorities carefully—and the principles on which we base them—is that they impact every important choice we make in life. Those choices further determine both the ultimate direction of our lives and the unique set of opportunities that will come our way.

Everyone has opportunities. I do not believe they are determined either by luck or by circumstances; they are determined instead by our priorities, principles, and choices.

Here again I will probably be charged with moralizing, but so many people in our society seem to have forgotten that all choices have natural consequences. Even the priorities we set and the principles we base them on have consequences.

We have also forgotten the converse—that most of what happens in life, whether good or bad, is (or could be) determined by our own choices. Remember, as human beings we do not just have to react to circumstances, we can shape them.

By this point some readers may conclude from all this talk about self-determination and the need to assume personal responsibility that I must be a conservative Republican. I'm not. But I would like to say something about political affiliation.

I am troubled by the growing rancor and divisiveness that has marked so much of our national political climate in recent years. Too many of us want to describe ourselves as Democrats or Republicans and never the twain shall meet. One says this and the other says that.

If one is for something, the other is against it. We get ourselves backed into corners simply because we define ourselves by the ideology of our parties rather than by what we actually think. Why do we even need our brains? We can just say "I'm a Democrat" or "I'm a Republican" and "This is the way *we* think." That's crazy. That does not even give ourselves credit for the ability to analyze and interpret and make choices about individual issues in light of our own experience, priorities, and principles.

Therefore, I describe myself as an independent. I consider it a waste of our human brainpower to be otherwise. Of course, that is just my own opinion. Some of my best friends are still Republicans and Democrats.

THREE SIMPLE QUESTIONS

Earlier I asked, "How many people do you know who actually sit down with a pen and paper and plot out a strategy for where they want to go in life and how they intend to get there?"

Here at the end of this chapter I would like to suggest that we might all benefit if we would periodically stop and ask ourselves three simple questions:

1. When my life is over, what do I want to be remembered for?
2. What do I want to be doing five, ten, and twenty years from now?
3. What do I want to be sure I am not doing five, ten, and twenty years from now?

If we engage our brains to answer these questions, we will be forced to consider our priorities, our principles, and the choices they lead us to make. Just asking these questions will not guarantee we all will reach the destinations we set for ourselves. But the answers can serve as a road map. They will show us the Big Picture and point us in the right direction.

Ten

BEING NICE, DOING GOOD

Not long ago I spoke at an insurance conference in the San Francisco Bay area. In my morning session I explained the acronym of my THINK BIG strategy—including of course the "N stands for Nice" idea. As I usually do, I told my listeners "If you're not a nice person, I challenge you to try it for one week. Be nice to everyone you encounter for one solid week.

"It's ten minutes before ten on Friday morning. Until 9:50 next Friday morning, be nice to everybody—everyone you encounter ..."

Then I gave some quick examples of what that would mean. Helping people who need help, speaking to people, letting others go first, and so on.

After I finished that speech I had several hours of free time before I was to address the conference again at an evening banquet. At about 5:30 in the afternoon I was walking through the busy hotel lobby when I heard a woman calling, "Oh, Dr. Carson! Dr. Carson!"

I stopped and turned to find a fashionably dressed, obviously well-heeled woman in her fifties zigzagging her way toward me through the crowd and waving for my attention. "Dr. Carson!" I stopped.

She introduced herself and said, "I want to tell you how much I appreciated your talk this morning."

I thanked her.

"You actually made me cry. What you said touched me

so much—especially that part about being nice." She told me she had taken my challenge. All day her focus had been on trying to be nice to everyone she encountered. "I feel like a new person!" She not only felt good about herself, she had been amazed by people's reactions. It was as if suddenly life became an adventure as she wondered, *Who can I be nice to?* As we parted company she thanked me again and said, "I think you've changed my life!"

I never cease to be amazed at how people react to the simple suggestion that they try to be nice. While I was working on this book I spoke at a church conference in British Columbia where I issued the same challenge. At the banquet later that evening I noticed a major logjam of people at the buffet tables. No one wanted to be first in line; everyone was waiting for someone else to lead things off. "I guess we took what you said to heart, Dr. Carson," someone announced rather loudly.

"Then I'll go," I responded, stepping to the front, and everyone laughed as they fell into place behind me.

Be nice. It is such an elementary concept, but I probably get as much reaction to this topic as anything I speak about—which underscores the importance of this seemingly simple idea.

WHY BE NICE?

OVER THE YEARS, I have discovered several reasons for being nice:

1. You can get more done by being nice

I mention this first because it is so pragmatic. And it is true. If you are nice to people you get more accomplished—whether you are merely trying to communicate or you are actually trying to accomplish a major task. Two brief examples:

A couple of years ago, Candy and I made a trip to France. Before we left we brushed up on the language, which we hadn't spoken since our college French courses. Neither of us was fluent, but we thought we should at least make an effort to converse with our hosts in their native tongue. Though we did it to be polite, we quickly discovered the greater benefit for ourselves.

Wherever we went in France, we tried to begin our conversations in French. Most of the French people we met spoke much better English than our French, so invariably, after listening to our feeble attempts to converse in their language, they gladly began to use ours. We were then able to have much more helpful and interesting conversations with people than would have been possible had we simply expected them to communicate in our language from the start. Our goodwill was more than repaid in kind.

Being nice also pays off professionally. I cannot do my job as a surgeon without the help of many other people. If I am nice to them — whether that person is a fellow surgeon or a filing clerk in radiology tracking down a lost X-ray — they tend to be nicer back to me. They cooperate faster and try harder. Their positive attitude helps improve their performance and mine.

2. It feels good

The lady who caught me in that San Francisco hotel lobby discovered this in just a few hours. It is simply a better way to live. So being nice is its own reward.

3. Everyone is worth it

Being nice is a simple, practical, concrete way to acknowledge the uniqueness God created in every individual and to show each person we encounter the respect and dignity he or she deserves. It demonstrates a spirit of democracy that says we think other people matter.

We like to think of America as a classless society, but if we are honest, we have to admit that we are divided into many categories — ethnically, economically, educationally, socially, geographically, and in other ways. Being nice to everyone is the simplest way I know to effectively lower the artificial barriers human beings have erected.

4. Being nice is much easier in the long run

Sometimes being nice just makes life simpler. We have all heard that smiling requires less energy and fewer muscles than frowning. The same economy-of-effort idea holds true in most human interactions. Being nice is often easier than the alternative.

It is clearly true when you factor in the long-term ramifications. People's reactions are simpler to deal with. Reduced tension and increased goodwill add up to greater efficiency.

You seldom make enemies by being nice, and life without enemies is always easier. Doctors whose patients think they are nice do not get sued as often—and that makes life a lot easier.

5. You never lose by being nice

It seldom costs anything, except for, perhaps, a little time, thought, and energy. Sure, you occasionally run into people who will take advantage of your kindness; they might even consider niceness to be a weakness. But in the end, niceness wins out.

Yes, Leo Durocher said, "Nice guys finish last." But Jesus disagreed. His take on life was that, in the end, "many who are first will be last, and many who are last will be first" (Matthew 19:30). Nice guys might finish last in the big leagues, but they finish first in the Big Picture.

BEING NICE—WHAT DOES IT MEAN?

IN EVERY AUDIENCE I speak to, some people need help understanding what I have in mind. I have tried to define *nice* with any number of synonyms: thoughtful, gentle, considerate, caring, pleasant, polite, agreeable, congenial, helpful—all of which may add up to something close, but none of them quite equals it.

The best way I have found to explain what I mean is to give a few concrete examples of actions and behavior that qualify as *nice*. As I told the United Way audience in Birmingham, being nice means "not talking about people behind their backs ... not talking about people in front of their backs ... if you see somebody struggling with something, help him or her with it ... putting yourself in the other person's place before you begin to criticize ... if the elevator door is open and there is only one space left, let someone else get on ... when you're driving your car and someone puts a blinker on, don't speed up; slow down and let them in ... speaking to people; when you get in the elevator say 'Good Morning.'"

Most people know exactly what I am talking about when I put niceness in those terms. Knowing *what* is not the problem. The bigger challenge is *how*.

BEING NICE — HOW IS IT DONE?

IF YOU HAVE NEVER been a nice person, or you have just gotten out of the habit, try the following steps. They might just transform your life.

1. Take yourself out of the equation

Whatever the setting — home, school, work, church, community — one of the keys to being a *nice* person (and being perceived as one), is to take your self, your ego, out of the equation. This is crucial whether the equation is a conflict, a casual exchange, or a deeply personal relationship you have with any other individual.

As a medical doctor working at an academic institution, I have noticed that the addition of M.D. or Ph.D. to the end of some people's names seems to elevate them above everyone else — at least in their own minds. So this may be a particularly difficult and pertinent strategy for highly trained individuals to employ. It is human nature to think the world revolves around us. It doesn't. And learning that is a giant step in being nice.

2. Try to look at the other person's point of view

This helps some people accomplish step one. For others, step one is a necessary prerequisite. Either way, they seem to work best in tandem. We can almost always gain a better perspective on the Big Picture if we look at life not just from our own vantage point but from the other person's position as well. When we consider their feelings, ideas, motives, it becomes much easier to be nice.

3. Just listen

If you are having trouble with steps one and two, then start here. Listening is not just a way to be nice; it is nice. Listening takes you out of the center of the equation and helps you see the other person's viewpoint. I have already said that being nice means validating a person's worth and recognizing the respect and dignity they deserve. The simple act of listening demonstrates that better than anything else I can think of.

I learned early in my medical career that the single most valuable thing I can do for patients is to listen. Many of them are too young to tell me anything, so I listen to their parents. When it comes to sick children, mothers are the best experts because they know their kids better than I ever will. I cannot count the number of times a patient's mother has told me something important about her child, some medically significant clue I would not have learned from any examination or test—a clue that enabled me to successfully diagnose and treat the problem.

Although it takes longer to listen to patients, it pays off in the long run—and not just medically. It is the primary reason my patients and their families think I am *nice*.

4. Put personal preference aside

People who cannot be nice remind me of children in the back of a car, bickering over who gets to sit by the window. Fortunately, most children develop a more mature perspective as they grow older and the conflicts diminish. Still, some adults never want to give up the window. They have never learned that being nice sometimes means putting your own preferences aside. I can think of one instance in which I have had to learn to do this.

For twenty-three years, I have been a vegetarian. Within the past few years, however, I have begun to notice that my personal preference has caused some consternation for others. They may be offended when I do not eat meat, or they feel embarrassed when they realize, despite all their careful preparations, my needs have not been provided for. So, out of consideration—in other words, to be nice—I have learned to eat chicken or turkey in situations where I cannot gracefully manage to have a vegetarian meal. Because my speaker's bureau and my office provide dietary information when they set up my engagements, this is not usually a problem. But occasionally it is.

My wife and I still laugh about the time we were invited for dinner at the home of some friends—who had evidently forgotten we were vegetarians. The main course that night happened to be pork chops with pineapple topping. This presented an awkward situation for me because I have never eaten pork, and among so few guests, I knew my avoidance of the entree would not go unnoticed. So I served myself rice and vegetables, then scooped some of the pineapple onto my rice, hoping it might look as though a pork chop were lurking under there somewhere. I also hoped the hostess would not notice.

No such luck. Unfortunately, the flavor of the pork that had soaked into the pineapple made me so nauseated that I could not eat. When our hostess realized the problem, she was embarrassed anyway. She too tried to be "nice" by not calling attention to me, but she appreciated the fact that at least I had tried to avoid hurting her feelings.

5. Learn to love people

If you really love people, being nice to them is almost second nature. For me, this strategy is closely connected to my own personal faith. I believe what the Bible says in I John 4:19–21: "We love because he first loved us. If anyone says, 'I love God,' yet hates his brother, he is a liar. For anyone who does not love his brother, whom he has seen, cannot love God, whom he has not seen. And he has given us this command: Whoever loves God must also love his brother." If I say I love God, I have no choice but to show it by loving and being nice to other people.

6. Do unto others ...

We can forget all five of these strategies if we just remember the best strategy of all: the Golden Rule, which Jesus gave his followers. He boils the "be nice" idea down to one simple sentence: "Do unto others as you would have others do unto you." That is the most comprehensive plan for being nice I have ever seen.

BEING NICE — WHAT IT DOESN'T MEAN

1. It doesn't mean being a wimp

Being nice is a choice. It cannot be dictated by circumstances or forced on you against your will. It is a conscious decision, requiring determination, conviction, and strength of character.

2. It doesn't mean letting yourself be hurt or taken advantage of

Some time ago my wife and I hired a young man we knew who had just started his own handyman business. We needed some things done around our house. Our attempt to be nice backfired when we lost several thousand dollars as a result of his inadequate workmanship and his unreliability. Our contract with him gave us legal recourse, but we chose not to sue him. But there was a limit to how nice we were going to be, and we made it clear that we would never hire him again.

Being nice doesn't mean you cannot or should not use common sense. I have learned through unhappy experience that when friends or acquaintances approach me for monetary loans, if I am not willing to write it off as a gift, the "nicest" thing I can do for them (and for me) is refer them to a bank or credit union.

I have already mentioned the woman who falsely accused me of fathering her child. In that case I chose to be forgiving and not pursue legal action. But there was another case recently where I decided I could not risk being so nice. A woman from New York whom I had never met developed an infatuation for me. She wrote me countless letters and enclosed nude pictures of herself. When I did not respond, she began to make wild threats. Her letters became so irrational that, on the advice of a psychiatrist who read them, and my own legal counsel, for a time I had to make arrangements for special security whenever I traveled to speak in the New York City area.

I decided in this case the danger warranted legal action. But the state's attorneys from Maryland and New York had to get involved and threaten this woman with imprisonment before she finally realized the gravity of the situation and quit harassing me.

3. Being nice doesn't mean always agreeing with others

I concluded long ago that if two people always agree on everything, then one of those people is probably not needed. So I neither expect nor want the people I work or live with to always agree with me. But that does not mean we cannot be nice to each other. You can even be nice when you are expressing an opinion you know the other person does not want to hear. I think of an incident that took place on a speaking trip to a medical school in the Midwest.

The older I get, the more young people I meet (especially minority young people) who have read my books and followed my career and tell me that my personal story has inspired them to choose a career in medicine. While it is heartening to hear that I am looked to as an example, it is also a humbling and weighty responsibility. Especially when these individuals I do not really know seek my advice on major career-related decisions.

On this occasion, a final-year medical-school student asked to speak to me. He quickly told me his story. He admitted to feeling a kinship with me; despite growing up in poverty, he too had set himself the lofty goal of becoming a doctor. Throughout his academic career this young man did well in the classroom but always struggled with standardized tests. That pattern held true in medical school as well.

That was at the heart of what he wanted to talk to me about. He had completed all his course work, passed his classes with flying colors, but after four years of hard work, he had done so poorly on his comprehensive exams that the school had ruled him ineligible to graduate that year. He was advised that before he could receive his degree he would have to retake three courses and sufficiently demonstrate his mastery of that material. He had just learned the ruling and was embarrassed, frustrated, angry, and devastated. More than anything he was afraid his lifelong dream would be lost. He didn't know what he should do. Ultimately, he believed he was being discriminated against by this administrative decision. At the urging of some of his friends and family he was considering legal action. But he wondered what I thought he should do.

I listened to the story, empathized with this young man's anguish and pain, but I quickly realized he wanted my approval, both to validate his feelings and to justify his response. I knew exactly what he wanted me to say. But I couldn't do that. Instead, I pointed out that no one had said he would not be able to graduate. Neither had they said they thought he was incapable of becoming a doctor. The fact that he failed to make the required grade on his comps was more indicative of his own lifelong problem with standardized testing than it was evidence of any discrimination. No one had closed the door to his dream; they had actually found a way to leave the door open. All his advisor had said was that he would be required to retake three courses to prove that he knew what he needed to know to be a good doctor. His disappointment and embarrassment were understandable, but I told him what I thought would be his simplest and best course of action: "I think you should retake the courses."

My response was not what that young student wanted to hear. Yet the moment I said it, the emotion and tension drained out of that room like air out of a balloon. He did not argue. After thanking me for my advice, we parted company. Fortunately, he followed my advice, retook the courses, passed the test to everyone's satisfaction, and is a doctor today.

And whenever I think about that young man, I am reminded that being nice does not mean we always have to say what another person wants us to.

4. Being nice doesn't mean you can't be honest

Niceness and honesty are not incompatible. In fact, truthfulness plus kindness equals tact. This truth is wonderfully illustrated by my friend and colleague, Dr. Levi Watkins, a noted cardiovascular surgeon. The first black medical school professor at Hopkins, Levi's numerous professional accomplishments include the development of the implantable automatic cardiac defibrillator. Not only is he recognized throughout the world for his professional contribution to medical science but he is known throughout our Johns Hopkins community as being an exceedingly "nice" man. His tenderhearted, caring nature brings all kinds of people with all kinds of personal problems to his office for advice. And yet, Levi is known as much for his candor as for his kindness. Not long ago a resident who had a serious personality conflict with some of the attendings came to Levi to complain and seek his support in rectifying the situation. Levi checked into the situation and confirmed that the problem was indeed a personality conflict. But instead of trying to resolve the conflict, Levi suggested to the resident that his best course of action would be to transfer to some other hospital. He did so and did well in the new program.

Levi does not waste time hiding his feelings or opinions. He simply tells it like it is. That is why his counsel is so widely valued and why he has become the best contemporary example I know of a *nice* and *honest* individual.

5. Being nice doesn't mean compromising your standards

Our best model for being nice without compromising our standards is also our best model in every area of life: Jesus. He is not only the author of the ultimate standard of niceness—the Golden Rule—he taught and lived by higher standards than anyone else in history.

Everything we know about Jesus Christ indicates he was certainly a nice person.

But that does not mean he excused sin or lowered his expectations of himself or others. He proved for all time that it was possible to be "loving, thoughtful, gentle, considerate, caring ..." (and whatever other ingredient of a nice person can possibly be), yet still hold to and live by an unwavering belief that wrong is wrong and right is always right.

BEING NICE IS NOT THE SAME AS BEING POLITICALLY CORRECT

In America today we seem to have made political correctness (PC) the litmus test for civility. Politically correct people are by definition nice. Those who are not PC, cannot possibly be. Political correctness has become one of our culture's highest virtues and loftiest ideals. Yet I see this development as a serious threat. Let me elaborate.

Although political correctness is lauded by its advocates as a boon to open discussion and civil debate, the first big reason I view it as a threat to American society is because its offspring—PC speech— has proven to be a formidable hindrance to improved communication. We have become so cautious, so careful about the exact words we use, that we miss the larger meaning of what is being said. We hear only the words and miss the message entirely.

I remember once in a speech I referred to fashion models as looking "so skinny they look like they just escaped from a concentration camp." After my talk I was accosted in the hallway by a young Jewish woman who chastised me for daring to compare rich, glamorous models to concentration-camp victims. How could I be so insensitive as to belittle holocaust survivors in that manner? This sensitive, well-meaning young lady had entirely missed a point I suspect she would have endorsed. I was talking about what a tragedy I thought it was that so many people unthinkingly allow themselves to be mentally and physically destroyed in order to conform to an arbitrary and artificial societal standard of beauty. She never heard that because the words "concentration camp" raised the PC flag in her mind.

Another time, one individual became irate with me after a speech in which I had compared the human brain to that of a dog and talked about the advantage we humans have with our highly developed frontal lobes. This deeply offended gentleman let me know in no uncertain terms that he thought my conclusion unfairly denigrated dogs. I got the idea he considered me little, if any, better than your average animal abuser. He too entirely missed my point, which was the incredible intellectual capacity God has entrusted to human beings that enables us to actually shape our circumstances and make the world a better place in which to live—for animals as well as people.

Reactions like these point out another way political correctness hinders communication. We have made certain ideas and words seem so sacred—capable of eliciting deep emotional responses and arousing much indignation—that we then justify personally condemning any and all transgressors. If simple observations on the size of models' bodies and dogs' brains can raise the specter of anti-Semitism and animal abuse, how much more wary would I need to be in trying to discuss controversial issues like abortion or gay rights?

I am convinced our obsession with politically correct speech has reduced the quality of meaningful dialogue on many critical issues—because it fosters fear. People see how others are attacked for a wrong choice of words, so they decide not to risk offering their own opinions. If enough people become so gun-shy they do not dare open their mouths, the quality of public discourse in this country will surely suffer.

In a real sense, political correctness discourages honesty. It places a higher value on making everyone feel good than on stating what we really believe. That does not seem honest to me. Since I do not see how individuals or groups can ever have a meaningful dialogue without honesty, I think political correctness is making it harder, rather than easier, to address the greatest problems and resolve the deepest differences our society faces.

Another way political correctness hinders communication is by dividing, rather than unifying, our society. We proclaim it as evidence of our culture's tolerance, but we use it as a primary screening mechanism for quickly and easily separating, categorizing, labeling, and judging people — good or bad, enlightened or bigoted, sensitive or boorish, reasonable or unbalanced, liberal or conservative, even educated or ignorant. No matter how we dress it up or what we call it, stereotyping people seldom improves communication.

WHEN BEING POLITICALLY CORRECT CONFLICTS WITH OUR PRINCIPLES

I REALIZE MANY PEOPLE consider political correctness a matter of principle. Sometimes it is. But there are other times when principle matters more than political correctness — that is, when PC is in conflict with what we believe. That, ultimately, may pose an even larger threat to society than the barrier PC is to productive communication.

Indeed, when we make "not offending" the highest commandment in our political-correctness creed, we automatically devalue all other principles. When we make it a major taboo to say someone else's beliefs may be wrong, we belittle our own. When society says we are politically incorrect to point out that someone else's lifestyle is wrong, we run the risk of losing our culture's moral compass.

I was driving to an appointment in the Baltimore area just before the time of Louis Farrakhan's Million Man March on Washington, D.C. Scanning the FM radio in search of classical music I stopped when I heard a voice on the radio use my name. Two men, one liberal and one conservative, seemed to be debating the merits of the rally. While I am fairly well-known among the African-American community in the metro D.C.-Baltimore area, I have no idea how my name came up in a discussion about whether I would support such an event. The pro-rally man insisted that my belief in the importance of family and the need for people to assume personal responsibility for their own lives would fit right in with the themes of the march. So, of course, I would support it. The critic of the rally was just as convinced that my outspoken Christian faith would mean obvious disagreement with so much of Farrakhan's rhetoric and his Nation of Islam agenda that I could not possibly endorse the march.

I laughed and wondered if the time had come to rethink my reluctance to go into politics. *If both sides are so convinced I am in agreement with them, how can I lose?* That thought lasted only as long as it took me to realize that although public approval often seems to be the highest goal of many politicians, in my personal value system, it certainly is not the highest good. When you believe strongly in something, the chances are that you will offend those who believe something different. If everyone likes you it may, in fact, mean you do not stand for anything.

I do not trust politicians who have no trouble talking on three sides of any two-sided issue. Neither do I want to learn how to do that. While I see no point in going out of my way to disagree with someone, I believe there is always a good reason to stand up for my principles and what I believe in.

That does not mean, however, that I cannot be nice about it. If you are a straight shooter and live by your principles, some people may not like you, but they will usually respect you and listen to the reasons for your opinions. Then, if they can feel free to tell you where they stand, you have a basis from which you can begin to discuss differences.

To me, this philosophy always seemed foundational to our American standard of democracy—though it seems to be at odds with the current thinking on political correctness.

TO BE OR NOT TO BE PC — TWO TROUBLESOME ISSUES

Let us consider two contemporary issues that have been negatively affected by the politically correct climate of today's society. The first is abortion. The second is gay rights.

Perhaps no other issue illustrates how political correctness discourages honest communication than abortion. I am constantly amazed to hear politicians and others in the public arena attempt to be politically correct on this issue. When I talk to many of those same people one-on-one, I discover their private views are different than their public pronouncements.

Somehow we need to create a different atmosphere in which, if not politically correct, it is at least politically permissible to speak openly and honestly about difficult issues. While abortion is a deeply personal issue, society's current acceptance of abortion on demand has serious implications for our entire culture's attitude toward the sanctity of life.

As a scientist I realize I do not have the ability to create human life. For me, conception and birth remain in the realm of the miraculous. As a doctor familiar with human development, I know that within weeks of conception a fetus becomes a recognizable individual, complete with a heart that beats and a brain that reacts and responds to stimuli introduced into its environment. So I would not and could not ever take part in the killing of one of God's creations simply because its birth would be an inconvenience. And I feel very strongly about my convictions.

But I realize many people with different convictions feel just as strongly about their beliefs. I also believe that our country was founded on the idea that its citizens should be free to express their ideas and beliefs even when we do not agree — maybe especially when we do not agree. We need to get past the unfortunate PC idea that standing up for what we believe and strongly advocating our beliefs is the same thing as forcing our beliefs on other people. Speaking up in public for our deepest beliefs should always be correct. Our heritage of freedom and democracy demands no less. If we follow the guidelines earlier in this chapter, I think we can profitably discuss, and disagree about, a subject as emotional as abortion. And we can even be nice about it.

Recently a homosexual couple brought a child in to be examined on one of our neurosurgical clinic days. During lunch, after the couple had left, one of my fellow staff members commented favorably on the couple's obvious love and commitment to the child. He said to me, "I know you don't approve of homosexual relationships and wouldn't consider their home a healthy atmosphere in which to raise a child. But I was impressed by that couple. I think their sexual orientation is their business. Think what you want, but it's just your opinion."

My response wasn't nearly that politically correct. "Excuse me, but I beg to differ," I said. "How I feel and what I think isn't *just my opinion*. God in his Word says very clearly that he considers homosexual acts to be an 'abomination.'" Whenever I point out that God calls homosexual behavior a sin, I am usually quick to add that the Bible just as clearly calls a lot of other things wrong—lying, cheating, adultery, murder, gluttony—and I am not going to try to justify any of those things in order to be politically correct either.

Just because I believe homosexual behavior is wrong does not mean, therefore, that I think it is right to discriminate against gays. Gays should not have any more rights than anyone else, but neither should they have less. I work with people who are gay; as long as they do their jobs well, their sexual orientation is not an issue I concern myself with.

Sometimes when I speak in churches I tell my fellow Christians that I believe God loves gay people just as much as he loves any sinner—and we are all sinners. I believe God can forgive homosexual behavior just as surely as he can our sins of pride and self-righteousness, and I have the feeling some Christians are going to be very surprised when they get to Heaven and discover that some people we didn't expect to see are there and others we thought would be there aren't.

I often remind fellow believers that God did us a tremendous favor by assuming responsibility for making the final judgment. He never put that burden on our shoulders. Our primary assignment is not to be dispensers of judgment but dispensers of grace. One of the most effective ways I know to do that is by being nice.

This is not to say we should not use personal judgment to discern right behavior from wrong. God gave us his Word to help us do that. But only God himself knows the heart of an individual, and only God can judge a sinner. Christians would be perceived as being a lot *nicer*, a lot more grace-full, perhaps even a little more politically correct, if we made a clearer distinction between judging sin and judging people. There is a difference—even if it is not politically correct to think so.

BEING NICE SEEMS LIKE such a small, personal thing. But I have discovered the same thing the woman in the San Francisco hotel lobby told me she had learned: doing something nice may seem the least we can do, but when the ripples spread, being nice can not only change your life, it can change the world.

Part Three

THE WIDE-ANGLE VIEW
OF THE BIG PICTURE

Back when I was labeled the "class dummy," none of my fifth-grade classmates ever imagined I would become Director of Pediatric Neurosurgery at the Johns Hopkins Medical Institutions or President and Co-Founder of the Carson Scholars Fund. But then neither did I.

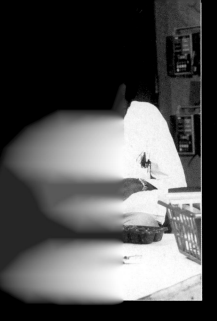
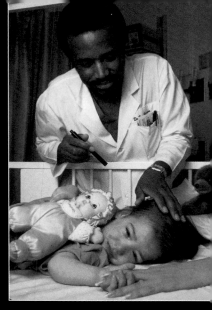

...ery on as many as 450 children a year. Nothing is ...or me than seeing a sick child restored to health.

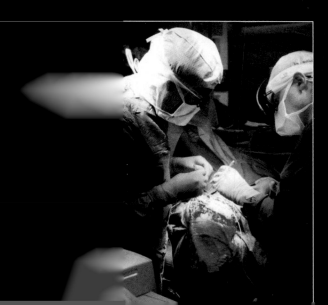

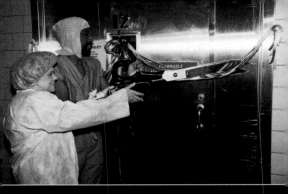

oneering work at Johns Hopkins wouldn't be possible
d skills of many people. (Above) Here I'm helping cut
f our new Pediatric Neurosurgery with my friend Shir
en's Cancer Foundation, (Below) A recent group pho
incredibly talented and hard-working staff.

d I will be forever grateful for the energy and enthusia
osen invested in helping get the Carson Scholar's Fur
sful start. Her sudden and tragic death just months be
on of this book forced all of us who loved Vicki to give
thought to the meaning of life and the big picture

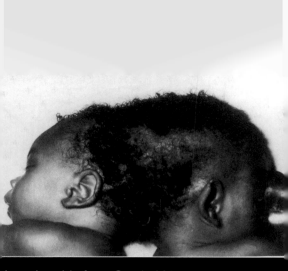

kwaeba girls from South Africa were the second
ese twins I separated. And for a long time afterw
ed why God allowed me to get involved in a cas
seemed like such a tragic failure.

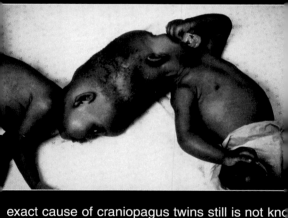

exact cause of craniopagus twins still is not kno
iese otherwise healthy and charming Zambian b
h and Luka Banda) had only one significant pro
vere attached to each other at the top of their he

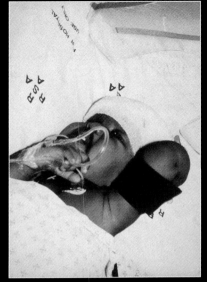

By the time the boys reached the intensive care unit they each had their eyes open and were trying to pull out their endotracheal tubes with both hands. After 28 hours of surgery, this was astounding.

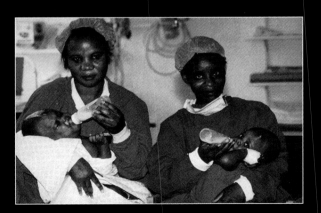

A couple of weeks after returning home, I received word from South Africa that the Banda boys were amazing their doctors by beginning to crawl. These two amazing boys were well on their way to full and normal lives.

While speaking to students across the country I noticed most schools have huge display cases for their sports trophies honoring their athletes. In contrast, honor students receive paper certificates and perhaps a National Honor Society pin label. So my wife, Candy, and I started the Carson Scholars Fund to better honor academic achievement.

Someday we'd like to name one Carson Scholar scholar in every school in our nation—a huge goal that would require a $1.5 billion endowment. But I want to practice what I preach when I challenge people to "THINK BIG!"

peak two or three times
r Breakfast in Washingto
nt in East Baltimore (mi
a special kick out of the
in Wax Museum" a fe

I believe parenting is the most important job in the world—and it's tougher than brain surgery. Which is why, when I consider the big picture, home and family has to be a true priority.

My mother, Sonya Carson (above), provided me with a wonderful parenting model. (Below) Candy and I are with my mother (seated) and our sons Murray (left), B.J. (right), and Rhoeyce (seated).

Pool and foosball games with my family help maintain my eye-hand coordination for surgery. But we also enjoy the mental challenge of chess. Clockwise (from the left) that's B.J., Rhoeyce, and (in the foreground) Murray.

Eleven

WHAT AILS AMERICA? RACIAL DIVERSITY IS A STRENGTH

IF SOMEONE GAVE YOU the chance to speak to the president, vice president, and most of the country's senators, representatives, and Supreme Court justices all at one time, what would you say to them? I had to ask myself that question when I was invited to be the keynote speaker at the 1997 National Prayer Breakfast in Washington, D.C.

I began, as I usually do, by sharing my own story with that august audience. I told them about my childhood ambition of becoming a missionary doctor, my early struggles as the "dummy" in the class, and how my mother's God-given wisdom and reading had led to my discovery of the amazing potential God provides all of us in our remarkable human brains. I even shared how I had turned to God for help in overcoming the youthful anger that almost destroyed my life and my dreams.

But I did not just want to talk about my life—I wanted to challenge those leaders to consider what I think is one of the most serious crises facing us all today. I said, "There is a segment of our society that I'm particularly concerned about, a group that seems to be affected by all the things I've talked about this morning—the dreams, the outrage, the lack of intellectual development. This group is young black males— whom we've all heard is an endangered species.

"Why do people say that? Because there are more young black males in jail today than there are in college.

"Why do we have this dismal situation? Some people say, 'I'm not a black male, so it doesn't affect me. It's not my problem.' I beg to differ. All our ancestors may have come to this country in different boats—but we're all in the same boat now. If part of that boat sinks, eventually the rest will go down too. We have to understand that."

Looking out over all those tables spread across that big hotel ballroom, I saw many heads nodding. "The interesting thing is that this doesn't have to happen," I went on. "Those of you in education know that young black males in kindergarten, first grade, and second grade are as good as students anywhere else. But then something happens.

"What? They start studying in American history about our great nation, and they discover that there's nobody who looks like them in those history books who ever did much of significance. They think, *Well, maybe next year, when I take world history, it'll be different.* Then they discover that nobody in their world history book who did anything of great significance looks much like them either. When they come home from school and turn on the TV they finally say, 'Oh! There I am—playing football or baseball or basketball, rapping in baggy pants that look like you could fly in them, or acting the fool on some sitcom.'

"So these young men begin to develop a certain self-image—about themselves and the world they live in. *That's how I'm going to make it,* they decide. *I'm gonna be the next Michael Jordan.* The media doesn't tell them that only seven out of a million make it as starters in the NBA or that only one in ten thousand make it in any lasting way in sports and entertainment.

"We need to emphasize the right things... We need to emphasize the intellect. Most of these young black men don't get that emphasis. When they don't find out until much later that they are never going to be a sports or entertainment star, what's left? Up drives a big black BMW with tinted glass. Out steps this tall, handsome gentleman wearing jewelry and furs, with women hanging on his arm. And he says, 'Wouldn't you like to have what I have? Society sold you a bill of goods. Let me show you how to get everything you'll ever want or need.' And hence, we have people who do things none of us can ever imagine a human being would do—because they feel betrayed by society.

"Of course, that's only part of the sociology involved. But it's something that should give us all pause. Because it didn't have to happen.

"Any of us could have taken that young man at the age of six, walked him down the streets of Washington, D.C., and given him a black history lesson that would have thrilled his heart. It could have changed his life.

"We could have started our walking lesson by pointing at our shoes and saying, 'It was Jan Matzliger, a black man, who invented the automatic shoe-lasting machine, which revolutionized the shoe industry throughout the world.' We could step out onto a street clear of debris and tell him about Charles Brooks, who invented the automatic streetsweeper. Down the clean street comes one of those big refrigerated tractor-trailer trucks—so we'd tell him about Frederick Jones, who invented a refrigeration system for trucks, later adopted for airplanes, trains, and ships. When the truck stops at a red light, we can tell him about Garret Morgan, a black man, who designed the stop signal, and also invented the gas mask, which has saved many soldiers' lives.

"We could then tell him about Henrietta Bradbury, the black woman who invented the underwater cannon, making it possible to launch torpedoes from submarines. And we could talk about Madame C. J. Walker, the black woman who invented cosmetic products for women of dark complexion, the first woman of any race in this nation to become a millionaire entirely through her own efforts.

"When we walk our young friend past a hospital, we could tell him about Charles Drew and his contributions to blood banking or about Daniel Hale Williams, who performed the first successful open-heart surgery. We could look up at a surgical light and tell him about Thomas Edison—you didn't know he was black did you? Well, he wasn't, but his right-hand man, Lewis Lattimer, was. Lattimer was the person who invented the filament that enabled Edison's light bulb to burn longer than a few days. He also pioneered research in incandescent lighting. He even diagrammed the telephone for Alexander Graham Bell. He was one of our country's greatest inventors, and yet most people don't even recognize Lewis Lattimer's name.

"We could walk along the railroad tracks and tell the boy about Andrew Beard, inventor of the automatic railroad car coupler, which helped spur on the industrial revolution. Or Elijah McCoy's many great inventions—like the automatic lubricating system for engines. When any big new mechanical development came along in the early industrial era, people used to ask, 'Is that a McCoy? Is that the real McCoy?' He was the origin of that phrase.

"I'm just scratching the surface here," I told the prayer breakfast audience, " . . . and you know, I can take that same walk down the street with a child from any ethnic group in our nation and point out tremendous accomplishments . . . because we have all made enormous contributions. That's how America got to be number one faster than any other nation in history—because we have people from everywhere, from all corners of the earth.

"Some people in America only see our differences as problems. But our racial and ethnic diversity should not be a problem. It is a good thing."

Then I reminded my ethnically diverse and distinguished audience how boring it would be if all the animals in the National Zoo were Thompson's Gazelles, if all the fish in the National Aquarium were goldfish, and everyone in the world looked just like everyone else. I told them, "We should praise our Heavenly Father for giving us diversity. And please, let's never let people with small minds make that into a problem. We don't have to do that."

I quickly ran through my T-H-I-N-K B-I-G points before concluding my comments to the National Prayer Breakfast audience by saying, "And we've got to get it across to our young people that it's okay to be nice to people, to care about your fellow man, to develop your God-given talents to their utmost, to have values and principles in their lives. If we do that, I believe we can help lead the rest of the world to a level of civilization this earth has never known.

"We should not castigate each other; we should love each other. We should follow the example of our Lord Jesus Christ. We should make sure that in all things we honor him. And one of the best ways we honor him is by honoring each other."

Then I sat down, and the president stood to speak.

PERHAPS CALLING ANYONE WHO considers ethnic and racial diversity a problem "small minded" seems harsh. But clearly such people fail to see the Big Picture.

I SAY "REMEMBER"

THOSE PEOPLE (AND THERE are many) who argue that racial attitudes are not significantly better today than they were a generation or two ago, that there is just as much intolerance and injustice in America now as there was before Selma or before Brown vs. Board of Education, that our country has seen no significant progress in race relations in recent decades—those people are wrong. They are not looking at the Big Picture.

They certainly do not remember what I remember. Even though I was born in the first year of the second half of the twentieth century, I can vividly recall, on childhood trips to visit relatives in the South, seeing and using specially designated "Colored" restrooms and drinking fountains. Looking back, it seems unbelievable how casual Curtis and I were about the loud and angry "Nigger!" taunts we regularly endured walking through white neighborhoods to school in Boston and Detroit. On occasion we actually fled physical attack. We didn't think to tell Mother what was going on, partly because we didn't want to worry her, but also because we had learned and accepted the fact that discrimination was an unavoidable part of life.

I certainly would not argue that bigotry no longer exists. But such public demonstrations of discrimination, so recently considered part of the cultural status quo, would be unthinkable in today's society — to most people of all races. As President Clinton's special commission on race reported recently, "It is fair to say there is a deep-rooted national consensus [when it comes] to the ideals of racial equality and integration, even if that consensus falters on the best means to achieve those ideals."

For those of us old enough to remember the days of Jim Crow and "separate but unequal," that "consensus" seems a drastic and undeniable improvement. So if the inability to see progress is not indicative of a small mind, it certainly must be evidence of a forgetful one.

YOU SAY "FORGET"

ON THE OPPOSITE EXTREME there are people who advocate the need to forget. They believe racial diversity is a problem in our country primarily because some of us insist on remembering too much. They focus only on what they see as progress, conclude racial prejudice is primarily a thing of the past, and therefore seem to think the majority of remaining problems would disappear if black people would simply forget history and try to "put it behind us and move on."

These folks who say of racism, "It's past, get over it!" clearly do not have a clue how impossibly ludicrous that advice sounds to minorities who have been reminded of their racial identity every day of their lives. I could no more *forget* my race than I could forget I am a man. I have no more desire to get *over* being black than I want to get over being a husband, a father, a son, a brother, or even a doctor. It is part of who I am — and not so much because I think of myself as black but because the rest of the world does.

Some of these reminders of racism are painful; their impact lasts a lifetime. Others may be small and seemingly inconsequential, except for the fact that they are repeated again and again by different people, in different settings, at different stages of life. As surely as dripping water can carve out caves of solid stone, even the littlest slights, repeated endlessly over time, slowly but surely shape one's thinking and being.

A number of ready examples spring to mind. I admit that my brother and I did not encounter racism nearly as often during our childhoods as many of our contemporaries did—perhaps because our mother made an effort to shield us from it. For a number of years we lived in black neighborhoods, attended black schools and worshiped in black churches, so I did not have much interaction with whites until we moved back to Detroit from Boston and I enrolled in Higgins Elementary School for the fifth grade. There I encountered the pain of racism for the first time.

The educational expectations were obviously different for black and white students at Higgins in the early sixties. Most black students (probably ninety percent of us) were relegated to the school's special education classes. The only other black student in my regular fifth grade class had been held back repeatedly and was at least two years older than everyone else. While my performance had earned me my "Dummy" status, my basically cooperative and polite behavior may explain why I was "mainstreamed."

One student in my class, a white boy named John, had done such an outstanding job on a class science project that he had been given the honor of representing our class, and all of Higgins Elementary School, on a television science program that was broadcast into the schools three days a week. We were all intently watching the anticipated broadcast, which showcased student projects from many schools around the state.

I was sitting next to a girl named Christine. Anxiously wondering when our classmate would get his turn, she and I got into a guessing game as to just when John would appear. So when one project segment ended, in an attempt to be the first one to guess, I blurted out loud "John will be next!"

When a black student walked out onto the set instead, a number of people snickered. Christine actually leaned over to punch me and announce that she should "ring my neck" for implying that John, of whom we were all so proud, was "colored."

More than thirty-five years have passed since that day in my fifth-grade classroom at Higgins Elementary, but I still remember the terrible, sinking, sick feeling in the pit of my stomach when I suddenly realized Christine, and evidently the rest of my classmates, considered it an unthinkable insult to be like me.

I remember another episode that took place after school one day that same year. I was playing with some white children when their parents angrily called them into the house. One of them sneaked out and caught up with me, just as I headed home, to inform me that they couldn't play with me anymore, because I was a "blackie"—which I was beginning to realize was not a good thing in a lot of people's eyes.

By ninth grade I had experienced enough racism that it no longer came as a shock, though it was no less painful and infuriating. The last day of my first term in high school, I had to carry my report card around from class to class so that each teacher could fill in the grade for that course. I had straight A's in every subject going into my last class of the day—physical education. My white gym teacher looked at all my other grades. Then he looked at me. Despite the fact that I had done all the requirements to make an A in his class, he wrote B on my report card. He just grinned, for he and I both realized that he had ruined my chance to be on the "All-A Honor Roll," and there was nothing I could do about it.

Unfortunately, my exposure to racism was not limited to bigoted teachers, classmates, or the neighborhood kids. During my junior high years, when my mother transferred our membership from a smaller inner-city church to a larger suburban congregation of our mostly white denomination, we received a mixed welcome. Members' responses ranged from genuinely friendly and gracious to overtly hostile. Many people who fell somewhere between those two extremes made a special point of informing us of the location of our denomination's nearest Negro, or "colored" church, as some folks still called them at the time. Mother always thanked them for the information, sometimes smiling and saying, "We like it here."

Long after we established our membership in that suburban congregation, one woman always made a special point of letting my mother know when another black family visited that day, the implication being that Mother should rush right over to talk with them. My mother's usual response was, "That's nice. Why don't you go greet them and make them feel welcome?" On other occasions, when someone would inform her that "some colored people came to church today," she very innocently replied, "Oh, really? What color were they?" It did not take long before most people quit making such comments.

I was not as amused when I encountered some of those same attitudes at the first church I visited my freshman year at Yale, though I was actually more disappointed than offended. The sixties had seen a lot of social change, and I was, after all, in the "enlightened" Northeast. Yet on my first visit to a white church in New Haven, I was informed by several people that there was a black congregation (by 1969 they didn't say "colored") I might want to visit over in Hamden.

I mention these examples not to shame my fellow believers but to indicate that small-minded people can be found anywhere. I even met some on the Ivy League campus of one of this country's great bastions of academic freedom and open-minded intellectualism. For instance, one day, while standing in the hall outside a dormitory bathroom, I overheard a conversation inside. A white classmate who had always been cordial with me—a guy who went on to become a professional actor—asked one of my other white friends, "Why do you eat dinner with that 'blackie'?" Neither student ever knew what I had overheard. The second young man, who is now an accomplished orchestra conductor, basically blew off the question and never let anyone else's opinions diminish our friendship. The first one matured considerably over our college years together, and while I bear no grudge against him, I have never forgotten how much pain his words and hypocritical spirit caused me at a time when I was away from home for the first time, feeling out of place, vulnerable, and very much in need of acceptance and friendship.

I remember another "friend" from my freshman year at Yale—a fellow from an elite New York City suburb. When we would eat lunch together, he would have a wonderfully warm and chummy "let's-talk-about-everything" attitude. But when other wealthy students joined us at the table, I would be tuned out as though I had totally disappeared. When the others left, it was like "I'm back!" And you know, the guy never apologized, acted sheepish, or funny. I doubt he ever realized what he was doing. It was as if this was the way our relationship was supposed to be. I never confronted the fellow about it. I realized it was his problem, not mine. But I can't say that his seemingly subconscious dismissal of me did not hurt.

Over the years, those hurts add up. Even when the dismissals and the judgments are not quite so personal. When our boys were young, my wife, Candy, would often take them to the store when she went grocery shopping. On many occasions, while she was transferring her purchases from the shopping cart to the trunk of our Lincoln Town Car, people in the parking lot gave her dirty looks. She overheard comments from some passersby who assumed she was one of "those welfare mothers" with a passel of kids who was obviously "milking the system" and "driving a Lincoln," which they and all the other "hard-working taxpayers" helped pay for.

One more automobile story: I suppose it was inevitable that I like cars. I did, after all, grow up in Detroit. I worked for Ford Motor Company one summer during school, which is why I have always bought and driven American-made automobiles. Several years ago, however, not long after Ford bought Jaguar, I thought seriously about buying myself a sportier set of wheels to drive. So one afternoon I decided to visit a Jaguar dealership in downtown Baltimore to see what might be available.

As I walked into the showroom, three salesmen were chatting with each other off to one side. They glanced my way—but that is all they did. As I walked around and looked inside cars, they kept right on talking, having obviously decided that a young black man could not afford one of their cars. They clearly were not going to waste their time to help me or answer my questions.

I did not stay long. I drove straight to another Jaguar dealership in Laurel, Maryland. I had not known it, but the sales manager there was the father of a former patient of mine. He offered me a fantastic deal, and I ended up with a new Jaguar and the distinct satisfaction of knowing I had come out ahead, while the salesmen who had dismissed me with one look had lost both a customer and a hefty commission.

Early in my days as chief of pediatric neurosurgery at Johns Hopkins, before I was well known, I regularly walked into examination rooms to find surprised looks on the faces of new patients who had not expected such a young—or such a black—doctor. And I knew these patients were struggling not to make the same sort of judgment those Jaguar salesmen had made.

Fortunately, that kind of reaction does not happen as much anymore. Most of my patients know something about me before they make an appointment, though an exception occurred not long ago. An older out-of-state couple was referred to our office. The woman suffered from *trigeminal neuralgia,* a condition that causes such painful reactions in the facial nerves that many people with the condition have commited suicide rather than endure the agony of its attacks.

During my residency I learned to perform a delicate but effective procedure that requires the insertion of a six-inch needle next to the mouth, into the cheek, up between the facial bones, and through a very tiny hole in the base of the skull to reach the foramen ovale, where a tiny injection of glycerine actually deadens the portion of the nerves that are transmitting the pain. The low-risk procedure (*percutaneous stereotactic trigeminal glycerin rhizotomy* is the name of the operation) takes only minutes and is effective in eighty to ninety percent of cases.

When I learned this procedure I was one of only seven neurosurgeons in the country who performed it. I have since taught many others how to do it but still do fifty or more of these procedures each year myself. Because trigeminal neuralgia patients are often in such debilitating pain and this procedure takes only minutes, I sometimes juggle my schedule to fit them into my OR schedule the same day. Being able to take away crippling pain and literally change someone's life in a matter of hours is one of the most rewarding things I do— which is why I make trigeminal neuralgia patients the only adult exceptions in my otherwise pediatric neurosurgical practice. And so this elderly couple had come to see me.

Carol James, my longtime friend and physician assistant, who happens to be white, conducted the preliminary interview with these folks, who evidently hailed from a small community that gave them little or no exposure to minority groups. As Carol took down the patient history, they admitted their uneasiness being in downtown Baltimore and seeing so many black people walking along the streets. They complained to Carol that when they had to stop for a traffic light at a corner near the hospital, they had been frightened because they felt as if "everyone was grinning at us, just watching and waiting for an opportunity to rob us or steal our car." The more derogatory remarks they made about black people, the harder it was for Carol to keep from chuckling out loud. When she finished her interview, she came out to give me a quick summary of the patient history and to warn me about their mind-set as well. We laughed in anticipation of their coming reaction—and then she followed me into the exam room.

I made no reference to what Carol had told me, and I might not have noticed anything in their well-controlled reactions either, except for the rather sheepish looks this couple gave Carol as I carefully explained what we were going to do. Fortunately, the subsequent procedure went well. We were able to send this woman home having alleviated all her facial pain and perhaps even a little of her racial prejudice—the latter having presented the far greater challenge.

Unfortunately, small minds are not exclusively the bane of people with limited social experience. I often detect the deeply buried roots of that same racial prejudice among many sophisticated, socially liberal individuals who would certainly be deeply offended by my saying so. Such people give themselves away, however, when, every time they talk with me, they feel compelled to tell me about some black "friend" they know who they have always thought was such a wonderful individual. Or they mention some famous black person everyone would recognize, say a Bill Cosby or a Michael Jordan, and go on and on, extolling that person's virtues.

When I encounter folks like that, I smile sadly inside. I wish I could say, "'Methinks thou doth protest too much.' You are trying too hard to prove your open-minded tolerance. If you were truly liberated from the bonds of racism, we might be able to talk freely about any topic without constantly cycling back to some race-related subject."

I share these examples of my own encounters with racism not to evoke pity or guilt from white readers. Nor am I trying to incite more racial hostility among minority readers (most of whom could probably share experiences more painful than my own). My intention is not to be divisive. This is not meant as a recital of grievances motivated by unresolved anger, nor do I claim the effects of racism have somehow ruined my life. They clearly have not.

Instead, I have done what many think is the answer to racial problems in America. I have simply *gotten over it*. Still, despite any success I might achieve, I will never completely *forget* racial differences. Society, daily living, and a lifetime of experiences are constant reminders that make that impossible.

SMALL MINDS AND THE BIG PICTURE

IF THOSE WHO REFUSE to see the progress we have made, on one hand, and those who won't see the need for more progress, on the other, are not *small-minded*, at least both groups are closed-minded—and they contribute to an ongoing crisis in race relations. Each group reminds me that prejudice comes in all shapes, sizes, and colors, and that ignorance and insecurity are at the root of racism wherever, whenever, and in whomever it shows itself.

Let us be sure to acknowledge the fact that prejudice is by no means a one-way street. Racism is an equal-opportunity character flaw. Many black people harbor racist feelings toward whites. While most black racism I have witnessed is what I would term *reactionary*, an angry response to the discrimination they have experienced themselves, it is no less hideous and no less destructive than any other variation of this plague on our society.

Dr. Martin Luther King Jr. was assassinated the spring of my senior year in high school. The following day, white students at Detroit's Southwestern High School were systematically searched out, isolated, and beaten. I hid several of them in a science lab where I worked at the time—until we could sneak them out of the school and get them home safely. Their only crime was being white, and that suddenly made them the object of black prejudice, anger, and hatred. That was terribly wrong.

Some of the most racist people I have met over the years have been black people who hate other black people. I encountered several such individuals in college, in the form of students who would do anything to avoid speaking to or associating with other black students. Their only friends were white. They talked white, walked white, acted white, and by every indication may have even thought white. They did everything but look white, and you felt they would have looked white too if they could have. The black community sometimes refers to such people as "Oreos"—black on the outside and white on the inside. I ended up feeling sorry for those students. They tried so hard to escape the reality of their blackness, to try to make their skin color a nonissue, that they let the very thing they were trying to deny become the single biggest determinant of what they did, the people they did things with, and ultimately, who they themselves were. They were unwitting victims of their own racism.

SMALL MINDS ARE SCARED MINDS

CANDY AND I GAINED a new perspective on racism during the year we lived and worked in Australia, where we experienced no discrimination at all. Blacks are so rare in that country that we were always treated warmly, more as a fascinating novelty than anything else.

By contrast, however, some Australians felt differently about Asians. Given the fact that Australia (which is the smallest continent) and its white population are comparatively tiny next to Asia and its masses, this form of racism is not surprising. It clearly illustrates what I already knew—that racism is often rooted in insecurity. Some Australians discriminate against Asians because they feel threatened by them. There aren't nearly enough blacks for them to even be concerned about.

I see the same motivation behind much of the racism in America today. Racist blacks feel insecure and threatened by the majority. The blacks who would be white feel threatened on all sides. Racism among whites intensifies when they feel the power and privilege they have enjoyed in this country threatened by everything from affirmative action, quotas, and legislated set-asides to the prediction of population experts who tell Anglo-Saxon Americans that they may not make up the majority in our country much longer. Indeed, if the Hispanic population continues to grow at the current rate, I suspect we will see increased prejudice directed at them as they become a bigger minority "threat."

Too often insecurity begets ignorance which begets more insecurity and ignorance that only exacerbate racism.

Historically, many myths have surrounded the sexuality of blacks. Some have triggered a great deal of insecurity and fear among some white men who then donned the cloaks of racism as a means of protecting white women from black men. One of the most intriguing examples I have heard occurred in Germany during the post-World War II occupation. According to some German men, black American soldiers were said to be subhumans who actually had tails. This was an attempt to make European women fearful of black men, but it evidently had just the opposite effect. So many curious women wanted to see those tails for themselves that Germany ended up with a surprisingly large number of mixed-race children during that time.

Black people have been guilty of creating their own racist mythology about whites as well. Growing up, I remember that it was not unusual to hear it said that white people were dirty, hardly ever washed their hands, carried lice, and were guilty of any other number of other outrageous and stereotypical claims. Of course, all such racist statements, about any group, only prove that bigotry knows no bounds and feeds on insecurity and ignorance to survive.

WHOSE BOAT IS IT?

Because America's diversity is so unique, we have much to gain by viewing that diversity as a strength. We probably have more to gain in that way than any nation on earth. By the same token, if we continue to allow people with small minds to make diversity into a problem, we have more to lose than any other people in the world.

It was once a matter of national pride for Americans to call our country a "melting pot." We pay homage to that part of our history in the inspiring national memorial we have created at Ellis Island, where millions of immigrants landed with nothing more than hopes and dreams in their hearts and what few possessions they could carry on their backs. I am well aware that during that era, many people were not truly integrated (literally or figuratively) into the "pot" because we were not all viewed as equally important ingredients of that uniquely American blend. That was unfortunate and wrong. Those old racist attitudes divided and weakened us all.

But new racist attitudes, sometimes disguised as racial and ethnic pride, can divide and weaken us as well. I know of no other nation on earth whose people describe and divide themselves into so many different cliques, so much so that few of us even consider ourselves "Americans" anymore. It is more "politically correct" to say we are Irish-Americans, German-Americans, African-Americans, Mexican-Americans, Japanese-Americans, Hispanic-Americans, Chinese-Americans, Italian-Americans, or some other brand-Americans. If we are not careful we may fragment and hyphenate ourselves into oblivion.

Let me make it clear that I am not knocking cultural pride or criticizing our interest in our own cultural roots. It is wonderfully enriching to have a sense of heritage, to know and understand the ethnic and racial background that helped shape the individuals we are. That is why I said what I did at the National Prayer Breakfast about the need for young black males to know about more black Americans who contributed to our nation's development. I would go so far as to say that we could all benefit from knowing more about each other's cultural history. If ignorance is a common root of racism, more knowledge and appreciation of each others' history could not hurt.

We came to this land in many different ships, hailing from many scattered and distant ports. But we are, indeed, all in the same boat now. We need to realize that our American culture is an incredibly rich tapestry, woven together from many other cultures and backgrounds. Each strand is fascinating and meaningful in its own right. But only all the parts, woven together, can make up the amazing whole. Each of us needs to be careful not to allow our interest and concern about our own ethnic, cultural, and racial heritages to so narrow our focus (or our minds) that we lose sight of the Big Picture in the process.

VISION CHECK

I DO NOT GET to see many movies, but when I watched the video of *Independence Day* with my sons, I was struck by the portrayal of the resistance efforts mounted against the alien invaders from outer space. The frail and arbitrary distinctions so often made between various segments of society, even between different countries and ideologies, instantly melted away as the people of the entire world focused not on their differences but upon a common threat and the common goal uniting them—the protection of the planet from alien invaders. I know *Independence Day* is science fiction, but the same heroic emotional reactions it portrayed were very much alive after Japan attacked Pearl Harbor in 1941. Recruiting stations across the nation experienced a virtual flood of people from all ethnic backgrounds ready to sign up for the protection of our country.

Crises that threaten an entire nation, or the entire world, may be horrible, but they force us to embrace a common vision. They remind all of us, who may have forgotten, exactly what it is that unites us. In times of crises even small minds get a clearer view of the Big Picture.

Naturally, I do not suggest that America start a war or send out engraved invitations to a Star Wars-type invasion from some galaxy far, far away. I just wish I could convince more thinking people of what I believe is true—that continued racial divisions within our society pose every bit as great a threat to our survival as a nation as any outside attack, be it from earthly or other-worldly enemies.

Once again Solomon offers sobering wisdom when he warns: "Where there is no vision, the people perish" (Proverbs 29:18 KJV). We need true vision to see the whole beautiful, varied, multicolored tapestry that is America. Not a narrow, small-minded vision that sees different threads, different groups as problems. But a vision broad and brave enough to see, embrace, and harness the incredible strength in our diversity.

How do we regain that vision? What can we do to draw strength from our diversity at this time in our nation's history when such deep divisions exist in our land? That is what we will talk about in the next chapter.

Twelve

FINDING A CURE FOR RACIAL DIVISION

GROWING UP IN DETROIT, I regularly heard on the local news the name of Judge Damon Keith, one of the first black men appointed to the federal bench. So when the Honorable Judge Keith contacted my office to invite me to participate in a legal conference he was hosting in Detroit, I took a hard look at my September 1998 calendar and sent him my deepest regrets. I had a Yale board meeting scheduled the same day.

By now one of the most venerable African-American jurists in the land, Judge Keith clearly was not a person inclined to take *no* for an answer. He himself called and spoke directly to my administrative assistant, Audrey Jones, to explain that a thousand or more black judges and jurists, from every level of the judicial system throughout the United States, would be there to think about and discuss what they felt were the most crucial legal issues of our day. And he wanted the perspective of someone outside the legal community for the conference's closing panel discussion on the sometimes divisive issue of affirmative action.

I looked at my calendar again. I simply had to be at Yale on the twenty-sixth. The medical school subcommittee of the board was meeting that morning; as the only physician on the committee I needed to attend. Our board meeting would not be over until noon. The final session of Judge Keith's conference in Detroit was to start only a couple hours later. There just was not any way I could be in both places.

When I told Audrey, "I don't see how this can work," she once again conveyed my regrets to Judge Keith, saying I would like to participate, but my schedule would not allow it. At that point, Judge Keith put Audrey on hold. While she waited, Judge Keith used his considerable political clout to work out this solution: he personally talked a top executive of one of Detroit's Big Three automakers into sending a corporate aircraft to Connecticut to jet me directly from my board meeting to the Detroit City Airport, where a driver would be waiting to whisk me downtown to the conference at the Westin Hotel in the Renaissance Center, where I could join the panel in progress.

When Audrey told me what he had done, I shook my head in disbelief and laughed, "I guess I'll have to go; the judge hasn't left me much choice." Then Audrey and I laughed together, for we both knew my thinking on the issue of affirmative action, and it was not exactly what the folks at the conference would expect to hear. So I accepted the invitation and thanked Judge Keith for all the trouble he had taken to make it possible. I said, "I want to be there. I'm looking forward to it because I'm a by-product of affirmative action."

The panel discussion was in full swing by the time I arrived at the hotel that Saturday afternoon. What a panel it turned out to be! I could not help wondering, *What have I gotten myself into?* Among the other participants were respected historians and sociologists, authors of seminal books on civil rights laws, noted legal scholars, the president of the NAACP's Legal Defense and Education Fund, and a couple of giants who have been at the forefront of the legal struggle for civil rights over the last half of the twentieth century. One of the panelists was William Coleman, who had actually been one of the original signatories on *Brown vs. the Board of Education* back in 1954. Also present was the Honorable A. Leon Higginbotham Jr., a long-time federal judge from Pennsylvania, who had been everyone but Lyndon Johnson's first choice when LBJ appointed Thurgood Marshall as the first black Supreme Court Justice back in 1967.

Everyone on that distinguished panel spoke in support of affirmative action. Everyone, that is, except a University of Texas law school professor of constitutional law, Dr. Lino Graglia. The professor caused a stir and prompted more than a few scowls when he charged that affirmative action was nothing more than another name for racial preference, that it merely replaced one form of discrimination with another. Not only was it unfair and inherently wrong, he argued, but it was doomed to failure because it created more hostility and division than good. After his introductory remarks, a number of the panelists reacted to his charges.

Since I had slipped onto the dais late, I was the final person to make opening comments—after a short but gracious introduction from the moderator. "I want to begin by saying there was no way for me *not* to come today with a person like Judge Keith asking me to be here," I said. "Because I recognize that it was individuals like Judge Keith, and the black lady scrubbing the floors of this hotel at nighttime, upon whose backs I climbed to get where I am today. And that's something I never want to forget."

To provide my listeners a little background, I very quickly referred to my personal experiences in South Africa. "The first time I went there was during apartheid, and I could sense the difference, the aura of oppression, as soon as I got off the plane. I even felt self-conscious myself while I was there ...

"The last time I went was just this past December, when I was privileged by God to be the leader of a team that separated a pair of vertical craniopagus Siamese twins—attached at the top of the head. We performed the surgery at one of the country's black medical institutions, the University of South Africa at Medunsa. After twenty-eight hours of surgery, both twins appeared perfectly normal, and they remain perfectly normal today—the first time that has ever happened ..." The audience applauded.

"I say that not for applause but to point out the effect this achievement had. You should have seen the people in that institution and throughout the country; they were literally dancing in the streets. Their level of self-esteem was so high that when I left there it was with a very different feeling from my first visit.

"I believe God put me there and gave me that experience for a very specific reason, just as he has done in a lot of other situations throughout my life. So I don't want to leave God out of this discussion we're having today.

"But I want to go back to the time when I was a student at Southwestern High School here in Detroit. I compiled a very good record and received what I thought were excellent SAT scores. In fact there was an article in the *Detroit Free Press* which said, 'Carson Gets Highest SAT Scores in Twenty Years.' But then I went off to Yale. I remember sitting at a cafeteria table one day, listening to people talk about their SAT scores. "I got 1,600," one person said. "I got 1,560," said another. I started praying that no one ask me because, even though I had achieved a terrific record at my high school, my score did not compare to most other Yale students.

"That is something we need to recognize right up front. Anyone, whatever stripe they come in, even the most racist person in the world, would have to admit that what is demonstrated in this book is definitely true." I pointed to *The Shape of the River* by William G. Bowen and Derrick Bok (Princeton University Press), which was sitting on the table in front of another panelist. "A lot of people, including myself, have benefited from affirmative action, have made good on the promise, and have, in fact, taken advantage of the opportunity it afforded them. And I think that is the best possible reason for advocating the continuation of some program that allows minorities to have opportunities and improved access to mainstream America."

A lot of heads nodded at that point. I hoped at least some of them would continue to nod as I moved on to my next point. "But," I said—and this was going to be a significant *but*—"I'm a pragmatist. I understand that the landscape in this nation is changing. We all need to be pragmatic in the way we look at things. I would love to hear people engage in a very different conversation—on how we might maintain the benefits of affirmative action but change it and even call it something else." That brought some scattered laughter, which

I acknowledged by saying, "We have to be smart, you see. What I would like to call it is *compassionate action*.

"This is a compassionate country. America has long been a compassionate country, and we have to phrase things in a way that better appeals to this trait. Compassionate action would mean that consideration could and should be given in admission policies and in jobs to any person who has come from a severely disadvantaged background, whatever it might be. That may not include my three sons, because they have not come from a particularly disadvantaged situation. Not that they do not have some disadvantages, but they also have the benefit of my telling them, from the time they could understand English, that they are going to have to be twice as good to succeed. And they will have a lot of other advantages—financial, educational, and otherwise.

"But there are going to be other people of all racial and ethnic backgrounds, who come from disadvantaged situations but will benefit society if only we give them the chance. If we call this new policy *compassionate action*, and we find a way to standardize the guidelines, then the people who truly need it will still benefit from it.

"So we need to agree together on which things are truly disadvantages, and then find ways, using our collective minds, to work them into a compassionate action program that is fair and just. We need to utilize the brains God has given us to recognize the landscape and to make appropriate adjustments in order to come up with something more palatable to our whole society, while continuing the benefits we've seen in the past from affirmative action."

The discussion moved on with other panel members, many of whom took aim at Professor Graglia and his earlier condemnation of affirmative action. The debate grew heated. Despite an overwhelmingly negative, might I even say *rancorous*, audience reaction to his position, the professor held to his contention that affirmative action would never work and was far too flawed an idea to be fixed simply by renaming it as I had proposed.

I jumped back into the discussion at that point. "I think Professor Graglia has been misunderstood. I'm not talking just about changing the name of affirmative action. I'm suggesting a major change in the way things are done. I appreciate his articulating the concerns he did, and I don't think we should attack him. One of the things we have to understand is that we come from different places..."

Once again I made the point I had raised at the National Prayer Breakfast. "This is America. And although our ancestors may have come here in different boats, we're all in the same boat now. If part of the boat sinks, eventually, the rest of it is going down too.

"So we need to develop a new vision, with goals that will work for everyone. The concept of compassionate action could do that by saying that qualified individuals, regardless of their ethnicity, race, or gender, who have come from difficult circumstances (whatever those might be), should have that taken into consideration. I'm talking about giving deserving underdogs a helping hand. That's the American way ..."

With eleven people on the panel, none of us got the opportunity to say all we could have. But when each of us was given two minutes for closing comments, I made one further point: "The landscape has changed. But one thing that has not changed is that people have a lot of potential, a lot of drive within them. Think back to Montgomery, Alabama, in 1956, when people who were not empowered — who possessed nothing but faith in God, belief in themselves, and courage of their convictions — were able to bring that bastion of racism to its knees. It took a long time, but it happened. And black people in this nation have a lot more power than that today, and more resources.

"Yes, this can be a compassionate country. But there are also people in America who respond to money and power more than they respond to people with their hands out. So we have to be smart. We have to look at the cards and decide where we go from here. One place we must go to is learning how to develop economic power in the black community — how to turn over dollars in the black community.

And how to be supportive of each other—and I'm not talking about doing that to the exclusion of anyone else.

"We're God-fearing people. We believe he created all of us. He loves us all. He gave all of us brains, and he gives us the wisdom to open our eyes to see that this is not necessarily a friendly environment, but it will become more friendly when we become more powerful—I guarantee you that. He also gives the insight and wisdom to realize that what worked in the past, and what we're doing today, may need to be replaced with a new vision for the future."

So many people wanted to talk to me after the panel, and their response was so positive, that Judge Keith pulled me aside and asked if I would be willing to sit on the dais for the conference-ending banquet that evening—and maybe elaborate on my ideas with "a few more remarks." By this time, I knew better than to try to say no to Judge Keith.

At the banquet I shared my concern about young black men and the need for all of us to instill in them a self-image that will enable them to see how their intellectual and educational success could fit into a broader view of the future, and I expanded on what I had said on the panel that afternoon.

Still, there was no time to say everything I wanted to say about compassionate action, the thinking behind it, or the reasons it might be an important part of our Big-Picture strategy for addressing the deep racial divisions in our nation—divisions epitomized by the loud and bitter disagreements over race-related issues in our society in recent years.

O.J. JUSTICE

THE FIRST CONCERNED THE O. J. Simpson trial. Who would have thought that a single crime involving a retired professional athlete—no matter how popular—could interest so many millions of people? Who would have imagined that one court case—no matter how sensational—could mesmerize a nation for so many months? And who would have predicted that one verdict—no matter how controversial—could trigger an emotional reaction that deeply divided our society along racial lines?

Like many people in America I was as disturbed by such disparate reactions—both during the trial and in its aftermath—as I was by the verdict itself. The whole thing reminded me how far we have to go yet if we ever hope to blend the perspectives of black America and white America into a common vision with common goals.

If there is any hope of creating a shared vision, we have got to begin by doing something I talked about earlier—that is broadening our perspectives by trying to understand and see both sides of any problem or situation. Doing that helped me get a little better handle on the black versus white reaction to the O.J. trial.

Most white people were absolutely horrified that this man, or any man who very probably was guilty based on the preponderance of evidence against him, could be acquitted for such a heinous crime. I realize some of those white people may have seen the case in racial terms—a black man viciously murdering his white ex-wife and the mother of his children. But I am not convinced most whites viewed this through a racial lens at all—at least not consciously.

O. J. Simpson was one of those rare individuals in our usually color-conscious culture who had seemed able to transcend race. Like a Bill Cosby, an Oprah Winfrey, or a Michael Jordan, O.J. was known and loved and accepted more as a celebrity than as a "black celebrity," remembered more for his endorsements than his ethnicity. That may have contributed to the sense of horror some whites felt, in that O.J. had broken a special trust and acceptance accorded him.

But because most whites thought of O.J. more in terms of his celebrity than his color, the real issues, the basic questions in their minds, had to do with "fairness" and "justice." Which made the racially divided reactions to the case that much more incomprehensible and upsetting to so many white folks.

Black Americans, on the other hand, find it almost impossible to think about "fairness" or "justice" in anything *but* racial terms—because of our nation's historical record of unfairness and injustice to our race. As I said in the previous chapter, no matter how often we are told we need to "get over" the past, white people need to understand these things are not easy for us to forget. White people think of racial violence in a modern context—such as the black riots that erupted in the wake of the Rodney King verdict. They have no grasp on the history of racial violence in this country—as illustrated by their total unawareness of what *Newsweek* (December 8, 1997) admitted were "two [facts] that every American should know. Between 1885 and 1900, at least 2,500 blacks were lynched or murdered as the KKK consolidated its hold on the post-Reconstruction South. In 1741, 14 slaves were burned at the stake and 18 others were hanged because of fears of a slave revolt—in New York City."

Too many other incidents of injustice are not merely ancient history, but personal history, even current events, for the majority of black people. I remember in Boston when I was a child, my older cousins, sons of the aunt and uncle who took our family in, were arrested and thrown into jail for some minor infraction of the law. When one of my cousins protested that abuse, he was beaten so severely by the police that he almost died. I vividly remember seeing the results of that beating.

A few years ago, when my own mother questioned a policeman who stopped her for a routine traffic violation in a Detroit suburb, the officer angrily told her she met the description of a woman wanted for abducting an elderly couple. He promptly arrested her, had her car impounded, and threw her into jail. I had to call a lawyer friend of mine, a fellow Yale alumnus, who used his contacts as a senior partner in a major Detroit law firm to get her released and to see that the bogus charges were dismissed.

Most black people can cite similar personal experiences of injustice. President Clinton's commission on race specifically cited the injustice of "racial profiling," which many police use to identify *potential* criminals. It is employed most often in traffic stops, for a crime sometimes derisively referred to in the African-American community as "driving while black."

Statistics support what many blacks have never doubted, that our justice system metes out different treatment to blacks and whites. The disproportionate percentage of black murderers versus white murderers who receive the death penalty is just one example. The 1998 race commission report cited another when it urged the president to reduce the disparity in sentences for crimes involving powdered cocaine and its concentrated form, crack. The board said longer sentences for crimes involving crack, largely involving poor, black, or Hispanic offenders are "morally and intellectually indefensible."

Adding all this experience with the American justice system together gives perspective then on the not-quite-so-surprising reaction many black people had to O.J.'s acquittal. The issue for them was not so much the guilt or innocence of one man; indeed, many, if not most, assumed his guilt. What the black community was celebrating was a historic turning of the tables. They could not help being elated to finally see the legal system work in the favor of a black man when it has worked against so many black people in the past. They were not thinking, "Good for O.J.!" as much as they were thinking, "Good for us!" and "It's about time!"

My intention in offering this rather quick and limited analysis of black and white responses to the Simpson verdict is not to justify either reaction. This case, rather, simply illustrates, in a remarkably clear way, the common difficulty we have in seeing the Big Picture—and the importance of looking at a problem from all sides. We may not always agree. But if we are at least able to hear and understand the reasons other people react differently, maybe those reactions themselves would not have to divide us further.

AFFIRMATIVE ACTION DEBATE

THE SECOND WIDELY DEBATED hot-button issue that has separated us along racial lines is affirmative action. During the campaign for and against Proposition 209 in California, the eventual passage of which effectively ended affirmative action programs in that state, the subject was fodder for talk shows across the country. When I listened to the anger and pain on both sides of the issue, I saw the same basic problem I had seen in the O.J. case—with equally divisive effects. It troubled me so much that I began thinking and praying about a solution—some plan broad enough to address both sides' concerns.

To do that I had to first try to understand both sides.

I could understand the hard feelings of the angry white male who feels like he is suddenly being shortchanged through no fault of his own. He says, "I never owned slaves. No black people alive today in America ever lived in slavery. So why should I be discriminated against by affirmative action laws that give blacks a leg up when it comes to getting a job or being admitted to a school I want to attend. Our laws need to be fair to everyone. Two wrongs don't make a right. If I have the qualifications, I should be given the same chance as the next person. This is America; we're supposed to believe in 'liberty and justice for all.' "

For most people opposed to affirmative action the debate focuses on merit and fairness. With such traditional concerns at the center of their argument, they are convinced the very spirit of democracy has to be on their side. What could be more American than individual achievement and fair play? Who can argue against merit or fairness?

At the same time those in favor of affirmative action argue that they too want only fairness. They say, "Yes, this is America where we believe 'all men are created equal.' But we're born into very different circumstances that quickly make some of us more equal than others. We'll never have true equality or any real hope for fair play until we're all playing the game on a level field. As long as the field is tilted in favor of those who are advantaged—be it economically, socially, racially, or any other way—the only means of insuring fair play is to give disadvantaged people some extra help. But all we're really asking is an equal chance for success, a level playing field. What could be more democratic? What could be fairer than that?"

If you listen to their reasoning, you can understand why each side feels so strongly. But when each side is convinced they have justice on their side, you have a serious and deep division. Trying to see both points of view convinced me of that much.

Affirmative action started in the late sixties and early seventies, after the Civil Rights Movement had already won many, if not most, of its landmark legal victories. Revolutionary civil rights laws had been passed. Yet there remained some segments of society that felt a minority population was not capable of producing—intellectually or otherwise—and were reluctant to give them any opportunity to prove otherwise.

Affirmative action policies forced open a lot of doors that allowed Blacks and other minorities an opportunity to demonstrate their capabilities. As I indicated on that panel in Detroit, I personally benefited from affirmative action when I was accepted into Yale. And I am only one of countless minority individuals who have been able to benefit, and also provide benefit back to society, as a result of affirmative action policies. We have proven that given a real chance, we are capable of significant accomplishment in virtually all arenas of our society. I think most Americans would agree that our society is much the richer for those contributions.

But admittedly, affirmative action has had its downsides as well. One I experienced may come as a surprise to a lot of people. When I first joined the faculty at Johns Hopkins, I saw patients from all over the country. Not only did some of them fit the stereotype Jeff Foxworthy jokes about, but they obviously came in with a bias against people of my race. I tried to watch their demeanor and gauge their attitudes. In the end, almost all of these folks decided that any black man must know what he was doing if he was already chief of pediatric neurosurgery at Johns Hopkins by the age of thirty-three; because of my position they gave me a grudging respect.

I actually had more trouble earning the trust of some of my black patients. No sooner would I walk into the examination room than I would see the wheels starting to grind inside their minds. (It is a special gift some neurosurgeons have.) I could tell they were thinking, *I'm not going to have some affirmative action benefittee operate on the brain of my child.* They automatically assumed I had gotten my position not because I was qualified but because I helped meet some quota. So for some black people, affirmative action actually created a bias against members of their own race whom they immediately suspected were less qualified than whites.

But perhaps the biggest downside of affirmative action is the resentment it has fostered among whites who genuinely see it as government-sanctioned reverse discrimination. That resentment seems to be building in recent years.

So has affirmative action worked? I would have to say, "Yes it has!"

Is it still working today? With some obvious drawbacks, "Yes." Should we continue affirmative action into the next millennium? That is a hard question.

Some opponents argue that it is no longer needed, that we have grown beyond it as a society. Indeed, the last two or three decades have seen an impressive increase in the number of minority individuals successfully contributing in virtually all professions; that would indicate progress. Still, when California and Texas voted out their affirmative action programs, the numbers of minority law, medical, and other graduate students dropped significantly in both states. If that trend continues in those and other states, the playing field may soon tip further out of kilter.

A telling incident occurred not long ago in California — after the approval of Proposition 209, which effectively ended affirmative action admission policies in all state colleges and universities. One premise of that proposition was that such policies were no longer necessary to ensure fairness. Yet parents in one white California neighborhood have since mounted a legal fight to keep a new school in their district from being named the Dr. Martin Luther King Jr. High School. They said they were afraid college admissions departments would see that name on an application form and wrongly assume their white children were black.

You do not have to be a rocket scientist — or a brain surgeon — to see the irony. Obviously, not all Californians who voted for

Proposition 209 did so because they really believe discrimination is a thing of the past.

Honesty compels us to acknowledge that racism still exists today. I have no doubt it will always exist as long as people with small minds have a devil to stimulate them. So we need to realize that arguing for affirmative action because we still have not ended discrimination essentially means favoring affirmative action forever. I fear that would present some serious dangers. The first danger we have already acknowledged. Resentment. That will only get worse over time.

The second danger in extending affirmative action indefinitely is what I call the "grizzly bear phenomenon." What I am referring to is the situation that occurred in Yellowstone and other national parks in our western states. When the park bears approached cars or campsites, the friendly tourists would always feed them, and people thought they were being nice to the bears. But over time those bears not only became fat and lazy, they became dependent on the tourists for their food as they lost all interest in hunting for themselves.

When the rangers finally recognized the harm being done, they enacted new rules against feeding the bears. Unfortunately many of the animals did not take kindly to people who refused to feed them; in some cases angry bears tore up camps, damaged cars and created a fair amount of havoc before they could be reintegrated into the wild and learn to fend for themselves again.

There is a growing danger of a similar thing happening the longer we continue affirmative action. I say this because I believe it has already happened with some well-meaning welfare programs.

No doubt, some readers are now ready to tell me I am not being politically correct, or particularly nice, to compare welfare recipients and people who benefit from affirmative action to wild animals. Please hold all the cards and letters. This is just an analogy. But I think it's apt.

Speaking of being nice. I do not think it is particularly nice to rob people of their dignity, destroy their self worth, and make them dependent on others—which some welfare programs have done and affirmative action could also do if it is continued forever. I think we have to consider that possible danger.

So what do we do about affirmative action then—taking into account its pros and cons, its history, and the mixed reactions it triggers throughout society today?

As I wrestled with my own personal response to that question, I did what I often do when I encounter troubling questions in my life. I ask myself a simple, but often very helpful question: *What would Jesus do?*

From everything I have read about him in the Scriptures and know about him personally, I am certain he would be especially sensitive and concerned about any groups in society who were suffering disproportionately. Yet I do not think he would ever advocate doing something that would penalize other innocent people. Surely he would want a solution that could benefit everybody. But what might that look like?

As I began to think and pray about this, the idea of "compassionate action" began to take shape in my mind. I pondered the practical implications for a while. Then I began bouncing the idea off others, first in casual conversation and then in some of my talks. I think the first time I posed the idea publicly was in a meeting I had with minority students at Stanford University sometime in 1996 when Proposition 209 was a major issue. Since then, the response from black and white audiences alike has been overwhelmingly favorable.

The idea continues to evolve in my mind, but the fundamental idea remains essentially as I described it on that affirmative action panel in Detroit. Compassionate action could benefit anyone in our society, regardless of race, national origin, physical limitations, or whatever. But it would take into consideration any special obstacles a person has had to overcome, making that just one of the criteria for choosing between otherwise equally qualified candidates—whether they are applying for jobs or academic opportunities. Sometimes race might be a factor considered, but it certainly would not be *the* determining factor. A poor white boy from Appalachia who has worked extremely hard to help support his family yet has excelled academically might get the nod over the black son of a middle class professional who had more financial advantages, because race would not be the deciding factor.

I do not doubt that the concept could use some further refinement. It might take some serious time and effort to reach consensus on what is truly a "disadvantage" (especially if more people begin to see the advantage and opportunity in hardship) and just how much weight should be given to overcoming each one. But the positive response I have gotten whenever I talk about it, plus the advantages I see in the compassionate-action concept, convince me that the basic idea could work.

One beauty in the plan is that it still helps the people who need help most—which includes most of those who have received some benefit from affirmative action. As long as blacks or other minorities are disadvantaged—economically or otherwise—they would qualify for compassionate action at a greater rate than the rest of the population.

Yet the fact that compassionate action could benefit individuals from any segment or strata of society should cut down the resentment toward the idea. As a rule, Americans love the underdog. Compassionate action would benefit underdogs wherever they are found.

The other big plus compassionate action has over affirmative action is the way it completely changes the focus and broadens our perspective by giving attention not just to race but a variety of challenges. It then further expands our vision by placing as much, or more, emphasis on personal achievement and success in overcoming hardship as it does on any obstacles that had to be overcome.

PARENTS CAN NEUTRALIZE PREJUDICE

I CONSIDER THIS LATTER change in focus so important that it is one of the things I emphasize when I talk to black parents. I regularly advise black families, and particularly mothers and fathers, not to be terribly hung up about being black in America. I warn them never to allow the fact that racism still exists to alter their course of action in teaching their children the things that are necessary to become a success in life.

I frequently remind black parents: prejudice was here yesterday, it is here today, and it will be here tomorrow. If you let your life revolve around that fact, you have certainly shortchanged yourself and your children. In the Big Picture of life there should be far more important issues for you to deal with than other people's prejudice. As long as you focus on that, you are allowing them to dictate the primary agenda of your life. Ultimately their prejudice is their problem. Not yours.

No one can go through life constantly thinking about being a victim without all of his or her actions being colored and limited by those perceptions. It is like handing over the control of our lives to those small-minded people we have talked about. We must never do that. Getting that truth across to our children is absolutely essential to banishing a victim mentality, and this message is best communicated by parents.

One way do this is to point out to our minority young people successful people who have not allowed the focus of their lives to be limited to, or limited by, the color of their skin. For example: General Colin Powell is a wonderful role model. I first had the privilege of meeting him when he was still Chairman of the Joint Chiefs of Staff and have enjoyed getting to know him better in the years since. He is a man of true presence, who determined early in life not to focus as much on skin color as on developing competency and achieving excellence. His career epitomized that. Unlike some black people who have achieved enormous success, Colin Powell has not turned his back on the black community. Still, he has realized his importance to all of society and lends himself to causes and programs that empower and benefit people of all backgrounds.

Oprah Winfrey is another person who never allowed the prejudice she faced early in life growing up in the South to limit her focus. She refused to become bitter, concentrating instead on the development of her God-given talents, and becoming one of the best loved and most influential women (of any shape, size, or color) in our society. Yet she too remains an extraordinarily nice individual who uses her own success to speak out for and help less fortunate people of all backgrounds in this nation and around the world.

By no means should the examples we hold up before our children all be famous celebrities. Most of us can look around in our communities, our churches, and our professions to find admirable individuals who can illustrate to our children the importance of developing a vision that looks beyond skin color—people who illustrate how excellence crosses all bounds and can effectively knock down any barriers.

Aside from my good friend Dr. Levi Watkins, whom I mentioned earlier, I can think of two other examples from my own profession. Dr. David Nichols and I met at Yale our freshman year. He came from an academic background much stronger than my own; his father was a professor at Brown University at the time. Yet David never rested on his laurels; he was a studious, conscientious individual all the way through college and medical school. He actually joined the faculty at Johns Hopkins the year I went to Australia to continue my training. Recently, David became only the second black man to attain the rank of full professor at Johns Hopkins' School of Medicine, having never complained that he had not been promoted to that ranking earlier, when many colleagues felt his accomplishments might have merited it. David remains a splendid example to all our residents of a person of extreme competence in his field—who just happens to be black.

I have known many outstanding black academic physicians over the years, but few can compete with Dr. Keith Black, chairman of the neurosurgery department at Cedars Sinai Medical Center, known in Los Angeles as the "hospital of the stars." I have known Keith since he was in a combined bachelors and M.D. program at the University of Michigan, where he graduated at the top of his class. He joined the faculty at UCLA and quickly rose through the ranks to full professor while also conducting one of the most productive brain-tumor research laboratories in neurosurgical history. Keith is a splendid example of what can be achieved by persons of any ethnic background with perseverance, determination, and hard work.

VERY SMALL MINDS

WHEN I ENCOUNTER INDIVIDUALS who focus most of their attention on skin color, whether their own or somebody else's, I am reminded of red ants and black ants. You could invite both groups to the greatest picnic in the world, with more sandwich and potato chip crumbs than they could carry off in a million years. But once they saw each other they could not care less about what brought them there. They would soon be fighting each other to the death.

Talk about the limitations of small minds! And yet so many human beings, despite having brains far weightier than whole colonies of ants, so often succumb to the same silliness. Still, the fruit of racism is so horrible that calling it "silliness" hardly seems a strong enough condemnation. That human beings invest so much time and energy in something so meaningless as skin color really does seem exceedingly silly. If it were not such a sad waste of human potential it would be laughable.

As human beings we are free to decide what is important to us. Deciding that a person's skin color is ultimately important is as silly—and as irrelevant—as deciding that a person's eye color is important. Or the texture of their hair. Of course, none of these things defines a person's worth or their ultimate value to society.

What if we were to decide, instead, to be more interested in a person's intellect and personality and spirit? What if we were to decide, as Martin Luther King Jr. once said, the overall "content of their character" is what is of value in people? Well, that would be smart. That would be using the brains God gifted us with. So, what is keeping us from doing it?

Maybe this whole idea seems easier to me because of the work I do. As a surgeon I literally get past people's skin every day to see — and try to fix — what is inside of them. For me as a brain surgeon, a person's skin is almost always irrelevant. It is just something I cut through, peel away, and often have to clamp back to keep it out of my way in order to reach and work on what is truly important.

When I am done with an operation, whether removing a malignant tumor or inserting a tiny pump to drain excess fluid off a child's brain, and after I have pieced together the protective shell of a skull and we are finally ready to close, the stretching and restitching of the skin is almost an afterthought. Indeed, if I do not get back to my desk to dictate my surgical notes right away, and sometimes even when I do, I will not be able to remember a patient's skin color unless there is something about their name that provides a clue about their heritage. The fact that race is so often irrelevant for me as a brain surgeon probably makes it easier for me to feel the same way as a man.

It also makes it easier to relate to what the Bible says when it tells us, "The Lord does not look at the things man looks at. Man looks at the outward appearance, but the LORD looks at the heart" (1 Samuel 16:7). That is what we all need. We need God's Big-Picture perspective on our lives and our world. If we could see ourselves as he sees us, that would be a vision that could truly unite us and enable us all to be the people he created us to be.

Thirteen

EDUCATION: THE GREAT EQUALIZER

THE YEAR WAS 1996. Not only did this particular day promise to be one of the biggest of my life, but the morning turned out to be gorgeous as well. Seventy degrees. Blue skies. Bright sunshine. The green lawn of the old campus never looked more lush than it did that day from the front of the academic procession that marked the beginning of Yale University's 291st annual commencement exercises.

As I marched in the president's official entourage, down the long grassy center aisle past 20,000 chairs, and then slowly ascended a short flight of steps onto a large canopied platform to take my honored seat, I could not help reflecting on the lifelong journey that had brought me to this day — and I remembered the first and only time I had sat there.

The graduating class of 1973 gathered on this same lawn, amid these same historic buildings, with the same bright sun shining from the blue sky, with the Yale University band playing the same number — William Walton's *Coronation March* — as brightly colored flags fluttered overhead in the gentle spring breeze. That too had been a hugely important day in my life.

Since my brother Curtis' education had been temporarily delayed by a four-year tour of duty with the U.S. Navy, I was the first in my family to graduate from college — and not just any college. I was now a Yale man! That had made me almost as proud as my mother.

Back in 1973 I had soaked in all the glorious pomp and circumstance of my college commencement thinking, *My dreams have come true at last.* I couldn't imagine they were only beginning. I sat with 1,200 fellow classmates and looked up in awe at the canopied platform where sat the president of the university, all the members of the school's board of trustees, and other distinguished dignitaries of the day—including the great concert pianist André Watts, who received an honorary doctorate that same morning.

Now, twenty-three years later, I sat on that platform looking out over that great expanse of green lawn at all those graduates so full of potential and at the proud family members and friends who had come to celebrate the occasion with them. Though I sat among the dignitaries this time, I was still in awe. This day too seemed like part of a grand dream. I received my honorary doctorate shortly after Eunice Kennedy Shriver and just before singer Paul Simon received theirs.

Immediately after the ceremony, the president of the university, Dr. Richard Levin, hosted an elegant luncheon in nearby Woolsey Hall for the board and other high university officials in special recognition of those of us who had received honorary degrees. I was asked to speak on behalf of all of us being honored that day.

I talked briefly about what education—particularly my Yale education—had meant to me. I told the story of my decision to come to Yale in the first place. During the spring of my senior year in high school, I still had not decided where I would attend college that fall. The University of Michigan had offered me a scholarship, but I wanted to go farther from home. I had narrowed my options to Harvard and Yale. Then, one Sunday, teams from those two schools actually competed on *The GE College Bowl,* the weekly television game show on which student teams from different universities engaged in academic competition. I was so impressed to see the Yale students blow away Harvard, by a score of something like 510 to 35, that my decision was instantly sealed. Forget Harvard! Yale it would be!

Of course, the Yale crowd at the luncheon loved that story. I also shared a few of my wonderful memories from my undergraduate days before concluding by trying to express what Yale University had meant to me over the years: "My acceptance letter from Yale was my written permission to pursue my dream. That day in 1973, when I received my bachelor's degree, was the beginning of that dream. And today I've come back full circle at Yale again, to receive an honorary doctorate—which is the realization of that dream. Thank you."

FIELD OF DREAMS

IF YOU LEARN IT, they will come—because education can turn dreams to reality. That is my primary message any time I speak to kids. And I do that a lot.

Many Monday mornings during the school year, I host seven hundred to eight hundred students from area schools, who visit our campus on educational field trips. I meet with them in the school's Turner Auditorium, where I always try to inspire a few dreams of my own. I usually start by showing them slides about neurosurgery, Siamese twins, and some of the other things we do at Johns Hopkins. I try to impress upon these students the incredible potential of the human brain and the ability we all have to turn our disadvantages into opportunities. As an example, I often tell them the incredible story of Chang and Eng, the original Siamese twins. I always share my own story about how reading and education turned my life around, provided an escape from poverty, and enabled all my dreams to come true.

I tell students that it does not matter who they are, what color their skin is, where they come from, or how much money their family has: education is the great equalizer. For example, to become a licensed physician I needed one thing and one thing only: the required education. It would not matter whether my father was Bill Gates or a penniless bum on the street. Education is the only requirement that matters.

I stand before them—a one-time class dummy, now director of pediatric neurosurgery at one of the greatest medical institutions in the world—as living proof that with education anything is possible. I want them to know that education can make their dreams come true too.

I feel so strongly about the role and importance of education that I never have time to get across all the points I would like to make in any one speech. Usually, I barely touch on a few highlights.

TO STUDENTS I SAY: YOUR DREAMS, YOUR CHOICE

In our country, public education is free. So the quality varies. Some teachers, some schools, some school systems are better than others. But if you decide you cannot get an excellent education because your teacher is not effective, your school does not have high enough academic standards, or your school system is poorly funded, you are in danger of letting a victim mentality limit your future.

Ultimately, the quality of your education is up to you. It is a choice only you can make. You decide how much you are going to empower yourself through learning and knowledge. How far you go is determined, largely, by how far you are willing to go.

Any student who so desires can achieve a high quality education, whoever or wherever he or she may be—as long as the student can read, because once you can read, you can achieve the world's greatest education.

Many students tell me, "I'm not a good reader" or "I just don't get much out of reading." Some have even told me, "I fall asleep when I read." Yes, of course, some people do have legitimate learning disabilities such as dyslexia, which seriously impact reading skills. But there are examples of people who have learned and achieved success in other ways.

Tom Harken, another of my Horatio Alger Society friends, is an amazing case in point. When he started out in business as a vacuum cleaner salesman, Tom was illiterate. But he had such a tremendous memory that when he got home each night he would recite the details of every single order to his wife (whom we all call Miss Melba). She would record the information and write up the invoices for delivery the next day. Tom's attention to detail made for a keen mind that soon enabled him to build a successful business—at which point Tom went back to school to learn to read. Today he is an extremely articulate, effective, and literate public speaker, and he is CEO of Harken and Associates, which owns and operates a number of restaurants.

Tom is just one of many people I have met who have refused to let learning disabilities or even illiteracy prevent their success. Still, I have concluded that the biggest reason most people have trouble reading is that they do not do enough of it—and they do not do it fast enough. If your mind is revving at Indy 500 velocity while you are actually reading at go-cart speed, it is only natural for you to feel bored. No wonder your thoughts veer off course. So do whatever it takes to pick up the pace, and do not let yourself become too comfortable.

I had this problem in medical school. I would fall asleep when I began reading my assignments. I soon discovered an effective solution: I would stand up—or actually walk around my room—while I read. The standing and walking kept me awake. I also learned to pace myself by reading just forty-five minutes at a time and then rewarding myself with fifteen minutes to do anything I wanted.

What is true of so many things in life is definitely true of reading: the more you do it, the easier it gets. And the easier it gets, the more efficiently you can extract relevant data from the printed page—not just breadth of information but also depth.

A good example of this can be found in my own medical specialty: most neurosurgery departments at major medical centers designate only a couple of doctors to handle all the neuro-vascular surgery cases. They are the ones who clip aneurysms, deal with arterio-venous malformations, and handle complex peripheral nerve surgery. The thinking is that these problems are so rare that if everyone on staff handled such cases, no one individual would ever acquire enough practice and experience to become proficient. This is not to say that anyone in the department could not learn to do a good job, but by allowing one or two people to become more experienced, we provide better patient care in the long run.

Reading is mental exercise for the mind and imagination. As with physical exercise, the more you repeat it, the more agile and flexible you become. So whether you read or do brain surgery, the same principle applies: practice makes perfect.

Education is where students have the opportunity to practice and apply everything we have talked about in this book. It is the laboratory where they refine their choices and priorities. It is the test track for learning to turn obstacles into opportunities. It is the proving ground for such lessons as delayed gratification, being nice, and racial tolerance.

And if that is not enough to convince kids to see education as an important priority, there is this: their education, more than anything else, will determine whether or not they will ever see the Big Picture.

TO PARENTS I SAY: LAY THE FOUNDATION FOR EDUCATION

When I speak to parents I make a number of points in regards to education.

1. Start rewarding and encouraging learning early in life — and don't stop

From the time children are little, parents need to look for ways to make learning a positive, fun thing to do. Parents need to show children that knowledge is empowering. Most parents do this naturally. They clap and cheer when their baby learns to take those first steps. What parent does not encourage a baby to repeat its first words over and over again? Consider the rapt attention given a first-grader who hesitantly reads a picture book for the first time. But somewhere along the line most of us quit giving that sort of positive attention to our kids' learning. And that is unfortunate.

In our home, we have a daily ritual. Each of our three sons is required to come to the supper table ready to share one fact he learned that day—any fact, on any subject, from any creditable source, as long as the information was previously unknown to any other family member.

This simple exercise accomplishes several things. It not only encourages learning as something that needs to happen every day, but it also triggers some unusual and interesting table conversations. Candy and I find it helps us know what the boys are reading and better enables us to keep up with what subjects are currently of interest to them. Not to mention the fact that it is fun, as the boys often try to outdo each other in their attempts to surprise, amuse, or impress us.

Any number of creative exercises, educational games, and family traditions can serve the same purpose—just by letting kids experience learning and the pursuit of knowledge in a positive light. Hopefully they will reach a point where they understand that for themselves, and you no longer have to create artificial incentives for them to learn.

2. Do whatever you must to encourage reading

If you start reading to your children as soon as they are able to sit up in your lap, then by the time they are old enough to start reading themselves, they will already associate books and reading with fun and enjoyment. Read often and read for variety. Strike a balance between reading some books kids get to choose and others you select for content and literary merit. Make trips to the children's section of your local library part of your family routine. And when children get old enough to read on their own, do whatever you can to make sure they do so. Even if that means restricting other activities.

My brother and I were not at all happy when our mother began to limit our television viewing to two pre-approved programs a week and required us to write two weekly book reports. But she saw her decision as a means of establishing our family priorities. I well remember the speech she gave when we complained. She said, "Why do you want to spend so much time watching television anyway? If you'd use that time to develop your mind and your God-given talents, it won't be long until people are watching you on television." That seemed pretty far fetched at the time. But it turned out she was right—as I am reminded every time I am interviewed on television or some producer calls about doing a documentary on some facet of our work at Johns Hopkins.

Kids who read are kids who learn. Reading is the best foundation you can give them for ensuring a successful lifetime of learning.

3. Get involved in your children's formal education—at home and at school

You can do this in a number of ways: by actively monitoring homework, and helping when you need to; volunteering at your child's school; supporting the PTA and other educational programs; letting your kids see that their education should not only be a priority for them, but that it is one of your biggest priorities as well.

4. Point your children to successful individuals who have been empowered by education

Kids need heroes—role models whose examples they want to follow. These days most of those heroes come from sports and entertainment. You can help counter these often less-than-positive influences by calling children's attention to people who have achieved success through education and the development of their minds.

5. Be an example yourself

Parents, or guardians—whoever you might be—have a real responsibility not to just think and talk about education for your children. You need to set an example by continuing to educate yourself. Make learning a clear and observable priority in your own adult life.

No matter what your profession or job in this fast-changing world, you cannot hope to get ahead or even stay abreast without making significant and continuing attempts to learn and read about your field. It makes a convincing statement about the importance of learning when your kids see you improving your mind instead of just watching television night after night.

Some parents do not feel they can be a good example of education. Perhaps they do not have good learning skills themselves. Maybe they did not have the opportunities to succeed through education when they were younger. Perhaps they failed to avail themselves of the opportunities they did have. To them I say, "It's *never* too late to learn!"

Another of my Horatio Alger friends, Wendy's founder Dave Thomas, is a good example of this. When he started out in business, Dave did not have much in the way of formal education. Through good common sense, a commitment to hard work, the support of a loving wife, and everything he could manage to learn for himself on the job, he built an international fast-food empire. And yet, he placed such a high priority on learning that, after he became enormously successful, Dave took the time to go back and get more formal education. Today he is a bright and knowledgeable man who can converse intelligently on any number of subjects, because his appetite for learning has always been every bit as great as his appetite for those spicy chicken sandwiches his restaurant sells.

But my best example of "It's-never-to-late-to-learn" is closer to home. When our mother told Curtis and me that education would enable us to better ourselves, she believed that could be as true for her as for us. Though she was always smart, her lack of education held her back. She told *Parade* magazine that when we were growing up, "My boys were ashamed of me—yes, they were. They would say 'Mom, why can't you speak in such-and-such a way.' I would say to them, 'Teach me. If you can't teach me, don't criticize me.'"

She was never too proud to learn from her sons. While Curtis and I were in college she went back and earned her GED and eventually graduated from junior college. She left her menial jobs behind and became an interior decorator. While she was in school she would write papers and ask Curtis or me to critique them. She says we taught her a lot. But it was not nearly as much as we learned from her example and the emphasis she placed on education—not just for us, but for herself.

TO EVERYONE I SAY: MAKE EDUCATION SOCIETY'S PRIORITY DREAM

STUDENTS AND PARENTS ARE not the only ones who need to commit to education. I believe our society has reached a critical crossroads. Having only recently experienced the beginning of the information age, we are now poised on the brink of a brand new millennium. We have some important choices to make—some serious questions to ask.

Will America continue to be a world leader or will we as a society be content to be world followers?

In my talk to the United Way conference in Birmingham, I cited the 1992 survey measuring the ability of eighth-grade students in twenty-two countries to solve complex math and science problems. The United States ranked twenty-one out of twenty-two, just barely nosing out one nonindustrialized Third World country.

Some people complain that the survey compared apples and oranges, that it unfairly judged a broad cross-section of American eighth-graders against only the top students in other countries. But the results of a 1998 survey gave lie to that complaint. It matched our top high school students with the "cream of the crop "in several industrial nations. We ranked dead last in advanced physics, next to last in advanced mathematics, and close to the bottom in most other categories.

Are we content with this showing? If not, we have a lot of other questions we need to consider.

Do we want to pay now or pay later?

Some statistics indicate that at least ninety percent of prison inmates come from dysfunctional or fatherless homes. The vast majority of those people struggled in school. Plenty of other indicators can identify at-risk children in our society long before they run afoul of this country's criminal justice system.

But what are we as a society doing to reach clearly troubled children? Most of us seem to be doing little besides advocating the building of more prisons—a strategy, by the way, that is doomed to failure. We could build a prison on every other street corner without solving any problems, and we would drain our national resources in the process.

I am convinced it would be smarter (not to mention more cost effective) to focus on the reasons young people are at risk and to address those problems with our time and our money. We must realize that every kid we keep off that road to destruction is one less individual we will have to protect ourselves and our families from in the years ahead, one less person we will all have to pay for in the penal or welfare systems, and one more productive person who will benefit society.

Education is key.

Some people feel overwhelmed by the challenge facing us here. They think, *I'm just one person, what can I do?* A practical place to start would be with mentoring. Groups of men in every community could mentor young boys from fatherless homes, providing them with long-term role models they can relate to and emulate. We should be able to find such men in churches, schools, neighborhood groups, and civic organizations.

There was a time in America when everyone took responsibility for the young people who lived in their community. In too many cases today, that concern has turned to callousness and even to fear when we see the behavior and tough exterior of these troubled young men. Yet experience has convinced me that these seemingly hardened young men need love and acceptance and affirmation just as much as anyone else in our society does—and possibly more. Because genuine caring will almost always win out in the long run, our time and concern will have more impact than all the money we could invest.

But will encouragement and education really work to change lives?

Based on my own experience, I think it can. I remember that once I began to believe in myself, read, achieve good grades, I also began to gain the confidence that, despite my poverty, I had control over my own destiny. I saw that with hard work and educational improvement I could go virtually anywhere I wanted to go and be anything I wanted to be. With exposure to learning through libraries, museums, and universities, I gained a broader vision of what my future might hold. It made poverty a lot more tolerable. I could deal with present hardship because I could envision a different future, and I saw education as the most viable road to get me there.

I believe the difficult lives of countless underprivileged young people today would seem a lot more tolerable if they just had someone who cared enough to spend time with them—someone who could exemplify that success through education makes all the difference.

How can we make teaching a more respected vocation?

What job could be more important than overseeing the development of the minds of tomorrow's leaders? Almost everyone claims to believe teaching is a worthy profession.

But that is just lip service. The average major league shortstop receives more in salary than a hundred starting teachers. Our kids are not dumb. They know what that says about the importance we place on education.

Although teacher salaries have risen substantially over the past decade, they still do not reflect the importance of the job to our society, and they could probably be improved by simply reducing the top-heavy administrative structure in our public educational system.

What if we created a system by which private corporations could offer recognition and financial reward for master teachers who consistently achieve excellence in providing noteworthy educational opportunities for their students? What might be the impact on education in a city like Detroit if the Big Three automakers got together and each year made $5 million available to provide financial supplements of, say, $10,000 to $20,000 each to outstanding teachers.

At the same time I think teaching could be a more honored career if we raised both the qualification standards for the profession and made teachers more accountable for their mastery of the subject matter they teach by administering periodic proficiency tests. Just as I favor accountability for physicians, I expect high standards from the teachers we trust with this nation's most valuable resources—the lives of our children.

How do we begin to reorder our society's priorities?

If we are serious about emphasizing the importance of education, I am convinced we must start by de-emphasizing those things that do not contribute to the building up of our society. Our glorification of self-indulgence, materialism, and consumerism stands in opposition to any appreciation for philanthropy. Our cultural obsession with celebrity leads to the neglect of selfless service.

So many things divert our attention from the things that make a society great—fashions, sports, and entertainment. I am not saying we should ignore these things, but they currently occupy such an enormous part of our culture's attention that other things—like education—do not stand a chance. Because every part of society is affected by this problem, the solution must involve us all.

Sometimes I feel like a broken record when I try to assure people I really do not have anything against sports and entertainment. I find personal enjoyment in both. I have great respect for sports and entertainment figures. Michael Jordan is a good example. Not only is he arguably the greatest basketball player who ever lived and one of the world's most recognizable celebrities, he has invested a significant part of his fortune in helping less fortunate kids around the country. He comes across as such a genuinely nice guy that millions of kids want to "be like Mike." And millions of parents feel fine about that.

But let me ask you a question: If you were stranded on a deserted island, would you rather be stranded with Michael Jordan or a run-of-the-mill civil engineer? Michael might be great company. He could certainly improve your one-on-one game. He is a smart person who might even know some valuable survival skills. But I would opt for the civil engineer—someone who could help construct a sturdy shelter, know how to find a water supply, design tools that would make daily existence easier, and perhaps even construct a seaworthy vessel that might sail us to safety.

Of course, we do not know what challenges we will face as a nation in the coming years and decades of the information age, but we can bet that our society's survival will depend more on intellectual than on athletic prowess.

Let me say one more time: I am not slamming Michael Jordan or any other famous athlete. In fact, I would like to enlist their considerable influence and popularity in behalf of our making education a priority. I was pleased a few years back when Michael shot a television spot encouraging young people to pursue intellectual careers rather than basketball. The pro basketball players' "Stay in School" campaign was also a step in the right direction. Still, if more players had earned college degrees before jumping to the NBA, that campaign would have seemed far less hypocritical.

It is easy to pay lip service to the importance of education. But what if professional sports interests actually put their money where their mouth is? What if heroes like Michael Jordan and Mark McGwire, individually or as part of their players' unions, devoted just a small percentage of their salaries to fund academic, not just athletic, scholarships to be used by disadvantaged students? What if the owners of professional sports teams decided, "We get so much from this city that we consider it our civic duty to give something back. So we're going to donate a percentage of our payroll for the next ten years to hire extra math teachers for the local schools instead of one more relief pitcher for our bullpen"? What if government officials and civic leaders who solicit hundreds of millions of dollars for new, state-of-the-art sports stadiums they promise will revitalize inner-city economies, said, "We're also raising matching funds to be used for the building of modern libraries and state-of-the-art learning centers where the promising children of this city can begin building their own fields of dreams"?

What would that say to our children, society, and world about the importance of education?

Or what if one of the networks created a new television program along the lines of *The GE College Bowl* to celebrate and reward exceptionally bright young people for their learning? What if Hollywood decided to broadcast a weekly television series based on such inspiring stories of overcoming and achievement as the ones I have heard from fellow members of the Horatio Alger Society? (While working on this book, I mentioned this idea during an interview I gave on the PAX channel, a relatively new cable network that purports to be committed to positive, family-oriented values. Afterward, the producer approached me to say PAX might just be interested in such a program and asked how to contact the society. So who knows?)

Of course reordering our educational priorities is going to have to involve more than just sports and entertainment. I speak at conventions and conferences all the time where I hear business leaders lamenting the poor quality of job applicants being produced by our schools and universities today. What if they determined to help solve that problem? What if more American companies established business partnerships with local schools to share some of their resources to help in the classrooms and to offer field trips that could give students a Big-Picture preview of the working world? What if businesses gave time off to employees to serve as guest lecturers or even to teach classes in their fields of expertise? What if companies selected academic superstars to endorse their products? Or, as I asked our nation's leaders at the National Prayer Breakfast, "What if everybody in this room, with all your influence, went home today and wrote a letter to the Kellogg Company and General Mills suggesting they put people of intellect on their cereal boxes instead of athletes and entertainers? What message might that convey to our young people as they eat breakfast before heading off for school every morning?"

Any society's priorities ultimately reflect the personal priorities of those individuals who make up the whole. If we are serious about reordering our country's attitude toward education, we need to acknowledge our own culpability in the current state of affairs.

Let me share one example: everywhere I go to speak, I meet attractive, young, educated, professional black women who express frustration and disappointment at the caliber and quantity of qualified young black men in the dating market. I have seen the statistics showing the disparity between young male and female college graduates in the black community. So I can empathize with these women. But I also usually ask them this question: "Whose arm were you hanging on in high school? Was it the nerd's or the cool guy's?"

From the beginning of time, men have done what they think will impress women. So a lot of the "too cool" behavior of teenage boys is driven by their desire to attract teenage girls. If, in fact, these young women had had the foresight to understand the future implications of their influence, they might have encouraged the nerd and seen a significant difference in the way a lot of young men felt about their academic pursuits.

I remember the outrage caused back in 1994 by the release of *The Bell Curve,* a book that claimed to prove that black people are intellectually inferior to whites, though superior to whites in other areas, such as athletics. I actually did an interview at the time for *ABC Evening News* in which I gave my reaction to the book's basic premise. One of the things I said, which was cut from my comments as aired, was this: "I have a strong suspicion if all black girls suddenly began telling all black boys, 'Sure, I'll go out with you, but only if you make an A on your next calculus test,' you would see, over the course of time, a marked difference in calculus scores among young black men. And the authors of *The Bell Curve* would need a revised edition to point out how young black men show a remarkable potential for higher mathematics."

My point being, of course, that human beings tend to excel in those areas that have been emphasized by their society, family, and peers (including members of the opposite sex), subjects in which they then take a special interest. Interest and emphasis have far more to do with achievement than any genetic predisposition.

All this to say that before we can reorder the national mind-set about education, we need to change our own attitudes.

Where have all the dreamers gone?

At the outset of his presidency, John Kennedy challenged the nation with the goal of landing a man on the moon by the end of the decade. Practically the whole of American society embraced the challenge and committed its vast resources, particularly the country's intellectual energies, toward the accomplishment of that objective. I doubt it would have ever happened without that dream.

The sixties were a decade of idealism. There was also the "The Great Society," with its purported goals of fairness and equality for everyone, and regardless of what you thought of the wisdom, specifics, or ultimate effectiveness of LBJ's overall plan, his Great Society dream framed the debate so that discussion could focus on a broad range of ideals and policies.

One of the natural by-products of such noble, visionary, societal goals is that they automatically channel energies and attention back onto education, because education plays a vital role if we are ever going to achieve our goals. Such broad challenges engage intellectual passions that then refocus the study of history and philosophy, create new urgency in the study of science and math, and stimulate more creative thinking about problems and solutions. All of society, but particularly our educational systems, benefit from the reenergized intellectual fallout.

What I am talking about here is a shared societal vision—something many nations only manage to achieve in times of war. Rare are the leaders who can effectively articulate such challenges in times of prosperity and peace. Perhaps rarer still is the society that will embrace them. America needs that kind of vision again. If we had it, we would find it a lot easier to make education the priority it needs to be.

MY DREAM FOR EDUCATION: THE
CARSON SCHOLARS FUND

ONE OF THE MOST effective ways our society can make education a high priority is to recognize and reward students who are educational superstars. Not only do exceptional students need to feel as important as the sports superstars, but all their classmates and the people around them need to see education as an important and worthwhile goal as well. Then, even more students can aspire to educational excellence.

That is the philosophy behind a program I started in 1994, the Carson Scholars Fund. I had been speaking to students around the country for years, and I noticed that most schools have huge display cases in the front hallways to hold the trophies that pay tribute to their students' sports achievements. In contrast, honor students traditionally receive a paper certificate of some sort and maybe a small pin from the Beta Club or National Honor Society.

I saw the rankings of American students in science and math. I knew from personal experience, supported by research, that children who learn to excel early and stay motivated have a higher chance of educational success. So Candy and I decided to start a program we hoped could recognize and elevate academic performance to the level it deserves.

Our program's mission was unique. We wanted to offer college scholarships, regardless of financial need, to outstanding students based solely on high academic achievement and a demonstrated commitment to serving their fellow man. Whereas other scholarship programs often focus exclusively on high schools, our scholars can be nominated as early as the fourth grade.

In the short time we have been running our pilot program in Maryland, Delaware, and Washington, D.C., we have awarded $1000 scholarships to more than seventy proud Carson Scholars from sixty different elementary, junior high, and high schools. (All scholarships are invested in trust funds until the scholar enrolls in a four-year institution of higher learning.) We are now seeking additional support from private and corporate sources in hopes of awarding an increasing number of scholarships each year.

Our ultimate goal is to name one Carson Scholar in every school in the nation. It is a huge goal that would require an endowment of $1.5 billion dollars. But I want to practice what I preach when I tell people to "THINK BIG!" This is the course I have chosen to try to help change society's priorities and to turn attention away from things that do not matter in the Big Picture, to those things, like education, that will help our country and world be the kind of place our Creator created it to be.

DREAMS COME TRUE

THE REASON I FEEL so strongly about education should be obvious by now. Education enabled all of my dreams to come true.

Once again, Solomon's wisdom tells us, Gold is nice, silver is nice, rubies are nice. But to be cherished far above those are knowledge, wisdom, and understanding. Because Solomon knew that with knowledge, wisdom, and understanding, you could get all the gold, silver, and rubies you wanted. More importantly, he knew that with knowledge and wisdom and understanding you will come to understand that the gold, silver, and rubies are not really that important in the Big Picture.

Far more important is developing your mind and your God-given talents to the point where you become valuable to the people around you.

For that we need education—because it helps us understand the past, cope with our present, and determine our future.

Fourteen

DIAGNOSING THE CRISIS IN HEALTH CARE

ONE DAY DURING THE course of writing this book, I had two medical students observing our pediatric neurosurgical clinic when parents bring their children into our hospital offices for examination, which happens both before and after their operations. Somehow I got into a discussion with these students about managed care and how it affects the way we can take care of patients today—particularly the problem it presents in trying to get things done efficiently and expeditiously.

That very day we had appointments for two children with very similar cases. I could feel through their scalps that they each had lesions on their skulls. I suspected little benign tumors. But I also needed to be able to see what those growths looked like.

The first child's family had a commercial insurance policy—Blue Cross/Blue Shield—which still allows physicians to make decisions. So we sent them down to radiology without calling anybody, the X-ray was taken, I confirmed my diagnosis, we set a date for surgery, and the family was gone in no time.

The second family belonged to an HMO plan. My secretary spent three hours on the phone with the company trying to get a gatekeeper's okay for a simple X-ray. Long before the ordeal was over the poor child was crying, the parents were upset, my staff was frustrated, and my medical students got a memorable object lesson in the aggravation commonly experienced by both patients and providers as a result of today's health-care system, which no longer has patient care as its primary goal.

Not long ago, I also evaluated a six-month-old baby with *achondroplasia*—a genetic condition resulting in the most common kind of dwarfism. Many of these children develop neurological problems with compression of the junction of the spinal cord and the brain stem at the base of the skull because the hole at the base of their skull is too small.

We have devised surgical methods for alleviating this problem, but it is highly specialized and requires multidisciplinary evaluations and a team effort to successfully manage these children. At Hopkins we've established a center for skeletal displasia with the kind of expertise necessary to care for these complex cases; we probably have more experience dealing with achondroplastic children than any other hospital in the nation.

We weren't covered by this particular family's managed care plan, but because of our reputation, the parents had decided to pay the out-of-pocket costs for an initial examination. I knew right away that their child would need a complex surgical procedure called a *cervical medullary decompression*, which I have performed numerous times. It's a very dangerous and complex operation in which we open the hole at the base of the skull and also remove part of the first cervical vertebra to make more room for the spinal cord.

Because of our experience with cases like this one, the parents petitioned their insurance carrier for permission to have their son treated at our center. The request was denied, and the parents were told they would have to see the pediatric neurosurgeon in their network. Unfortunately this surgeon, who was otherwise well qualified in his field, had little or no experience with achondroplasia. He operated—unsuccessfully—not because he wasn't a competent surgeon, but because he had never before performed the procedure this child needed.

When the parents contacted me afterwards to say the operation had not relieved their child's symptoms of decreased mobility and loss of reflexes, I warned them something had to be done as soon as possible. The longer the spinal cord remains compressed, the greater the chance of permanent damage. It is like heavy furniture on a piece of carpet; the longer it sits there, the harder it is to get that imprint out. I told them, "Hire a lawyer and write some very strong and demanding letters to your HMO to insist on further treatment immediately."

They followed my advice and their HMO relented. We were able to work the child into our operating schedule within a matter of weeks. The operation was successful. And the child did very well.

But the managed-care organization paid for two operations instead of one. And what is even more outrageous was that they put that baby and his family through the trauma of a second life-threatening surgery, which could have been avoided if they would have had the best interest of their patient in mind from the start. I feel certain if the child had been the son or daughter of one of the executives of that well-known managed-care organization, he would have been sent to an appropriate, experienced center without any hesitation.

At Johns Hopkins we worked with another family prenatally after their baby had been diagnosed with *hydrocephalus* in utero. We counseled the devastated parents ahead of time, going over the kinds of treatment that would be necessary. The day after birth we were ready to implant a shunt into the child's head. This kind of shunt drains the excess fluid off the brain and channels it through a tube beneath the skin all the way down into the child's abdominal cavity. The baby did well—growing and developing normally for months.

At about a year of age, the shunt malfunctioned as a certain percentage do. But we fixed that. The baby was doing fine on all the subsequent check-ups until the family was told by their HMO that they would have to switch their surgical care. The mom was so distressed she came into our office crying.

I suggested if she felt that strongly about continuing her daughter's relationship with us, she should make phone calls and write letters to her insurance carrier citing the family's history at Johns Hopkins. But her correspondence only delayed the inevitable. The family was finally told, "You'll go to the doctors we tell you to go to." They were emotionally distraught when they left, but they were given no choice.

The basic reason given by this HMO for their decision was that the daily cost of any necessary hospital stay at Johns Hopkins would run a little higher than at the hospital used by the HMO's neurosurgical provider. But there are other numbers that might have shed a different light on that decision. If they had looked at success rates in dealing with shunt complications of hydrocephalic patients at every hospital in Maryland which handles such cases they would have found an average mortality rate of 4.5 percent. At Johns Hopkins our mortality rate for hydrocephalic patients with shunt malfunctions is 0.45 percent—ten times better than the statewide average. But far too few managed care organizations ever factor in the outcome numbers. Dollars and cents are the only numbers they consider.

As a result, I am all too frequently faced with crying mothers whose children are badly in need of serious medical attention who, in addition to experiencing the stress of dealing with a neurologically ill child, are also being forced to jump through numerous hoops by uncaring insurers who give no consideration for a family's wishes, the patient's history of treatment, or even a doctor's professional experience.

I relate these three stories not because they are the worst I've seen but because they are so typical of what we experience in health care today. Are things really that bad? Is there any hope for improvement?

To answer those questions we need to take a much closer look at the Big Picture of health care and how we got to the point we are today.

HOW DID IT GET SO EXPENSIVE?

FROM THE BEGINNING HEALTH insurance has had the commendable goal of providing more people with affordable and higher quality health care. Like the fire and life insurance industries that developed earlier, the health insurance industry was established on the assumption that a group of people assuming relatively small degree of shared risk and costs will prevent individual policy owners and their families from suffering financial ruin in the event of catastrophic misfortune. The idea was, and is, both laudable and sound—which explains why the concept caught on and grew steadily throughout the 1900s. People saw that it worked.

But other modern developments greatly impacted both health care and health insurance. The tremendous technological and pharmaceutical strides medicine made in the middle decades of the twentieth century wreaked havoc on the numbers in many of those probability/actuarial tables upon which insurance costs, benefits, profits, and premiums are figured.

For the first time in history, we were routinely able to save extremely premature babies by placing them in incubators, then combining complex chemical and drug regimens with never-before-imagined procedures and equipment. When these babies finally went home with their grateful parents, we would hand over to insurance carriers a bill totaling six, sometimes even seven, figures. And many of those most premature babies faced a lifetime of continuing health problems with the prospect of even more expensive future treatments.

At the same time, we developed the ability to operate on an eighty-five-year old woman with diabetes, thyroid disease, and hypertension and successfully remove a life-threatening brain tumor to provide her with another few months (maybe even an extra one or two years) of life. Here too we would hand over a bill for hundreds of thousands of dollars to the insurers.

Understandably, insurance companies had to adjust the price of their premiums to pay for the cost of our increasingly sophisticated and expensive medical progress. As those premiums and medical costs steadily escalated, fewer and fewer individual families could afford to carry their own insurance. But they didn't want to risk going without coverage. So a growing number of employers began to include health insurance as a standard part of employee benefit packages.

In accepting the development of employer-managed insurance plans to relieve individuals of the growing burden of health insurance premiums, we also relieved many patients of any personal sense of concern or responsibility for health-care costs. At the same time we also removed a large measure of the medical community's accountability to individual patients. No longer having to consider the direct cost of their care on their patients, doctors had little incentive to weigh issues of cost versus quality of care. The patients weren't paying; the health insurance companies were. Add to that the evolution of a medical mindset operating under such well-intentioned assumptions as "better safe than sorry" and "the more information the better," and doctors feeling fewer financial constraints began routinely ordering unprecedented numbers of costly tests and procedures.

These and other factors sent medical expenses and health insurance costs spiraling upward at a dizzying rate over the following decades. Now, at the end of the millennium, health-care costs account for one-seventh of the entire U.S. economy.

HEALTH CARE CLIMATE CHANGE

NATURALLY, AND RIGHTFULLY SO, the skyrocketing price of medical care gave rise to enormous public, governmental, and insurance industry concerns about cost containment. One result was the recent proliferation of managed care organizations such as PPOs and HMOs—concepts that had been around for fifty years without ever really catching on or playing a major role in health care.

The sudden popularity of managed-care organizations made an immediate and undeniable impact. They quickly achieved their declared goal—severely curtailing the rapid escalation of medical costs in a relatively short period of time. That impact continues to this day with the cost of providing medical care now rising at a much slower rate than it did before the recent rise of managed care.

Patients' premiums, however, have not followed the same curve. Indeed, insurance costs continue to rise at a steady rate. Few of the dramatic savings seen in medical-provider costs have been channeled back to the consumer or into medicine to improve care. The money has simply shifted into the pockets of shareholders and into the bank accounts of managed-care executives. It turns out what we have is not so much *managed care* but rather *managed finance*.

Throughout this time, the insurance industry has very cleverly and effectively directed the focus of concern over costs onto the providers, so that the average consumer/patient believes that it is the enormous fees paid to medical providers that not only escalated the costs in the past but continue to keep the cost of medical insurance coverage so high today.

Few people realize that only nineteen cents of every health-care dollar goes to pay for professional services while twice that amount (approximately thirty-eight cents) goes to pay administrative fees— which means if we want to bring the rising cost of health care under control, we need to turn our attention to all the factors in the equation and not lay total blame at the door of doctors.

Having said that, I want to quickly acknowledge that in some cases the medical profession should make some concessions and may even need to be taken to task for the current state of affairs. And I'll cite some specifics before I'm through.

SYMPATHETIC "VICTIMS"?

At the risk of sounding defensive and self-serving, however, I would point out here that doctors as a group make irresistibly easy scapegoats. And a lot of that has to do with the way we are trained and socialized.

Let me explain.

With few exceptions, people who become doctors were diligent and disciplined college students who would forego the immediate gratification of partying, social life, and so on, in order to study and achieve the kind of grades necessary to get into medical school. Then, during the first two years of medical school, they kissed their friends and relatives good-bye to submerge themselves completely in their studies. They were forced to do this because there is so much knowledge to acquire in med school that the first two years are sometimes likened to the challenge of learning eight new foreign languages simultaneously.

If they make it through that, the third and fourth years of med school introduce students to a new lifestyle where working incredibly long hours and being on call twenty-four hours a day is the rule rather than the exception. This sort of austere life is reinforced through internship and residency, during which the vast majority of your waking hours are spent dealing with other people's problems. By the time you survive that to become an attending physician, you think nothing of missing your child's birthday party, standing your spouse up for your anniversary dinner, or being awakened at 2:30 in the morning to answer some patient's questions over the phone. You simply get used to dealing with other people's issues immediately, while putting your own concerns, and often your family's concerns, on the back burner.

Over the years you develop a certain mentality that precludes your complaining about things that impact your own personal life or your own well-being. Indeed, it is usually considered unprofessional to do so.

Consequently, when insurance companies and managed-care organizations began limiting doctors' traditional rights to make decisions on behalf of our own patients, unilaterally reducing our fees, and otherwise dictating how we practice medicine, we as a group offered only minimal protest. Finding so little resistance from the medical community, some of the more ruthless business types in managed care kept pushing and shoving doctors into a health-care scenario that is less and less desirable for us and for our patients.

So it is these days I often hear doctors griping among themselves about working harder and harder for less and less money. But I'm growing tired of such complaints and don't want to hear any more about it until doctors are ready to stand up and speak out for themselves and their patients.

I have often likened what we have in health care today to a customer going into a car dealership and seeing a brand new car with a sticker price of $25,000. But he tells the dealer, "I'm only going to pay you $10,000. Here's the money." And then he takes the keys and drives out.

If the dealer does nothing about it, the customer will eventually come back to look at another car and say, "I think I'll only pay $5,000 for this one." And the next time he comes he will say, "I believe $1,000 should cover it this time." Until he eventually decides he can have any car he wants for nothing at all.

As long as the dealer does or says nothing, there's no incentive for this sort of behavior to stop. And that is just what seems to have happened in medicine today.

A lot of doctors hesitate to complain for fear the public will charge them with selfish motives — thinking they are simply concerned about their own income. I believe those doctors, and the public, need to stop, step back, and try to consider the bigger picture.

Look at the cost of four years of college. And another four years of even higher costs for medical schools. Add years of internship and residency at very limited salaries. Note the high costs of practicing medicine (including malpractice insurance), which continue to climb. Factor in the high stress levels associated with many medical careers and the expected sacrifice of family time.

When you consider all these elements of the Big Picture, it is a lot harder to justify the argument that these same people should also sacrifice their income. In fact, if we want people of high intellect and general excellence to continue to be attracted to the field of medicine, we cannot continue to tolerate a health-care environment in which we routinely beat up on the practitioners.

You think I am exaggerating to try to make doctors more sympathetic "victims"? Consider this.

In past generations, a large percentage of doctors seemed to have one or more children who considered it almost a noble family calling to follow their parent's footsteps into the medical profession. Today I encounter more and more doctors who feel so hassled that they are not only pointing their sons and daughters toward other careers but actively discouraging them from going into medicine.

Some of the same frustrations are prompting more doctors themselves to reexamine their careers or to drastically alter the way they practice medicine. I know a number of capable OB/GYNs in their forties who have quit delivering babies because they are legally liable for birth-related traumas suffered by their patients until those children reach eighteen years of age. These doctors know there is absolutely no way they will be able to continue to afford the astronomical price of their malpractice insurance once they are living on their retirement income. So they have decided to limit their practice by staying out of the delivery room for the final eighteen years of their medical careers—rather than risk financial ruin in their retirement years. As a result, we are losing the services of some of our most experienced doctors at what should be the prime of their professional lives.

Traditionally some of the brightest people in our society have chosen to go into medicine. But they didn't choose their profession to be told how to practice it. Or to have their decisions routinely second-guessed and overruled by people with considerably less training, or none at all, in their field—people with little understanding of, or interest in, patient care. It is a formula for short-term frustration, a recipe for long-term disaster, which will drive more of today's best and brightest out of medicine and may discourage tomorrow's best and brightest from ever seriously considering a medical career. If that happens, the impact on the quality of health care we now enjoy in the United States may be horrendous.

CALLING ALL DOCS

DOCTORS THEMSELVES NEED TO look at the picture I have sketched here and see it as a call to action. We all took the Hippocratic oath. Part of that oath charges us to accept responsibility for the health care of our patients. It did not say we should abdicate that responsibility to third parties who are willing to take the health care of our patients and make it a commodity on the stock market.

Not that the medical community is blameless for the current state of affairs. When the recent rise of HMOs and PPOs began, insurance carriers recruited doctors, enticing them into managed care plans by telling them, "If you'll agree to become a part of our network and accept reduced fees for your services, we'll make sure all our clients come to you. We can promise that because we won't even cover them if they go to anyone else."

A lot of doctors took that bait—hook, line, and sinker. They saw the dollar signs in an exclusive guarantee of additional patients; clearly there was going to be a lot of money at stake for those who got in early. Other doctors weren't motivated so much by greed as by their own survival instincts; they didn't want to be the one who would not be reimbursed by patients' insurance. They realized if enough of their patients left them for "approved" network physicians, it could seriously damage or destroy the practices they worked so long to build. So many of them also bought into managed care.

By the time all the dust had settled, few physicians had not become affiliated with one or more managed-care organizations. And fewer still mounted serious resistance to, or even spoke out in protest against, even the most negative implications this system has had for doctors and patients alike.

Those of us in medical professions share culpability for the situation we all find ourselves in today. Yet it is not too late for us to realize we should not be competing with each other. Rather we should be pooling our intellectual and moral resources to reclaim both our advocacy role and our primary responsibility for the health care of our society.

ISOLATIONISTS OR HEALERS AND HELPERS IN SOCIETY

To reclaim our role in health care, we doctors need to acknowledge and correct our mistakes. For starters it would help if we, as doctors, recognized how we have weakened, and sometimes even abandoned, our relationships with our communities over the years. At the outset of the twentieth century and for decades thereafter, doctors still played integral parts in the broader life of society. Using their superior training and knowledge along with the pragmatic problem-solving skills learned in medical schools, physicians helped address the biggest issues facing the communities in which they lived.

But as medicine, like society, has grown more sophisticated and specialized, we have slowly but surely isolated ourselves in our professional societies, our operating rooms, and our clinics. We live and work in what amounts to a "gated" medical community whose literal and imaginary walls have limited our interaction with, and our involvement in, the broader world.

This trend isn't just sad; it's a tremendous tragedy—not just in terms of health-care issues but because of what society as a whole has lost.

Things haven't always been this way.

Not long ago I was invited to the Cove, Billy Graham's retreat center in the North Carolina mountains, where I spoke to health-care professionals about some of my concerns. There I met United States Senator Bill Frist, a cardiovascular surgeon from Tennessee who was at that time the one and only M.D. serving in the Senate.

Senator Frist gave me some historical perspective on physicians in Congress. He had done his research and told me that if you go back through American history in twenty-five year increments, you would see a steady increase in the number of doctors serving in Congress. When you go all the way back to the first U.S. Congress you will find more than forty physicians.

I'm not arguing that our legislatures ought to be comprised of more doctors than lawyers, but I can't help believing our modern culture would be better served if more doctors were better public servants, if we recognized our potential to influence the world we live in, and if we felt a greater civic responsibility for the resources, training, and trust our society has invested in us.

Perhaps a Big-Picture view could broaden our perspectives on our societal role, convincing us that we should not just view ourselves as providers and protectors of health care but that we should involve ourselves in all those contemporary issues that affect the quality of life—mentally, spiritually and physically—in our society. Perhaps we, as doctors at the outset of a new millennium, can once again aspire to be healers of society, rather than very specific, narrow-minded practitioners of physical medicine.

To do that we might also need to remember and recapture the traditional heart of medicine.

Throughout history the prime focus of health care centered on the basic, two-party relationship between doctor and patient. Even after insurance companies inserted themselves into the mix as an interested third party, their stated intention was merely to facilitate the doctor-patient relationship and make medical care affordable to more people.

Unfortunately the system has evolved to the point that a third party has now become central to the equation. Indeed, the entire health-care universe often seems to revolve around an all-powerful insurance business whose interests sometimes supersede those of patients or doctors. We have forgotten that the doctor-patient relationship is at the heart of health care. In so doing, we neglected the interests of both. Sometimes tragically.

A case in point:

An eighteen-year-old hydrocephalic patient who had been treated for years by one neurological team was forced to change doctors when his parents' employer changed medical insurance plans. Shortly thereafter he experienced a shunt malfunction. His new doctor, an extremely capable surgeon whose work I am familiar with, revised the shunt and determined it was functioning. A subsequent CAT scan showed the ventricles were still enlarged, but the surgeon didn't have immediate access to baseline X-rays with which to compare the results. As far as he knew, what the CAT scans showed was normal for his new patient.

Every patient is different. Some people spring back quickly in response to a shunt revision, others gradually improve. You never know, unless you have a history with the patient, how he or she typically responds. It wasn't until later that his doctor was able to learn that this boy usually bounced back very quickly. This meant that his slow response after this surgery was not normal but indicative that he still had an unresolved shunt problem.

The night following the surgery the patient herniated and suffered a massive stroke as the result of increased cranial pressure. This boy, who had been able to live a virtually normal life for eighteen years, was suddenly left in a permanent vegetative state.

It is very unlikely that this terrible tragedy would have occurred had the patient been cared for by his original neurosurgical group who knew him and his history. Yet this is a scenario doomed to be repeated many times in a system that does not encourage, and sometimes actually prevents, the establishment of long-term doctor-patient relationships in complex medical cases where continuity of care can make a life-or-death difference.

The current system also regularly shortchanges patients by denying them personal control, individual freedom of choice, and access to the best available quality of care. It undermines the interests of doctors by usurping their medical authority to decide what is best for their patients and dictating how medicine will be practiced in our country.

As a result, in more cases than I want to think about, managed-care companies and their representatives are, in effect, practicing medicine without a license.

THE DEVASTATING EFFECT ON RESEARCH AND EXPERIMENTATION

BEYOND THE SERIOUS IMPLICATIONS for patients and doctors of nonmedical authorities dictating choices for treatment, there is yet another troubling concern that will negatively impact the future of health care for decades to come. That is the effect managed care is having on the development of new medical treatments and procedures.

From the time Johns Hopkins was founded back in 1876, medical research has been central to our institutional mission. In order to financially support Hopkins' research and teaching functions, our costs, like those of other similar academic institutions, have traditionally run a little higher than community hospitals.

Most patients who have sought care at Hopkins over the years, however, have understood that regional research hospitals cost a little more because they absorb a whole range of expenses local hospitals never have to worry about. Traditionally, our patients—and their insurance companies—have always accepted a trade-off. Along with higher prices, they have expected cutting-edge medical treatment, doctors at or near the top of their fields, easier access to multidisciplinary treatments, and a greater level of expertise and experience in dealing with complex or unusual diagnoses.

The bottom-line mentality demonstrated by most managed-care companies today too often ignores or discounts such trade-offs. By focusing so much of their attention on the dollars and cents, they have lost sight of the bigger picture.

They forget, or place little value on the fact, that a disproportionate percentage of training and medical advances take place in teaching and research hospitals. If the current trend continues and fewer patients are allowed to choose treatment at these institutions, there can't help but be serious implications for the future progress of health care across America.

Many research hospitals are struggling desperately to survive in the stormy financial climate of health care today. Unfortunately, for some it will be a losing battle.

Just one of the examples I am familiar with is the University of Minnesota Hospital—long noted for its outstanding vascular-surgery department. Surgeons from around the world came to Minnesota for specialized training, and the new life-saving techniques pioneered there became standard procedure in operating rooms everywhere.

But that respected department has been devastated over the past few years by managed-care organizations deciding higher costs ruled out the University of Minnesota for their patients requiring vascular surgery. The sudden reductions in patient numbers meant a serious drop in income for the program. The department had to cut some of its first-rate staff and could no longer offer the same amount of quality training or fund all the research projects that had made their vascular surgery department the asset it had been to the University of Minnesota and the world of medicine. As a result, we are all the poorer.

WHO PAYS?

LIKE EVERY RESEARCH INSTITUTION in the country, Hopkins faces similar struggles in virtually all our departments. The budgetary challenge I face every month in the pediatric neurosurgery department is a daunting one.

In order to compete at all in the managed-care marketplace, we have had to drop our charges to the point where, despite personally performing twice as many operations a year as the average neurosurgeon, despite the selfless dedication of a staff who works far more hours than they are paid for each week, I regularly have to make agonizing budgetary choices. Do we cut or underpay valued staff? Do we go without useful equipment? Or must we tell the families of desperately ill children who need our skills and experience that we can't afford to help them because the amount of money their insurance will pay for an operation won't begin to cover our expenses? Some days it seems we must do all this and it still won't be enough.

The ramifications of all this became disturbingly personal in the weeks before the completion of this book. The budget crunch at our hospital has forced us to trim the number of OR personnel to the point that some afternoon and evening shifts are reduced to little more than skeleton staffs. This means that on days when we have an unusually high number of surgical cases, or when emergencies need to be scheduled, we have very little flexibility. We don't have enough surgical support personnel to simply run more operating rooms simultaneously—as we might have done in the past. Instead of moving efficiently from one OR to another, surgeons have to wait for one procedure to be completely finished before the same few on-duty nurses, technicians, and other professional staff can even begin preparation for the next case. This means on heavy surgery days I'm routinely beginning complex surgeries at 6:00 or 8:00 or even 10:00 in the evening and then working late into the night—just to perform the same number of surgeries I used to be able to finish up by suppertime.

Not only is such a schedule terrible for young patients and their families who have to spend the entire day not knowing exactly when surgery will finally begin, it is also a terrible strain on the medical staff. So much so that it almost cost me my own life—*twice* within a matter of days.

The first incident occurred driving home at 2:00 A.M. after just completing my seventh operation that day. I had begun in surgery before 7:00 that morning. As I was heading home at seventy miles an hour on Interstate 70 in light traffic, I dozed off. For how long I don't know. When I suddenly awakened, I instinctively jerked the wheel of my Buick to the left just in time to avoid drifting under the wheels of an eighteen-wheeler I didn't remember starting to pass.

The very next week I fell asleep a second time, on the same familiar stretch of road—once again heading home in the wee morning hours after an eighteen-hour day of surgery. That time I actually drove off the pavement before I awakened and steered my car safely back onto the road.

Having that happen a second time within a week scared me so badly that I wrote a letter to the administration of the hospital the next day. I recounted those two experiences. Reminding them of why I had been operating at that hour of the day, I informed my superiors if the situation didn't change immediately, I could no longer continue the surgical load I had been carrying. If surgical cases kept getting pushed back into the night, they were going to have to find someone else to do the operating. I no longer thought it was worth risking my life.

To the hospital's credit, my superiors all reacted with alarm and genuine concern about what had happened. They immediately vowed to look for ways to resolve the problems. But I realized so many factors are totally out of their control. The root of the problem is the system itself—a system where all the providers, hospitals as well as doctors, are being squeezed harder and harder by an insurance industry that too often makes profits a higher goal than quality health care.

FORTUNATELY FOR ME, AND for our hospital, William Brody, the president of Johns Hopkins University is a resourceful as well as visionary administrator. Before coming to Hopkins, Dr. Brody had been vice-chancellor at the University of Minnesota to witness what impact the managed-care environment had inflicted there. His leadership and experience has played a major role in helping us not only preserve our mission as a research institution but to maintain our reputation and *U.S. News and World Report*'s rating as the number-one hospital in the United States for eight straight years. I'm hopeful we will work out the OR staffing challenges to the benefit of our doctors and our patients alike.

But what can be done to preserve other research institutions that don't have the leadership or the resources we have at Johns Hopkins? How do we create a national health-care climate that is healthier for doctors *and* patients? If so many people on so many sides of this issue can agree that we have a serious medical-care crisis in America today, why can't we begin working together to find some creative solutions?

In the next chapter I will try to answer these questions as I propose some solutions to the thorniest health-care problems facing our society today.

Fifteen

REVOLUTIONIZING HEALTH CARE:
ONE DOCTOR'S PRESCRIPTION

SOME TIME AGO OUR pediatric epilepsy team at Johns Hopkins evaluated a four-year-old girl from South Carolina with intractable seizures. They recommended her to me as a candidate for a *hemispherectomy*—a drastic procedure in which one entire half of the brain is removed.

I told a rather extended and dramatic story of my first hemispherectomy in the book *Gifted Hands*. I have since performed this procedure successfully numerous times, usually in cases where debilitating seizures (sometimes occurring hundreds of times a day) are steadily destroying the health and life of a young child. Since this sort of seizure activity invariably affects only one side of the brain, and because the still-developing brains of children amazingly retain enough plasticity for one hemisphere to adapt and take over function of the other, we've been able to restore many of these children to near-normal lifestyles by completely removing the entire diseased hemisphere. In fact some of my earliest hemispherectomy patients are in college now and doing well.

Obviously, we perform hemispherectomies only as a last resort. But our evaluation team concluded that there were no viable alternatives left for this particular child. She was deteriorating rapidly.

Still, the child's family's managed-care organization protested, saying they thought medications and a less radical treatment were warranted. Because hemispherectomies are still a fairly new and very radical surgery not performed very many places, this HMO deemed them "experimental" and said it wouldn't pay for the procedure. Considerable time and effort were invested in phone calls and letter writing by the office and medical staff members at Hopkins who related our success with such cases in the past. We finally received a written response informing us that despite the "unorthodox and experimental" nature of this procedure, they would approve it "this one time. But if the patient requires another hemispherectomy we will not pay for it."

We passed that letter around our department and laughed a long time. Since the human brain is composed of only the two hemispheres, taking out a second one would leave the patient with no brain at all. The very idea of any patient having a second such operation was not only absurd, it was impossible.

(Although I have wondered at times if some of the managed-care bureaucrats I have encountered over the years had been subjected to a bilateral hemispherectomy. It would certainly explain some of their rulings.)

I COULD GO ON and on telling not-so-funny stories of distressing situations that have occurred not only in my experience but in cases other physicians have told me about. Colleagues and professional acquaintances regularly relate their insurance horror stories to me because they know I have been concerned and outspoken on this subject.

I remember one of my own first encounters with managed-care decision-making. This case, which may prove instructive for families who find themselves bogged down in health-care bureaucracy, involved a young patient of mine from California with a complex brain tumor. A five-year-old-girl developed a rapidly growing lesion at the top of the brain stem near the pineal region. The family contacted us, and I confirmed the earlier opinions they had received. I told the girl's parents that their daughter definitely needed surgery, and when they asked if I would perform it, I assured them I would be glad to do so.

Their managed-care organization, however, told them they couldn't take their daughter outside the state of California for treatment. They definitely wouldn't pay for her to come cross-country to Hopkins.

Fortunately, this family was very media savvy and had carefully read the fine print of their insurance coverage, which stated they could go outside the network for treatment of complex problems requiring specialized expertise. They told their story to one of the most popular radio stations in Southern California, and people began talking about their case on the air. Before long there was such a public outcry about the company's reluctance to live up to its contract that this well-known managed-care organization recanted and agreed to let the girl come to us. They even tried to play their change of heart to their own public-relations advantage by announcing that the patient was indeed going to Hopkins and the insurance company would be covering all costs.

We successfully operated on the tumor, and that little girl continues to do well—eight years later.

It is cases like hers that have convinced me insurance companies believe most people will meekly submit, instead of protest, when any sort of bureaucratic obstacle is placed before them. And the insurance companies are right.

However, the small percentage who hire a lawyer and keep pushing are much more likely to eventually get a ruling in their favor. This is particularly true when a significant degree of publicity might surround the case. Only the squeaky wheel gets the best care. And insurance companies continue to reap profits from the other ninety percent who don't question them about anything.

I HAVE COME ACROSS other cases where managed-care organizations do not seem to be as concerned about money as they are control. One case in particular involved an infant with a grossly misshapen head, whose physician-father served on staff at another university hospital.

This concerned doctor-dad wanted me to assess his son because he knew of my experience caring for children with craniofacial problems. But his managed-care organization refused him permission to come to Johns Hopkins for a consultation. When I heard the story I agreed to see the child for a nominal fee, which the family willingly paid out of pocket.

Upon examining the child, I quickly diagnosed the problem as *positional plagiocephaly,* a mechanical deformation that occurs when the position of a child in the womb prevents the skull bones from forming properly. I wasn't immediately convinced the child's condition warranted surgery; time and less drastic therapies sometimes correct such problems enough to avoid the physical and emotional trauma of operating.

Still, I informed this father and his managed-care organization that if something had to be done surgically, I was willing to perform the necessary procedure for exactly the same charge they would pay at a facility in their network. I explained I was doing this as a personal favor to the family. Nevertheless, the company refused permission, denying any coverage if the child came to Hopkins.

That ruling seemed incredible to me at the time. But in sharing the experience with other physicians, I have learned the same thing frequently happens with other companies. Obviously this is an issue of control as well as a clear indication of managed-care companies' disregard for their clients' concerns.

I have since developed a fairly effective strategy for dealing with such situations. When a company refuses to pay for care outside their network, despite our assurances that we will not charge any more than their usual providers, I ask them to explain that decision in writing. Most of the time I find they back down. They worry about the publicity that could result from putting such an irrational, insupportable decision down in black and white.

I have concluded there are far too many people in the current managed-care environment who love the feeling of being in control. Not all HMO gatekeepers are like that, but unfortunately, not enough effective checks and balances are in place to insure fairness or rationality. Too often it is a matter of who happens to handle your case; if you get the wrong person, you have a problem.

I, like many physicians, probably share some of the blame for the way things are. When we willingly offer to lower our usual fees to accept whatever they are willing to pay, we only contribute to the perpetuation of a system that constantly pushes health-care providers against the wall. Nevertheless, in many situations like this one with the doctor's child, I develop an emotional involvement with the family and really want to do something to help them.

I long for the days when medical practitioners could devote their energies to practicing medicine and not to worrying about the finances of our patients. I think we may be able to return to those days, but it will require some real determination along with a comprehensive, Big-Picture plan.

Not only must physicians stand up. But the general population must rise to the occasion and reclaim control of their health care and that of their loved ones.

OPENING SHOTS IN THE REVOLUTION

Motivated by all these experiences, I have been to Washington, D.C., to discuss health-care reform with legislators on Capitol Hill. I have met the President, and I was invited to a White House conference by Hillary Clinton, though I had to decline because of previous commitments. I am convinced that everyone concerned is honestly looking for solutions.

So why are we stuck?

Let me say I am not surprised that recent attempts at health-care reform have not been successful. The pool of resource people Mrs. Clinton assembled for her health-care initiative early in her husband's administration relied heavily on major players in the managed-care and insurance industries. And more recently, managed-care interests have also had the ear of conservatives opposed to such reforms as the

Patients' Bill of Rights and other consumer-friendly legislation, which among other things would have enabled patients to sue their insurance companies for damages when the companies' medical decisions result in harmful or tragic outcomes.

I know I approach this subject with a physician's bias, and I would never presume to have all the answers to such a complex issue. But I think a doctor's perspective on health care must be considered by anyone wanting an accurate and comprehensive understanding of the Big Picture. And it is absolutely essential if there is any hope for making the doctor-patient relationship central to American health care again.

I have posed the following ideas to a lot of different people over the past couple of years—fellow doctors, patients, managed-care officials, legislators, and even some malpractice lawyers. Those discussions have helped further refine some of my thinking on the following proposal.

COMPUTERS: PROMISING A COST-CUTTING EDGE

AS WE CONTINUE TO move from an industrial to an information age, we could improve both the quality of medical care and cut its costs if we simply made better use of the computer technology that already exists. Let me explain.

Virtually every medical diagnosis has a standard, nationally recognized, alphanumeric designation called an *ICD 9 code,* and almost every medical test or procedure is also designated by what is called a *CPT code.*

Both of these standard codes are currently used throughout the health-care industry for diagnosis and reimbursement purposes. They routinely appear on almost every page of the enormous mountain of paperwork surrounding the care and treatment provided to patients at every point in our modern health care system—from doctors' offices to clinics and hospitals, to medical laboratories, to the accounting department of every insurance company.

What we have not done, but what current technology and these already existing codes would easily allow us to do, is take the next, big, logical step. We could eliminate the incredibly expensive burden of paperwork that plagues our industry by utilizing computer data banks, Internet communication channels, and electronic transfer capabilities to streamline both our diagnostic and our financial reimbursement procedures in medicine. We could start today and see the difference almost overnight.

We should probably anticipate a great deal of opposition to any such plan from many of those in the insurance industry who make their living pushing papers or make their profits by creating complex bureaucratic schemes that ensure a place for them at the very heart of the health-care system. But we need to consider again the traditional model of health care, which was defined by and focused on the doctor-patient relationship.

In truth, you cannot have health care without a care provider and a patient. And the more layers of bureaucratic decision makers we allow between those two essential parties, the more we allow that essential relationship to be weakened.

STUCK IN A BUREAUCRATIC BOG

I THINK OF A recent case I had—an eighteenth-month-old girl with *metopic craniosynostosis*. With this condition the skull sutures at the front of an infant's head fuse too early. This often results in the still-growing head becoming pointed in front like the keel of a boat. In severe cases that may so decrease space anteriorly that the brain does not have enough room to grow.

In many, less severe instances there is nothing we need to do for the patients—unless the cosmetic problems are severe or they become symptomatic with severe headaches or developmental problems. Unfortunately, this little girl exhibited irritability consistent with headaches as well as delayed speech.

So we did a CAT scan to determine the pressure effects on the bone and immediately recommended surgical correction. Without that correction, I believed the mounting pressure and the worsening symptoms could result in permanent brain damage.

The girl's family was well-to-do and highly educated. They even had a relative who was a well-known neurosurgeon in another state; he concurred with our diagnosis. The family's HMO, however, refused to grant permission for the surgery because they said it was "cosmetic."

The parents argued with the insurance people. Then various members of my staff called to try to explain that this surgery was not being recommended for appearance reasons. They couldn't get it approved either.

Finally, I called the HMO offices myself. The first person I talked to about the case clearly had no medical background at all. When I couldn't get anywhere with her, I asked to speak with her supervisor. Still no luck. It didn't matter how I explained this little girl's condition and the need to operate to relieve the building pressure on her brain, the HMO classified this particular kind of surgery as "cosmetic" and said they would not cover it.

I kept getting passed up the bureaucratic ladder. I felt hopeful when the fifth person I talked to turned out to be an MD. But I soon discovered he knew nothing about metopic craniosynostosis either—though that didn't keep him from denying the recommended procedure.

When I continued to press my argument, this doctor finally told me he would refer the case to a consulting neurosurgeon and they would get back to me. I never heard from the company again. The next thing I knew, the girl's family engaged a lawyer and the HMO finally decided they would cover the surgery after all.

Working with plastic surgeons who are part of our craniofacial surgery team at Johns Hopkins, I operated on that little girl. She came through the procedure beautifully and is doing fine today—no thanks to the HMO that had wanted to deny her treatment.

Of those five levels of managed-care employees I talked to about this little girl's case, how many actually facilitated the relationship I had with my patient and her family? Do experiences like this explain why administrative costs now make up twice the share of professional fees in every health-care dollar?

COMPUTERS: IMPROVING PATIENT CARE

WE COULD ADDRESS BOTH the bureaucratic costs and communication problems with better, more purposeful use of computer technology. And I am convinced we could actually improve the quality and effectiveness of medical care in the process.

Some people may wonder, "Who's going to police the medical providers to prevent financial abuse of an impersonal computerized system?"

I feel certain we could limit that risk by establishing extremely serious penalties for fraud. We might learn something from Sweden's get-tough laws against drunk driving; with the threat of lifetime loss of driving privileges, confiscation of vehicles, and serious jail sentences, driving under the influence in Sweden has become a rare occurrence. We could just as easily make the punishment for medical fraud so substantial—permanent loss of medical license, confiscation of property, mandatory prison sentences—that no reasonably intelligent person would consider it. Few doctors would be willing to take those risks.

Computers could also assist physicians in other ways. Already we can create databases and program computers to enable doctors to access the very latest medical findings, to find up-to-date standard of care information for various diagnoses, and to reference the most comprehensive differential diagnosis lists. Such an on-line system could be instantly available to virtually every physician in the nation. And we would all reap two enormous benefits from utilizing the information highway this way.

The first and perhaps greatest advantage would be the patients'. On-line access would improve the quality of health care in this country by bringing every physician up to a critical standard in terms of the physician's medical knowledge and methods of treatment for standard problems. This in turn would have the secondary benefit of reducing the incidence of malpractice—which is already quite small. And with a little more refinement, such a system could be used to return some sense and sanity into the whole medical liability issue.

Let me say that I know something about malpractice cases—not from being sued myself but rather from testifying as an expert witness in court on several occasions. Most of my experience in such cases has been supportive of the defendants—professional colleagues I thought were unfairly accused. But I have also testified in court on behalf of plaintiffs who suffered from inadequate medical care.

As long as health care is administered by imperfect human beings, unfortunate, even tragic mistakes will sometimes be made. Injustices will occur. Diseases will be misdiagnosed. Some victims will deserve recourse for their suffering. But a measure of reason needs to be restored to our malpractice litigation process. Here again modern computer technology could help.

With the availability of on-line resources, laws could be passed stating that any physician who is adhering to the nationally accepted guidelines for the treatment of a certain diagnosis could not be sued—despite the results of the treatment. An enormous percentage of medical malpractice activity would disappear overnight.

Moreover, physicians, reassured by the knowledge of such a law, would no longer feel the need to practice defensive medicine. This would result in the elimination of countless unwarranted tests and other clinical activities routinely ordered by many gun-shy doctors these days simply to protect themselves from a malpractice suit. If we can replace this paranoid "I did everything possible" defense with an "I did what was reasonable" strategy, the health-care dollar savings could be astronomical.

I realize some physicians will bristle at the idea of standardized treatments, claiming it would infringe on their autonomy and reduce their chances of practicing the way they want to practice medicine. To them I would say two things: first, the current system already infringes on our autonomy by dictating much of what we do and don't do; and second, doctors will still be free to practice the way they wish. If they want to follow a nonstandard treatment plan they can. They just wouldn't be covered by the law protecting them from being sued — and that would be no different from the system as it currently exists.

This new system could be modified to allow a greater measure of individualization of treatment in unusual cases. A physician could enter into his computer the reasons for a deliberate deviation from the national standards in the treatment of a particular case. The reason for this deviation could be analyzed almost instantly by a nationally recognized group of peers in his specialty who would be on call on a rotating basis. If this advisory panel agreed with the reasons for the unusual treatment, the practitioner could still be covered by the law that prohibits the initiation of a malpractice suit in the event of a bad outcome.

I don't have the expertise necessary to estimate actual dollar amounts that could be saved with each of these suggestions, but it seems clear that the elimination of large mountains of paperwork by using computers for billing and reimbursement, along with any drastic reduction in medical malpractice litigation, would have to result in greatly reduced health-care costs in this country.

MORE ON MALPRACTICE, INSURANCE, AND PHYSICIAN INFORMATION REFORM

I HAVE HEARD ADDITIONAL suggestions for addressing some of these same issues recently. Many of them deserve consideration and possible inclusion in a comprehensive plan for health-care reform.

For example, in response to the current malpractice issue, many ideas for tort reform have been posed in Washington, D.C. One of those suggestions advocates that the loser pay legal fees and court costs in medical malpractice cases.

Although I have met some outstanding malpractice attorneys of great integrity, there are other lawyers who have no qualms about taking on frivolous suits in hopes of improving the odds that they will be able to win or settle a few cases with significant remuneration. It is this second group that would be largely eliminated by a loser-pay system. The idea has merits and should be seriously considered.

Before America's trial lawyers rise up in protest to this idea, let me hasten to say I have recently found myself agreeing with the legal community regarding other reform proposals. As long as managed-care organizations are allowed to make judgments on health-care treatments that amount to practicing medicine without a license, I think they should be legally liable when their medical decisions result in bad outcomes. As things stand now, when patients suffer as a result of managed-care companies' decisions to deny recommended treatment, the only recourse those patients or their families have is to sue the provider, who may have recommended the proper treatment in the first place. Obviously that's not fair.

This is why I actually supported patient-doctor-lawyer-friendly legislation to make insurance companies liable when it was proposed in the Maryland legislature recently. It came very close to passage before better-funded managed-care interests rallied their forces and defeated the bill by two votes.

Some people may be surprised to find me, a doctor, siding with lawyers in some instances. Others may be just as surprised to find me siding with patients in other instances.

I am a big advocate of what I believe is an equally important patient right. I think it is a sad commentary on our present health-care system that patients can find out more about the qualifications of the plumber they call to unclog a toilet than they can about a surgeon into whose hands they are expected to place their very lives.

Our society places physicians in highly esteemed positions of responsibility where they are privy to the most intimate details at the most desperate and vulnerable points of their patients' lives. It is not only unreasonable, it is wrong that doctors are able to hide their professional records.

Whatever reforms we adopt, I believe we need to move to an outcome-based system, which will not only provide better health care for patients but will also begin to help us as physicians identify those members in our ranks who achieve subpar results and may be a danger to society. We have an obligation to insure those individuals receive the remedial training they need—or that they stop practicing medicine.

We can no longer turn a blind eye and a deaf ear to medical practitioners who are not providing quality care—for whatever reason. As protectors of society our first obligation is to our patients. While we cherish our colleagues, we must understand that we can in no way tolerate subpar performance that endangers or compromises the care of those individuals who have entrusted their lives to us.

For this reason, any serious attempt at health-care reform should include easy public access to information regarding disciplinary actions or negative incidents surrounding any physician's practice of medicine. This should not include mere allegations of wrongdoing, but only official acts of discipline after due process. Because access to such information might prompt some patients to move from one physician to another, health-care reform would need to include total choice for every patient.

If a physician and patient establish a relationship that they wish to continue, a third party should never be given the power to break up that relationship. This would obviously be much more easily accomplished in a setting where every individual or family owned and managed their own policy—as opposed to having it managed by an employer as is usually the case today.

AN AMBITIOUS PLAN

But would such a change in our current system be economically feasible or even logistically possible?

Any number of reasons are put forth by some people to argue against serious reform. In fact, when I have taken part in various medical panels discussing health-care reform, I have been distressed by the predominance of negativity and cynicism. Too many people seem to devote most of their critical thinking to attacking each others' suggestions.

If we adopt a facilitator's mindset instead, agree that the health-insurance system in America once worked better for a large number of citizens, and ask what would need to happen to make it work better again, we just might find some reasons for hope.

A plan like we have already talked about that reduces paperwork, improves the standard of care, and discourages frivolous malpractice litigation could result in lower premiums. But we might reduce the cost of medical insurance a lot farther by taking an even broader approach to the problem.

A RADICAL IDEA FOR REFORM

I think it is generally assumed by those seriously involved in the discussion of health-care reform that most Americans would oppose the creation of a single-payer health-care system such as some other countries have established. As a rule I too am concerned about the growing intrusion of government into citizens' personal and professional lives.

Still, state and federal governments handle some well-defined programs reasonably well: for instance, disaster relief programs and the Federal Emergency Management Agency (FEMA), which has been streamlined and noted for increased efficiency and effectiveness in recent years.

If the government did not step in to provide aid to private citizens following natural catastrophes such as hurricanes, earthquakes, and floods (and even unnatural disasters such as the Oklahoma City bombing), hardly any of us would be able to afford homeowner's insurance. In an attempt to cover the eventuality of such disasters, insurance companies would either go out of business or be forced to raise premiums to astronomical levels. But because insurance companies can generally assume the government will absorb a large share of the responsibility after such disasters, almost every home and business owner in America can afford adequate insurance coverage for real estate.

What if we considered a similar model for health care?

Just suppose health-insurance carriers were no longer responsible for covering the costs of catastrophic health care (defined by a certain dollar amount, say $200,000 per illness). With this decreased liability, combined with the added savings of reduced paperwork and reduced malpractice suits, health-care insurance premiums could be reduced to the point where individuals could own their health-care policies just as they own their own life insurance and automobile insurance.

Once that was the case, both the individual and society as a whole would see many secondary benefits. We already know that prevention pays in health care. Financial incentives in the form of premium reductions could be offered for anyone who undergoes regular physical exams—making early detection and treatment more likely—and thereby saving the system and society even greater long-term costs.

Auto insurance companies find it cost effective to give lower rates to good drivers and provide discounts for taking driver-training courses. Homeowner insurance rates can be lowered by taking such safety precautions as installing deadbolt locks and fire extinguishers. In the same way, people who take precautionary measures and exhibit healthier lifestyles—who don't smoke, aren't professional lion tamers, etc.—could be given further reductions in health-care insurance costs.

People who were responsible for their own premiums would be more likely to question a health-care provider about certain tests and procedures charged to their insurance policy, and health-care providers themselves would be more sensitive about ordering questionable tests and procedures if they knew their patients were actually monitoring the billing.

Another significant benefit to consumers would be the portability of their health insurance. You do not change car or homeowner's insurance just because you change jobs. If you owned your family health insurance, there would be no reason ever to have to change coverage unless it was somehow to your advantage. It would put an end to that all-too-familiar "preexisting condition" rationale used to justify "ineligible for coverage" rulings affecting millions of people every year.

SO WHO PAYS?

How would we make up the difference? Who will foot the bill for catastrophic health-care costs?

This is where a government-run catastrophic health-care fund would come in. Such a fund could be supported by a mandatory contribution of say ten to fifteen percent of the profits made by each health-insurance company—including managed-care operations. Since those companies would no longer be required to cover the cost of catastrophic illness, they should continue to reap substantial profits even after a significant reduction in health-insurance premiums. And without the huge risk factor of catastrophic illness to allow for, the health-insurance business should be far more predictable. It would be much easier to predetermine the lower expected payout of insurance companies as compared to the premium dollars collected. So profiteering could be better controlled—either by governmental regulation or by public and marketplace pressures that force companies to return excess profits to clients or further reduce premiums.

Such major changes as the ones suggested here might well lead to new and different regulations written to address specific concerns about our present system. We might be able to draw up new industry guidelines that are more consumer-friendly. This would make it impossible for companies to exclude patients based on preexisting conditions, limit rate hikes so that companies could not effectively exclude people simply by raising premiums to prohibitive levels, and require insurance companies to reimburse clients or providers for the actual cost of treatment rather than limiting benefits to some arbitrarily established *prevailing rate,* which always seems to fall below the regional average.

I can hear the insurance industry screaming already. But keep in mind, if they are no longer required to cover catastrophic illnesses, insurance companies would cut their risks. They could no longer justify these unfair practices as necessary to provide such a huge financial margin of error.

TAMING THE MEDICARE MONSTER

THE ADDITIONAL POSITIVE RAMIFICATIONS of such a plan are numerous. For example, Medicare could be eliminated—or at least greatly reduced. Think about it. If individuals owned and maintained their own health-care policies, retirement from the workforce would not affect them any more than retirement affects homeowner's or auto-insurance coverage. (Although some mechanism or formula for lowering the premiums of retired people with fixed incomes should definitely be explored.)

Another advantage is this: the government's assumption of catastrophic health care would almost certainly and immediately prompt a national debate on what catastrophic conditions should be treated—and to what extent. We might even hope for some reasoned discussion on some difficult choices we will all face with the aging of our baby-boomer generation.

As our medical knowledge increases and our technical abilities advance, the modern medical community finds itself capable of successfully performing procedures never before considered—such as quadruple bypasses on eighty-five-year-old patients or extensive resections of malignancies in very elderly individuals who also have a host of other serious medical problems. As America's general population ages and our medical capabilities continue to expand, we will face more and more such scenarios. In fact, we may soon find it possible to keep most people alive, albeit at varying levels of activity, well beyond their hundredth birthday. The question is: Should we do it simply because we can?

Half of the lifetime medical expenses the average American incurs are incurred during the final six months of life. One reason for this is that, unlike many other advanced nations, American society has not yet accepted the idea of keeping someone suffering terminal or catastrophic illnesses comfortable at home rather than in a hospital. Our mind-set is to automatically pull out all medical stops—even if that means literally torturing loved ones during their last few months of life.

What if rather than always putting terminally ill patients in intensive care units—where we poke, prod, test, and operate *ad nauseam*—we allowed most people the dignity of dying in relative peace and comfort, at home, surrounded by loved ones, with hospice care or some other medical attendant if necessary?

Agreement on who should be treated and who should not be treated would require an extensive national discussion that could hopefully result in some helpful basic guidelines. Obviously any such guidelines should allow for flexibility and choice. And decisions should be based not merely on age but on the viability of the patient. I have seen ninety-year-olds who are healthier than some forty- or fifty-year-olds. So I would argue that medical treatment should not be withheld any time there is a reasonable chance of recovery and a resumption of a quality lifestyle.

If any patient insisted on having *everything* done, I think consideration of more aggressive treatment should be given. I also believe, however, that most reasonable, terminally ill patients would much prefer to die in comfort and dignity at home than be tormented until the end in a hospital setting. Especially if we can freely and honestly talk these issues out in a national discussion that would help us all rethink our culture's mind-set about death, dying, and terminal illness.

Let me make it perfectly clear that I am not talking about euthanasia or mercy killing—of any sort. As a surgeon and a committed Christian, I have the highest regard for the sanctity of life. But as a doctor who is convinced there is a spiritual dimension to life and believes in the potential immortality of the human soul, I have concluded that in many cases there are worse things than physical death.

Don't get me wrong. I always do everything in my power as a physician to save the lives of my patients. And I regularly ask God to bolster my limited efforts with his healing power. I believe in answers to prayer and miracles because I have seen them. So I don't give up easily. I have devoted myself professionally to the betterment of health and the preservation of life.

But I think too often in the face of terminal illness our attitudes and actions are colored more by a fear of physical death than by a belief in the spiritual nature and the sanctity of human life. This is true even for a lot of my fellow Christians.

Still, people of faith have much to contribute to any discussion about how to treat various terminal patients. We need to start that discussion now, before worsening economic factors begin to speak so loudly that faith-filtered perspectives are drowned out of public debate. If the reforms suggested here improve the economic picture in health care, they could help on both scores.

A BETTER SAFETY NET

IF WE CAN ADDRESS health-care reform from a broader, all-inclusive perspective, there could be another major benefit. Perhaps we could finally find a reasonable, workable, cost-effective solution for the 35 to 43 million Americans (depending on who is counting and how) who do not have health-care coverage.

Let's start by acknowledging a couple of important facts. A significant percentage of people without health insurance are between jobs or haven't been working at a job long enough for the employer-provided health care coverage to take effect. If we had a system that encouraged and enabled individual ownership of health insurance, most of these people could take their coverage with them when they change jobs and wouldn't ever have to be uninsured—even temporarily.

But perhaps even more germane to our discussion is the fact that under our current health-care system, no one in America is truly without access to medical treatment. Hospitals are prohibited, by law, from refusing medical treatment to anyone who comes through the doors of their emergency rooms, regardless of their lack of insurance or their inability to pay.

So, in a sense, every American is already "covered." On the surface this sounds compassionate—the least we can do. Unfortunately, it is too often less than we could or should do. Yet we all pay a terrible price for this minimal safety net. It is actually a part of the reason health care costs are so high in our country.

When people routinely take their children to the emergency room for such common problems as sore throats and ear infections because they can't afford, or don't have access to, a family doctor, that is an exorbitant waste of health-care dollars. By waiting until they develop an acute condition that may require more serious intervention, patients who regularly rely on emergency-room treatment for their primary medical care seldom experience the benefit of healthier and cheaper preventative care.

So what might we do for the indigent and others who require assistance in maintaining medical coverage? Again it might be wise to look at a current governmental program that could serve as a model: the food stamp program is not perfect, but there is a basic framework there that might lend itself to health care.

Instead of handing out medical assistance cards to the poor or indigent, they could be issued the equivalent of health stamps. These could be credit vouchers—perhaps in the form of electronic money—that could only be used to purchase medical services, in the same way food stamps are used to purchase food items.

Such vouchers could be allocated according to preestablished criteria on a monthly basis. If a person receiving such aid frequented emergency rooms for their primary care needs, their allocation of health-care voucher dollars would quickly be depleted and carry significant consequences. (In the same way spending food stamps for steak or junk food means less for the purchase of more economical staples at the end of a month.) On the other hand, if people used their health vouchers at a primary-care clinic, the resources would stretch much farther.

Not only would such a system foster more personal responsibility, it would encourage even the poorest individuals and families in our society to establish relationships with physicians. And that in turn would facilitate preventative-care measures.

Instead of a poor, elderly woman waiting until an ulcerated foot forced her to seek treatment in some emergency room, she could receive routine care from a health-care professional who could help monitor and control the diabetes that led to the ulcer. Not only would that be more cost efficient than the current system that we all subsidize with taxes and higher health-care prices, it would be far more compassionate because it offers hope of a much healthier life.

HIGH HOPES FOR HEALTH CARE

I REALIZE I HAVE thrown out a lot of thoughts here. Some are such radical departures from the status quo that I have no doubt they need to be refined and improved upon. But I believe that some variation on this framework could work effectively and be implemented quickly, and I suspect many of these things will be done eventually as a matter of survival. But the transition won't be carried out as smoothly if we wait until the worsening crisis forces their implementation.

I understand that working out the details of the various elements of this proposal would require a multidisciplinary team of health-care providers, economists, lawyers, insurance specialists, and interested citizens. I am hopeful that because we are all affected, many more of us from all sides of the issue will become vocal and involved in this business of health-care reform.

I am optimistic because of the interested and positive responses I have received from medical colleagues, legislators, patients, and friends in the legal community. I was even invited to speak at a managed-care conference last year where I shared some of my horror stories and challenged my listeners to consider the perspective of doctors and patients when they make their decisions. From the honest and sometimes emotional feedback I received during and after my speech, I know many of those industry representatives were not only challenged but felt convicted about the need to bring more compassion and change to the health-care scene.

Meaningful improvement in our system will require all of us to make some concessions. But even before we can begin, we will all need to step back far enough from our own selfish interests and our old familiar arguments about what will and won't work to get a new, broader perspective on the Big Picture.

EPILOGUE: THE TRULY BIG PICTURE

THE FIRST TIME SHANNON Jones' parents brought her to Johns Hopkins for an exam, I could see how much they loved their ten-month-old daughter. They told me they had been trying to have a baby for five years before God blessed them with this beautiful little girl.

Everything had seemed fine when she was born and for the first few months of her life. But then their pediatrician noticed Shannon's head was not growing. When she became cranky and exhibited other changes in behavior, he referred the Jones to me for further evaluation.

I determined that Shannon was suffering from *craniosynostosis* and explained to her parents that meant her brain was growing but that her skull was not. I told the Jones I felt confident we could help their daughter, but that she would need a cranial expansion — a major operation, but one we had performed successfully many times.

On the day of the operation everything seemed to be going well when Carol James, my physician assistant, noticed the anesthesiologist fidgeting a bit with his controls. "Are you having some difficulty?" she asked him.

"I'm a little concerned about the blood pressure," he told her. Maybe thirty seconds later he announced, "The patient has arrested! We need to resuscitate."

We still had the head open, a section of skull out, and the brain exposed. We hurriedly used some towel clips to pull the scalp back together and close the wound so that we could immediately flip the child over and begin cardiopulmonary resuscitation. In the process the endotracheal tube became dislodged and had to be reinserted while the CPR was going on.

Five minutes. Ten minutes. Fifteen minutes went by. When we were getting nothing but a flat line on the EKG monitor at twenty minutes someone asked if I wanted to call a code. "Let's try a little bit longer," I said. And I continued to pray. *Lord, this family has been trying to have a child for five years. And now their baby is dying on this operating table. Can you please do something!*

At the twenty-four-minute mark we finally got a little blip on the screen—and incredibly, shortly thereafter that little girl returned to sinus rhythm. We rushed her over to the pediatric intensive care unit to try to stabilize her. But when the anesthesia wore off Shannon's pupils were fixed and dilated, there was no movement, no neurological response at all.

And I remember thinking, *How am I going to tell these parents that the little girl they waited and prayed five years for is now brain dead?*

I walked into the smaller, private waiting room we have where we take families when we have to give them bad news, and I thought about how this was the worst part of my job—having to inform young parents that their child is dead or dying. I would rather do anything else in world.

The Jones reacted pretty much as I had anticipated. There was shock and disbelief. There was weeping. They asked if there was any hope. I had to be honest; I told them it did not look good. Since they had already talked about having prayed for so long that God would give them a child, I reached out to place my hands on their shoulders and added: "But even when we can see little reason for hope, we know God can do anything."

Shannon's father looked up and said, "I believe God can work miracles. And I'm going to pray for one."

"I'll be praying, too," I assured them.

"Let's see who can pray the hardest," he challenged me.

"It's a deal!" I replied. And do you know what? Within twenty-four hours that child's pupils began reacting and she started to move. Everyone in the PICU was flabbergasted but delighted. People all over the hospital were talking about this miraculous recovery, and I went from being extraordinarily depressed to feeling like I was on cloud nine. Shannon Jones had come back from the dead.

But before that second day was over, she began having trouble breathing. Segments of her lung were rupturing and bleeding, and Shannon began deteriorating rapidly. By the time I went home from the hospital that night the pulmonary specialist had told me he thought there was less than a 5 percent chance she would live till morning.

Driving home I prayed, "Lord, you answered prayer and brought the child back, just so she could die from a different cause? You were looking awfully good there for a while; everybody was talking about you and saying what a miracle it was. I just do not understand this!"

I was still upset when I got home. But I went on to bed because I was scheduled to catch a plane at seven the next morning — to speak at a medical school in Ohio. At 3:00 A.M. Candy and I were awakened when our youngest son, Rhoeyce, had a severe asthma attack. Soon after Candy left to take him to our local hospital's emergency room for treatment, I received another phone call from the PICU at Hopkins saying that the last functioning segment of Shannon's lungs had ruptured; she was going to die within the next few minutes. Could I come in and comfort the family?

It was almost four in the morning and my plane was taking off at seven. So I decided I would get up, pack my things, and drive to the hospital on my way to the airport. But before I could leave the house I received a call from the local hospital saying they could not get Rhoeyce's asthma under control, that he was in grave danger. So I made arrangements for him to be transported by ambulance to Hopkins. Once we got all that taken care of, it was time to head for the airport. By the time my plane took off, Rhoeyce was out of danger, but I had not had time to talk to the Jones. The minute I landed in Ohio I called the PICU at Hopkins, assuming Shannon had died, to see if I could at least talk to her parents before they left the hospital.

The intensive care doctor told me, "The child hasn't died. And not only has she not died, but for some reason, her lungs have actually improved. The child has rallied."

I got back to Baltimore about midnight and drove straight to the hospital to visit my son, who was doing much better. Then I went to the PICU to check on Shannon who was making such incredible improvement that within the next few days her lungs had healed to the point that she came off the ventilator.

First she had come back from a cardiac death. Now she had come back from a pulmonary death as well. I was so astounded that I praised God and told him, "This is fabulous!"

But that wasn't the end of the story.

The rehabilitation specialists and the pediatric neurologist came by to examine Shannon. They told the parents that their daughter had sustained so much damage to her brain during these two episodes that she was blind, deaf, and would never be able to do enough to justify any rehabilitation.

So later that same day, when I made my rounds, the clearly distressed parents were telling me all about this assessment they had been given. Shannon's father admitted, "I wanted to punch those guys in the nose! They obviously didn't know what they were talking about." And I did not blame him; after all that had happened we were not about to give up that easily.

I had to go to California the next afternoon to conduct site visits for the National Institute of Health. When I returned three days later I went to visit Shannon. The child now followed me across her room with her eyes. She could clearly hear again as well.

The rehab specialist turned out to have been right about one thing. Shannon wasn't a candidate for rehabilitation ... because she was able to go home without it.

The portion of the skull we had not had time to replace, grew back. Since we had never finished the original procedure, she did require a subsequent surgery to further expand her skull some months later; but everything went well the second time. And today Shannon Jones is completely normal.

To me, Shannon's story is an amazing example of God doing today what he did back in Bible times. He brought this child back to life twice, then restored her sight and her hearing. There was no medical explanation for what happened. I know I did not do it. So whenever I remember Shannon Jones, I am reminded of the lesson I learned from her. That even though I may develop my ability as a neurosurgeon to the highest levels, there is only so much I can do. I have to have a plan of action, I have to be able to articulate that plan, and I need the skills to execute it. But there is always more help available. Once I do my best, I can trust God for the rest.

That experience with Shannon Jones had a profound effect on my faith in God.

CHILDISH PICTURES OF GOD

WHEN I WAS A kid, I imagined God as an old, old man with a long white beard who lived up in the clouds and had a powerful telescope that could see through walls. And he was always peering down to see what you did wrong, so that he could make sure you got punished for it.

That concept was reinforced for me when I would hear people at church say things like, "God gave everyone a guardian angel. But if you go to the wrong kind of place, say a theater or a bar, your guardian angel won't go in with you. He'll wait outside until you come out."

All these childish impressions added up to an image of a God who was extraordinarily judgmental—a distant, uncaring, harsh being who invested most of his time and energy making sure no riff-raff got into heaven. And even though I attended church and read my Bible and professed to love God, I clung to the remnants of that childhood image of God as I grew up.

As a result, I found myself in early adulthood being extremely conservative about everything—to the point of being puritanical. I was judgmental of others' actions and attitudes, and I didn't always enjoy life as a result.

I even remember a discussion some years ago at church, in a Sabbath school class. There we were encouraged to talk honestly and openly about our feelings toward God and about how our faith relates to contemporary issues and the way we live our lives every day. One of the men in the class made a simple statement that so shocked me that it has stuck in my mind for years. He told us he had come to believe that, "God loves people so much that he will do everything in his power to save everybody."

I thought, *Whoa! That guy is just too radical!* What he was saying just did not jibe with the image of God I had gotten growing up.

But over the years, through professional experiences with patients like Shannon Jones, through reading and studying the Bible, through personal life experience, I have developed a very different perspective on who God is and what he expects from me.

ONE SMART GOD

As a doctor, the more I learn about creation and especially the human brain, the more impressed I am with how incredibly smart our Creator must be. Whether I look down through my operating microscope and marvel at the intricate complexities of creation inside a baby's brain or stand under the stars on a summer night, looking up at the mind-boggling magnitude of a universe made with such precision you can set clocks by it, I see evidence everywhere of a brilliant and logical God.

So why would he provide us with guardian angels, if those angels were not going to go with us and protect us when we went into dangerous places. Where is the logic in that? There is none. So ... maybe I need to rethink some of my other childhood impressions about God.

A GOD WHO LAUGHS

WHEN I WAS A kid, I never thought about God having a sense of humor, and yet, who but a joyful, fun-loving God would put a giraffe and a hippopotamus on the same planet, let alone the same continent? I see evidence of his humor throughout creation. I even see it in my own life.

I have to laugh, for example, at the irony of my own name. Benjamin Solomon Carson. When God inspired my parents to give me the middle name of Solomon he must have known I would have a lifelong love for the book of Proverbs, which King Solomon wrote. I also see the irony in the fact that Solomon, early in his reign, made his reputation for great wisdom when he settled that dispute between the two women arguing over who was the rightful mother of a child, by proposing they divide the baby in half. In my early career I too made a name for myself by dividing babies—when we separated the Binder Siamese twins.

So I feel a real affinity for Solomon. I only wish I could be half as wise.

Fortunately I keep learning and changing my perspective on God.

Remember the incident that occurred during the summer of 1996 when the Baltimore Oriole's second baseman Roberto Alomar got into a heated argument and actually spat in the face of an umpire? Remember the horror, indignation, and outrage that ensued, not just here in Baltimore but around the country? Remember the debate about how Alomar should be punished? Should he be suspended for the rest of year? Maybe even banned from baseball for life? The incident so offended everyone's sensibilities that countless editorials condemned it as symptomatic of an attitude toward authority that threatened the very foundation of our society.

I couldn't help thinking, *All this over a baseball rhubarb with an umpire?* Because the incident reminded me of the time the all-powerful authority and Creator of the universe humbled himself and came to earth to be spat upon, cursed, kicked, even beaten with a whip, before he was crucified on a cross for the very same people who did that to him. And I thought, *Maybe God* does *love people so much that he will do everything in his power to save everybody.*

That would mean God, instead of being quick to judge and anxious to condemn us for every little sin, was really an almost unimaginably tolerant and forgiving God who loves us so much that he puts up with anything and everything we do. Understanding and believing that led me to change some of my other ideas about him. It has taken me a while, but I have finally come to realize that God's first concern is not about whether or not we abide by his rules. His priority is not our *wrong behavior* so much as it is *right relationships.*

I think of my marriage as an analogy. If I truly love Candy, and I do, then I do not have to reread my wedding vows every day. I gladly keep those vows, almost automatically, because of the loving relationship we have. Those vows do not present a terrible hardship I have to struggle over; keeping them is merely a natural byproduct of the relationship.

The same principle holds true in our relationship to God. Too often people focus on the rules and never find the relationship. When the truth is that if we develop that relationship—if we concentrate on knowing, and understanding, and pleasing God—we will naturally become loving, caring, and obedient people as a result.

So it is not about *How many people did I help today? How much food did I give to the poor?* Or *Did I tell a lie last week?* We do not have to keep score—which is a good thing because we are human, we are fallible, we are going to make mistakes. End of story. We have to learn that what matters most in the Big Picture is not whether we view ourselves as Democrat or Republican, rich or poor, black or white, tall or short, young or old, smart or dumb, successes or failures. What truly matters most in this world is who we are in relationship to the one who created it. Then our right relationship with him will dictate our right relationship with others.

A PERSONAL GOD?

I KNOW A LOT of people in our society, maybe even a few readers of this book, get uneasy when they hear talk of a *personal relationship with God*. The idea sounds to them, if not downright fanatical, at least presumptuous.

And indeed it might be presumptuous and egotistical to think of ourselves as capable (let alone worthy) of a personal relationship with an almighty God who created us and everything else in the entire universe. Except for one thing. This personal-relationship idea was his idea in the first place. The Bible tells us it is what we were created for. It is all God has wanted from us since the beginning of time.

I see convincing evidence of this in the story of the thief on the cross beside Jesus. He was undoubtedly the scum of the earth — a criminal whose deeds were not just deemed worthy of death but deserving of the humiliating and painful death on the cross. Nevertheless, when this man voiced a simple belief in the power of Jesus to save him, Jesus did it. The thief did nothing to earn salvation or prove himself worthy of a relationship with God. He merely believed and accepted the gift.

The privilege of that relationship is always a gift. Actions do not really have anything to do with it. The question is whether or not we accept what God did for us. When we accept him and allow him a place in our hearts, we become a different type of individual. Our whole life is changed — not because of our behavior but by the relationship itself.

If the very idea of a relationship with God still seems incomprehensible, or just too fantastic to be true, think again about our deepest, most meaningful human relationship — marriage. It is true that before you are married, if you see an attractive stranger, it would indeed be more than a little presumptuous to imagine you were going to marry that person and think that you already knew exactly what that marriage relationship was going to be like. Obviously, there is no way you could realistically imagine a marriage relationship until you actually began to know that person. But if you ask the person out, begin to date and spend time together, learn everything you can learn about the person in order to please them, a true relationship begins to develop. What was once a mere fantasy, which seemed too good to be true, becomes a reality as the relationship and the love grow. Until you have been together so long that your marriage relationship seems the most natural part of your life.

I have discovered it is the same way with God, the all-powerful, all-knowing Creator of the Universe. What once seemed a privilege too good to be true now seems the most natural part of my life.

A BETTER PERSPECTIVE

Rather than seeing God as a celestial fun-spoiler who wants to punish people for every misdeed, I now see him as a God who wants what is best for all us of. I have drawn that conclusion from countless experiences in my own life, and from seeing how he works in the lives of others.

One of the most memorable examples was with a patient of mine name Cynthia Clayton. This nine-year-old suffered from a tumor called a *cranio-pharyngioma*. She had been operated on a number of times before she came to me. This tumor was just a monster. No one could get it out. They had tried radiation, but that did not stop it. Nothing was working. I operated a couple times to try to debulk it but still couldn't get it under control.

When we operated a third time we were able to get most of it and things were looking pretty optimistic toward the end of the operation when one of the other surgeons operating with me said, "There's just one more piece of the tumor over here." I told him to go ahead and get it out. But it must have been a plug, because when he gave a little tug, it was as if someone had opened a fire hydrant. Blood gushed from the base of the brain so fast that we couldn't keep up with two suckers going on high. We were losing the patient right there on the table.

I began stuffing cotton and whatever else we had into the hole to try to stop it. The brain was bulging clear out of the skull, so I literally stuffed it back in with my hands as we pulled the covering back over the wound. By the time I finished stitching it closed, the skin was bulging like a balloon about to pop.

We got Cynthia back to the intensive care unit where I expected her to die within hours, if not minutes. But I hoped that time would give me a chance to talk to the mother, to prepare her a little, so that her child's death wouldn't seem such a sudden shock .

I told the mother what had happened. I explained that the little girl's pupils were fixed and dilated. The brain had swollen until the skin was as tight as a drum. There was no circulation. And it didn't look as if her daughter could live very much longer.

At that point the mother began pleading with me. "There can't be *no* hope!" This was her only child. "There's got to be *some* hope! Can't there be just a ten percent chance?"

I shook my head. "No."

"Just one percent? Tell me there is a one percent chance. Just one percent!"

I said, "There's not."

"One-tenth of one percent?"

"Look," I said. "I'll tell you what—you pray as hard as you can and you get everyone you know to pray as hard as they can. I promise I will pray. And if we all do that, there may be the tiniest, possible chance."

And I remember leaving that waiting room, walking back to my office and closing my door and saying, "Lord, in the Bible you raised people from the dead. I've never asked you to raise someone from the dead before, but this girl is dead. She's the only child this mother has. If there is some way you can see to bring this girl back, even just for a little while, I would be so grateful." I prayed for that little girl for hours.

The next day I went to see Cynthia, but she was no better. The day after that I saw her again. By this time the staff of the PICU were saying to me, "We know you're a strong believer in God and everything. But, Dr. Carson, this girl is brain dead. The neurologists came by and they think we should take her off life support."

I said, "Look. Can we just wait until tomorrow?"

We all agreed we would do it the following day. I prayed again that night and the next morning as we were preparing to remove her life support, she moved a finger. The staff were astounded. So we left her hooked to the machines. And within days she was making more movement. Eventually she was able to go to rehab. And sometime after that she walked out and went home with both visual and mental capabilities.

She lived between two and three more years before the tumor recurred and she finally died. But during that time her mother had another child—a beautiful, healthy little girl. And she was more at peace and better able to cope with Cynthia's loss.

I often hesitate to tell stories like Shannon's or Cynthia's because I am afraid people will expect a miracle to occur every time. And there is not a miracle every time. I don't know why.

I do not know why Cynthia only lived a couple more years, why God did not heal her completely. I do not know why some patients die no matter how hard they are prayed for. But cases like Shannon's and Cynthia's, plus forty-seven years of life experience, have taught me I can trust God with all my unanswered questions.

I am just a brain surgeon. I cannot know everything. Thankfully I do not have to, because I have learned the wisdom of Solomon who wrote, "Trust in the Lord with all your heart and lean not on your own understanding; in all your ways acknowledge him and he will make your paths straight" (Proverbs 3:5).

In other words, we need to realize that God is in control. We need to seek his will and get his perspective by developing a relationship with him and his word. When we can begin to see the world through his eyes of love and compassion, we will also see ourselves in a true light, as part of his plan.

Then, and only then, can we really begin to understand the Big Picture.